MODINE MANUFACTURING COMPANY
LIBRARY
No. B 1399   Date Jan 10, 1972

Professional
Mail Surveys

Professional Mail Surveys

Paul L. Erdos

WITH THE ASSISTANCE OF   Arthur J. Morgan

McGRAW-HILL BOOK COMPANY
New York   St. Louis   San Francisco
London   Sydney   Toronto
Mexico   Panama

PROFESSIONAL MAIL SURVEYS

Copyright © 1970 by McGraw-Hill, Inc. All Rights Reserved.
Printed in the United States of America. No part of this
publication may be reproduced, stored in a retrieval system,
or transmitted, in any form or by any means, electronic,
mechanical, photocopying, recording, or otherwise, without
the prior written permission of the publisher.
Library of Congress Catalog Card Number 75-95800

ISBN 07-019570-6

234567890 HDBP 754321

Introduction

THE PURPOSE of this book is to describe the techniques used for professional mail surveys in sufficient detail to enable readers to conduct their own surveys, to evaluate those made by others, or simply to become acquainted with proven procedures used in mail surveys.

It has not been the author's aim to write comprehensively on the technical aspects of statistics, sampling, or electronic data-processing, although this book touches on all these fields. Since this is a book on mail surveys, related subjects such as sampling, data-processing, and report presentation are discussed in some detail when they have special application for mail surveys; otherwise they are described only in general terms.

As Chapter 3 will show, there are many types of mail surveys. Because of the specialized experience of the author, the techniques discussed in this book are based primarily on market research surveys. However, many of these techniques are adaptable to mail surveys conducted for other purposes.

The reader may notice that some of the examples and illustrations given describe media surveys conducted for magazines and newspapers. Other types of market research studies might have served as illustrations, but a good many of these are confidential, while most media studies are published and may therefore be used as examples. The author feels that wherever possible it is preferable to use actual surveys rather than hypothetical questionnaires or findings as illustrative material.

Should the reader come across an unfamiliar term in this book, he may refer to the Glossary for definition.

I would like to express my gratitude to Frank R. Coutant, first president of the American Marketing Association, who pioneered many market research techniques and who unstintingly shared his knowledge with a young employee.

For information, helpful advice, and criticism, I want to thank L. A. Capaldini of the American Bankers Association, Dr. W. Edwards Deming of New York University, David L. Kaplan of the Bureau of the Census, Ingrid Kildegaard of the Advertising Research Foundation, and Dr. William Neil of the University of Nottingham.

The book could not appear in its present form if I had not had the assistance of Arthur Morgan: our collaboration is now in its third decade, and our friendship is in its fourth.

While working on this book we received much needed help from our associates at Erdos and Morgan. Frank Boone read the whole manuscript and offered much sound criticism and a number of valuable suggestions. Roy Wollney executed many of the charts and figures. Other associates read parts of the book and gave helpful advice. We are indebted to Francis Justice, who edited the manuscript, for a great many constructive suggestions.

Let me close by expressing my appreciation to my wife Helen, who read and proofread the manuscript several times, made many suggestions, and was more than patient with a husband who had continuous homework for a year and a half.

I am grateful for the help of all, but I also wish to make clear that all errors and omissions are solely my responsibility.

Paul L. Erdos

Contents

	Introduction	v
ONE	The Development of Mail Surveys	1
	History and definition. The first "mail survey" in the New World. The progress of mail surveys.	
TWO	Advantages and Limitations in the Use of Mail Surveys	5
	Wider distribution. Less distribution bias. No interviewer bias—truthful reply. Thoughtful reply— time —control—cost. Limitations on the use of mail surveys—list problems. Interviewer needed—questionnaire problems. The respondent—the budget— timing.	
THREE	Types of Mail Surveys	15
	Uses of mail surveys. Industrial and consumer surveys. Media studies and surveys on advertising. Multiple surveys and panels. "Hybrid" mail surveys.	

vii

viii   Contents

FOUR **Survey Design**   22

A list of steps in planning. Problems—objectives—universe. Reliability—sample and scope. Techniques of data-gathering and data-processing. Timing and cost estimating.

FIVE **Mailing Lists and Notes on Sampling**   27

The advantages of card lists. Types of mailing lists. Frame bias. Sampling. Sample size. Considerations based on response. How many to mail.

SIX **Questionnaire Construction: What to Include and How to Get Answers**   37

A list of important considerations. Completeness and relevance. The "short-and-easy" look. Paper and printing. Layout. Check versus open-end questions. Grouping check answers. Pitfalls to be avoided. Saving the respondent unnecessary reading.

SEVEN **Questionnaire Construction: Interest, Bias, and Precision**   57

Interest and importance. Title and introductory question. Avoiding jargon—keeping the respondent interested. Bias: the sponsor and the subjects. Bias: the content and position of questions. Clear and precise answers. Helpful examples. Rating versus ranking. Logical order—detailed instructions. Questionnaire construction and tabulating. Built-in controls—courtesy.

EIGHT **Cost Estimating and Scheduling**   75

No cost item should be omitted. Individual item cost—timing as it affects cost. Scheduling.

NINE **Pilot Studies**   84

Categories of pilot studies. Basic principles. Purposes of pilot studies. Pilot studies are worth doing.

TEN **Advance Notice of the Questionnaire**   89

The advance postcard. The advance letter. Other methods of giving advance notice.

ELEVEN **Incentives**   94

Main considerations in the selection of incentives. Why money is an effective incentive. Money incentives and bias: executive response. Money incentives and bias: tests. Other advantages of money incentives.

TWELVE	**The Accompanying Letter**	101

Listing and discussion of 22 important considerations in letter construction.

THIRTEEN	**Mailing Procedures**	118

The outer envelope. The questionnaire. Letter, incentive, and reply envelope. A case history: past practice and changes. Testing improved methods. The sequence of mailing operations.

FOURTEEN	**Follow-up Mailings**	129

Why follow-up mailings are needed. The reminder postcard. The second wave. Letter and incentives. The third wave. Further efforts to increase response.

FIFTEEN	**The Nonresponse Problem**	138

Problems of achieving a high response rate. Completion rate in personal interviewing. The problems of nonresponse. An example of distorted results. A high percentage of response. Occasional usefulness of low-response surveys. The nonrespondents. What can be done about nonrespondents. Weighting the nonresponse. Conclusion.

SIXTEEN	**Checking in Returns**	152

Opening the envelopes. Pulling mailing cards. Orderly procedure.

SEVENTEEN	**Data-processing**	159

Methods of data-processing. Hand tabulating. How to tabulate by hand. Tabulating brands and reasons. Supervision and checking.

EIGHTEEN	**The Punch Card and Its Use**	167

Description of the punch card. Flexibility in the use of columns. Trailer cards. Preparing questionnaires for punching. Coded questionnaire and master.

NINETEEN	**Editing and Coding**	176

The purpose of editing. Editing for consistency and clarity. Editing incomplete replies. Clarifying entries. Proper editing. Establishing codes. How many to test tab. Test tabulation. Recapping test tabs. The code booklet. Numerical answers. Coding. Uniform coding procedure. Accurate, efficient coding.

TWENTY — Card Punching and Machine Tabulation — 192
Work of the keypunch operator. Card verification. Consistency checks. An example of consistency checks. Correcting errors. Machine tabulating. EAM and EDP. Tabulating specifications. The need for detailed, written instructions.

TWENTY-ONE — Recaps and Calculations — 203
Operations involved in recapping. "No Answer" counts. Percentaging. Averages and medians. Weighting and projection.

TWENTY-TWO — Final Checking and Presentation — 212
A list of important checks. Presentation of the findings. Contents of the report. Format of the report.

TWENTY-THREE — Recognition Studies and Corporate-image Surveys — 219
A note of caution. Areas of consideration. The universe. Timing and frequency. Structuring the questionnaire. General considerations. Case histories.

TWENTY-FOUR — International Mail Surveys — 236
International mailing lists. Problems of language and custom. Postage. Response rate and language. The income question. Open-end questions.

TWENTY-FIVE — Evaluating Mail Surveys — 243
A 56-point checklist. Sponsor, purpose, and survey design. The questionnaire. Data-gathering. Data-processing. The final report.

TWENTY-SIX — Ethical Standards in Mail Research — 250
The survey and the sponsor. Obligations to the sponsor. The public and the respondents. Proper use of the findings.

APPENDIX Percentage and Speed of Response   255
*Size and number of pages.   The second wave.   The
speed of response.*

Glossary   264
Books on Related Subjects   276
Index   279

Professional
Mail Surveys

ONE
The Development of Mail Surveys

THE HISTORY OF SURVEYS can be traced back thousands of years: The Bible speaks of the count (census) of the children of Israel; there are surveys of people and goods in Babylonian records; and the thread leads through the history of Western civilization, through the Roman census (the office of the *censores* was created in 443 B.C.), the Domesday Book (1086), Napoleon's surveys (1806), and down to the present.

There are three main types of surveys, depending on the method of data-gathering used: personal-interview surveys, telephone surveys, and mail surveys. The basic distinction between mail and other types of surveys is the fact that in surveying by mail there is no person to ask the questions and guide the respondent. This gives rise to important differences in survey design, questionnaire construction, and various other aspects of the survey. These differences result in some advantages and some shortcomings for mail as compared with other survey methods, and these will be examined in detail later.

Mail surveys are by no means a recent development. A detailed account of a mail survey conducted among Church of England clergymen can be found in an 1839 issue of the *Journal of the Royal Statistical Society.*[1]

THE FIRST "MAIL SURVEY" IN THE NEW WORLD

In the annals of the Western Hemisphere the history of mail surveys goes back much further than most of us would imagine. In the year 1577, King Philip II of Spain decided to conduct a census of his New World possessions. In effect this was a mail survey by official courier, since mail service in our sense was not as yet known. A questionnaire, in the form of a memorandum, and detailed instructions were sent to overseas governors and other top government officials with a royal request that "Said printed instructions and memorandums are to be distributed throughout all towns of Spaniards and Indians in each jurisdiction in which there are Spaniards, sending them to the Councils, or, if these are lacking, to the parish priests or the monks...."[2]

Here is a sample of the instructions accompanying the questionnaire:

> After carefully reading each paragraph of the memorandum, they are to write down separately what they have to say, answering each one of the questions it contains, one after the other. Those questions to which they have nothing to answer are to be omitted without comment, passing on to those that follow, until all are read. The answers given are to be short and clear. What is certain is to be given as such, what is not is to be recorded as doubtful, so that reports may be exact and in strict conformity to the instructions of the memorandum.

Since to complete the questionnaire was required by royal command, the incentive for answering was to avoid displeasing His Majesty. Not surprisingly, the percentage of returns was very satisfactory. The 38 questions are clear and penetrating, on subjects ranging from topographical to population characteristics, agriculture, taxation, and religion. Here are some of them:

QUESTION I: In the town with Spanish inhabitants the name of the district or province is to be stated, also the meaning of the name and the reason it is so named.

QUESTION III: State in general the climate and quality of said province or district; whether it is cold or hot, dry or damp, with much water or little and at what season there is more or less; and the prevailing winds, whether violent and from what quarter and at what season of the year.

QUESTION V: State whether the district is inhabited by many or few Indians and whether in former times it had a greater or lesser population; the causes for the increase or diminution and whether the inhabitants live in regular towns permanently or not. State also what is the character and condition of their intelligence, inclinations and modes of life; also whether different languages are spoken throughout the whole province or whether they have one which is spoken by all.

QUESTION XIV: State to whom the Indians belonged in heathen times and what dominion was exercised over them by their lords; what tribute they paid and the form of worship rites and customs they had, good or bad.

QUESTION XXIV: Mention the grain and seeds and other plants and vegetables which have served or serve as food for the natives.

QUESTION XXXIII: Describe the trade and traffic and dealings with which the Spanish and native inhabitants of the town support themselves and state with what produce and how they pay tribute.

We have the answers to these questions—they are clear and concise, containing a wealth of material.

THE PROGRESS OF MAIL SURVEYS

It is a long way from the 1577 survey to the 1960 Census in the United States. This was the first general census in which the mail survey method was extensively used. The aim was to obtain better quality data than under the previous method of personal interviewing, while keeping costs at a reasonable level.

In the United States, mail surveys have been used for marketing research and public opinion polls for several generations.[3] Newspaper straw polls were conducted early in the nineteenth century. Often quite crude affairs by our standards, they offered interested readers the opportunity to cut out ballots, which were printed in the paper, and which the reader could then fill out and return. Little or no thought was given to sampling theory or to percentage of response.

During the last quarter of the century, advertising agencies such as N. W. Ayer & Son became interested in market research, and with the aid of the academic world, research techniques began to improve. In 1895 Harlow Gale at the University of Minnesota conducted a mail survey on advertising. However, it is only in the last thirty years that techniques and standards have improved to a point where they may be called "professional." So late as 1937, a widely used college text on marketing research stated: "The percentage of replies received from mail questionnaires ranges from less than 2 per cent to as high as 30 per cent. A 10 per cent response is considered a very satisfactory result and is generally accepted as 'par' for this type of work—probably the average returns from all mail questionnaires are not much over 7 per cent."[4] A later edition of the book, published under a somewhat different title in 1955, omitted the above quotation but refers to 43 per cent as "a very high rate of return."[5] Today no responsible research man would consider a return of less than 50 per cent as very good, and returns of 75 per cent and higher are not unusual. For a mail survey to earn the approval of the Advertising Research Foundation a minimum response of 80 per cent is usually required. The need for an 80 per cent response in every survey can be argued, but this requirement demonstrates a dramatic change of standards made possible by the improvement of methods.

Of course the percentage of response is only one facet of a good mail survey. Many other aspects of this research technique show the same kind of improvement in the past twenty years. Sampling, questionnaire construction, printing, mailing, data-processing, report presentation, and interpretation—all show great progress since the "pioneer days" of conducting market research by mail. Early techniques appear somewhat amateurish when compared with the best work being done today.

An evaluation of the current mail technique has been given by the U.S. Bureau of the Census:

> Between 1960 and 1965, the Bureau made additional trial runs using the mail approach in four cities of varying sizes and a major metropolitan area.... Results were gratifying. As a result of these pre-tests, the Bureau concluded that a census by mail was practical for most parts of the country and that the use of this method in the 1970 Census would result in a better census than one taken by traditional methods, and including the non-recurring cost of developing the new system, would cost less than the 1960 Census when allowances were made for price and workload increases.[6]

REFERENCES

1. "Agricultural Queries, with Returns from the County of Bedford, Presented by the Rt. Hon. the President of the Board of Trade," *Journal of the Royal Statistical Society of London*, vol. 1, pp. 89–96, 1839.
2. Zelia Nuttall, "Official Reports on the Towns of Tequizistlan, Tepechpan, Acolman, and San Juan Teotihuacan Sent by Francisco de Castañeda to His Majesty, Philip II., and the Council of the Indies, in 1580," papers of the Peabody Museum of American Archaeology and Ethnology, Harvard University, vol. II, no. 2, pp. 45–84, 1926.
3. Frank G. Coolsen, "Pioneers in the Development of Advertising," *Journal of Marketing*, vol. 12, no. 1, pp. 80–86, July, 1947; also, Lawrence C. Lockley, "Notes on the History of Marketing Research," *Journal of Marketing*, vol. 14, no. 5, pp. 733–736, April, 1950.
4. Lyndon O. Brown, *Market Research and Analysis*, The Ronald Press Company, New York, 1937, p. 210.
5. Lyndon O. Brown, *Marketing and Distribution Research*, The Ronald Press Company, New York, 1955, p. 197.
6. U.S. Department of Commerce, Bureau of the Census, "Planning Notes for 1970 Decennial Census," no. 1, p. 2, Mar. 17, 1966.

TWO
Advantages and Limitations in the Use of Mail Surveys

AT AN EARLY STAGE of planning a survey, the research staff will have to decide which data-gathering method is to be used. They must choose among a number of possible techniques, such as personal interviews, telephone interviewing and mail surveys. Which of these methods is most appropriate and applicable to the particular piece of research on hand? Which will best fit the available budget and time requirements? Which can achieve the most complete and most reliable results? The purpose of this chapter is to list certain advantages of the mail survey method and, on the other hand, to show where it would be either inappropriate or not feasible.

There are ten major advantages of mail surveys over surveys using other methods of data-gathering:

1. Wider distribution
2. Less distribution bias in connection with the neighborhood
3. Less distribution bias in connection with the type of family
4. Less distribution bias in connection with the individual
5. No interviewer bias

6. Better chance of truthful reply
7. Better chance of thoughtful reply
8. Time-saving (under certain circumstances)
9. Centralized control
10. Cost-saving, resulting in more flexibility per dollar spent.

Let us briefly consider each of these points.

Wider distribution. Nearly all personal interview surveys are clustered in a limited number of cities and an even more restricted number of rural areas. If you are surveying a random sample of camera purchasers who sent in warranty cards, and the sample calls for one interview in Hungry Horse, Montana, and two in Kailua, Hawaii, it is obviously prohibitively expensive to send an interviewer to each spot. But the mailman has no difficulty in reaching them. This means we don't have to find "representative" cities, counties, or states. We can sample the "universe" (all people relevant to the survey) without introducing the complications inherent in clustering. Regional differences are adequately represented. There is no special problem in reaching rural as well as urban homes or in surveying any number of different countries.

The cost factor is not the only reason for the flexibility of the mail survey method in the distribution of the sample. Even if the unit costs of mail returns and of questionnaires administered by personal interviewers were the same, the researcher would still be faced with the problem of finding the necessary number of trained interviewers at a given time and at every location that happens to fall into his sampling structure. This is sometimes impossible, sometimes difficult, and often leads to compromises in sampling, the quality of interviewers used, or both.

LESS DISTRIBUTION BIAS

Bias connected with *neighborhood.* Rural homes are not the only ones which are hard to visit. Interviewers usually have a marked aversion to working in tenements and "bad" neighborhoods. It is not surprising that interviewers often miss a disproportionately large number of interviews among people living in neighborhoods they regard as undesirable territory. In such areas you need specially trained interviewers or even interviewers of a particular race, nationality, or religion. It is even harder, at times, to obtain interviews in the wealthier neighborhoods, where interviewers are refused admission to estates or apartment houses. The mail, however, gets through.

Less distribution bias in connection with the type of family. This kind of bias is of course connected with the previous point—reluctance to work in "bad" neighborhoods will cause an underrepresentation of poor families or families of specific racial, national or occupational backgrounds. The difficulty of reaching people in well-to-do neighborhoods may also affect the distribution of the sample. These problems can be aggravated within the same neighborhood by the special difficulty of reaching some families in *any* neighborhood. For example, it will be harder to make an appointment with the Governor of New York at the Executive Mansion in Albany or with a senior member of the du Pont family at Wilmington, Delaware, than with some of their neighbors. The result is that both the rich and the poor can be underrepresented in a survey using personal interviews, while in similar situations the mailed questionnaire will reach them all.

There is still another type of family or single individual who is hard to reach by personal (or telephone) contact. Suppose all members of the family work during the day and often go out at night—they are obviously harder to find at home than, for example, a retired family, a family where one or more members of the household do not work, or a family which spends most evenings at home. All this may cause possible bias for interviewers—but not for mail surveys.

Less distribution bias in connection with the individual. The mail is delivered to the addressee's home and will be there whenever he arrives. If the person the interviewer wants does not happen to be at home, he either has to come back or talk to another available member of the household. The individual sought may be working, or he may be in the hospital, on a business trip, or vacationing on the Riviera, but sooner or later the mail survey with its follow-up mailings will find him. Once, a survey conducted by telephone interview showed a surprisingly large female readership of business publications. As these findings failed to agree with all other research on the same subject, most research men were suspicious that a large number of the phone calls were made during the daytime while many men are at work, resulting in a preponderance of answers from women.

There is also evidence that personal interviewers sometimes select their respondents according to some conscious or unconscious bias.[1]

NO INTERVIEWER BIAS—
TRUTHFUL REPLY

Poor interviewers and interviewer cheating are indeed serious problems,[2] but they can be eliminated by careful training and supervision.

However, even in a well-trained group of honest interviewers all will not be equally capable. As Deming puts it, "Variation attributable to the interviewer arises from many factors: the political, religious, and social beliefs of the interviewer; his economic status, environment and education. Also, perhaps, most interviewers can not help being swayed in the direction of their employers' interest."[3] In cases when the interviewer does not know the sponsor's identity there is still the danger of "opinion bias," which occurs when ". . . interviewers report more responses in agreement with their own positions than do interviewers who disagree with that stand."[4]

Getting unbiased answers is very difficult after the respondent's opinion has been filtered through the mind and writing style of another person, the interviewer. The author once devised a check system for interviewer rating for a large cosmetics manufacturer. It was found that in one town where 6 interviewers were administering the same questionnaire to 400 people, 20 respondents stated that they liked a certain brand of soap because ". . . it has a fragrance like lilacs." All 20 interviews were made by the same interviewer. A check showed that she hadn't been cheating. She just happened to like lilacs and had introduced this particular question with a little aside about the lilacs then in bloom.

Even the appearance, clothing, tone of voice, urgency, and manners of an interviewer may influence the answers. The appearance of the interviewer—beautiful or ugly, white or colored, elegant or seedy, young or old—can introduce subtle biases into the mind of the respondent. This may explain why the U.S. Bureau of the Census ". . . believes the mail census (of 1970) would produce . . . more reliable answers supplied directly by respondents instead of through a more or less inhibiting intermediary, the enumerator."[5] The Bureau has published a study of its experiences with enumerator variance.[6]

Better chance of a truthful reply. The above quotation from the Bureau of the Census also underlines the inhibiting factor of another person's presence. The average man or woman does not wish to appear prejudiced, or stupid, or poor, or boastful to the interviewer. His psychological visor will be down when facing another person; it may be (and often is) up when completing an unsigned questionnaire addressed to an impersonal research firm in a distant city. The percentage of "No Answers" is often higher in personal interview surveys than in mail surveys. For example, an extensive survey measuring the differences between the results of mail surveys and of personal interviews (conducted among the same people) found the answers obtained by the two methods to the "family income" question quite different. In the words of Dr. Lazarsfeld and Dr. Franzen, who conducted this research, "Two differences are important here. First is the large percentage of persons who refuse income information in the interviews. Five times as many persons refuse income data to an interviewer as refuse to answer the same questions by mail."[7]

The interviewer can sometimes give an answer from observation, but this introduces another possible bias. However, the real problem is not the "No Answer," but the not-quite-true answer, triggered by the fact that the respondent is facing another person in general and a specific interviewer in particular. The absence of another person and careful phrasing of the questionnaire and its accompanying letter can minimize this kind of bias.

The anonymity of the respondent and the fact that his answers will be confidential can be made very clear in the letter accompanying a mail questionnaire. On the other hand the same respondent facing a personal interviewer in his home or office must be aware that his name and address can be connected with his answers.

THOUGHTFUL REPLY — TIME — CONTROL — COST

Better chance of thoughtful reply. The phone rings and an interviewer asks you to answer a few questions. You have a few minutes, and she sounds pleasant, so you don't mind obliging. She wants to know whether you watched TV during the past 48 hours, and the answer is that you did. Next she wants to know the stations you were tuned to and the programs you watched. You readily remember one or two of the half-dozen or more programs you watched, but you are not going to ask the interviewer to wait, while you try to recall all the shows which you watched yesterday and the night before. So the one or two easily recalled programs will be duly noted and the interview will continue.

A questionnaire which you get in the mail is different. You can throw it away (just as you can refuse to be interviewed), but if you decide to answer it, you'll do it at your leisure, you will have a chance to give it thought if thought is needed, and you can seek help from another member of the family if you get stuck. The big difference is that you do it at *your* convenience, and not when the interviewer happens to call on the phone or in person. In a survey conducted on TV viewing, radio listening, newspaper reading, and magazine reading, both mail survey and telephone interview methods were tested. The results agreed about the number of respondents who read, listened to, or watched these media, but there were many more programs, newspapers, and magazines listed on the mail questionnaires than on the phone interviews.

Time-saving. Using a single mailing and air mail both ways, a nationwide survey of a large sample distributed all over the United States can be completed in two weeks. (Usually this will get about 90 percent of all the returns which would come in if the survey were kept open longer. See "The Speed of Response" in the Appendix.) It is often impossible to get the results in two weeks by personal interviews. By the use of the mail technique, in 1970 the Bureau of Census expects "... better results, including a shortening of the period for collecting the data."[8] The time-savings can be even greater in international surveys.

Centralized control. Mail surveying can be done from one office, with built-in checks and controls for every phase of the operation. On a major personal interview job, hundreds of interviewers have to be instructed, supervised, and checked, with special controls by region, state, or city. It is much easier to keep the quality of data-gathering uniformly high by means of the centralized control possible in the mail survey.

Cost-saving resulting in more flexibility per dollar spent. The cost part of this point can be axiomatically stated: The services of mailmen in any state or country always cost less than those of interviewers of the same state or country. Obviously, not only is the time of the interviewer costly, but his training, briefing, supervision, and checking are expensive as well. On the other hand, the combined costs of a mailing piece, postage, and incentives offered to respondents are usually considerably less. Because of this difference in cost, on any given budget one can afford to produce a larger number of completed questionnaires through the mail method. As we shall see later, this will enable the researcher to have stable bases for various cross tabulations and special analyses, thereby greatly increasing the flexibility and usefulness of the survey.

LIMITATIONS ON THE USE OF MAIL SURVEYS—LIST PROBLEMS

In some cases the mail survey method is inappropriate, and at other times its uses are limited. A number of such situations are listed on the following page. Of course some of them may apply to other data-gathering methods as well.

1. No mailing list is available
2. The available mailing list is incomplete
3. The available mailing list is biased
4. Subject requires a specially trained interviewer
5. The questionnaire cannot be structured
6. The questionnaire is too long
7. The questionnaire is too difficult
8. The information required is confidential
9. The respondent is not the addressee
10. The available budget is inadequate
11. The available time is insufficient

Let us consider each of these points briefly.

No mailing list is available. If the research calls for a probability sample of the population of the United States, there is no readily available mailing list. To construct one (containing individual names) would be too expensive for most purposes. In some cases an acceptable, although more limited, substitute can be found, for example, a random sample of all persons listed in United States telephone directories, instead of a sample of the total United States population. If, however, no acceptable mailing list is available and the cost of creating one is prohibitive, the research cannot be conducted by mail.

The available mailing list is incomplete. Lack of individuals' names (as against names of companies), incomplete names, incomplete addresses, and the incompleteness and unreliability of old lists, all will result in an excessive number of undeliverable questionnaires or a higher rate of refusal. In some cases such incompleteness will make it impossible to conduct a reliable mail survey.

The available mailing list is biased. Lists can be biased either because they do not represent a proper sample of the universe or because they have previously been used for promoting an idea or distributing a product connected with the survey. Such a biased list will make it impossible to conduct meaningful research.

INTERVIEWER NEEDED—
QUESTIONNAIRE PROBLEMS

Subject requires a specially trained interviewer. In some types of surveys (for example, psychological motivation) the questioning may be the key to the whole research, and it may have to be done by a psychologist. Similar situations can arise in medicine and other specialized fields.

The questionnaire cannot be structured. In the case of depth interviews, where the information required from respondents cannot be structured, it is often impossible to construct a questionnaire. The interview has to take the form of a conversation between the respondent and a clever interviewer who is capable of drawing him out and getting a complete case history. In this situation a mail survey won't do.

The questionnaire is too long. In general we can say that a questionnaire that is longer than six to eight pages should be administered by a well-trained interviewer, who can keep the respondent going. Generally the percentage of response to a mailing falls off sharply when the questionnaire becomes too long. There are cases where respondents are willing to fill out ten- to twenty-page questionnaires and return them. These, however, usually concern the hobby or special interest of the group surveyed, as for example, a questionnaire on amateur radio sent to ham operators or one on cars sent to hot-rod fans.

The questionnaire is too difficult. It may not be possible to conduct a mail survey (and sometimes any other survey) if the questions and answers are too time-consuming or require too much concentration or checking of documents or consulting of other people. This is also true when an inventory is needed (such as a complete listing of the family medicine chest) and the researcher is reluctant to trust the respondent's thoroughness or even his willingness to do the job. In some other cases the "questionnaire" may include a whole kit; for instance, the issues of several publications in order to check the readership of their editorial or advertising contents. In many such situations an interviewer is needed to collect the data. There are questionnaires which are administered by personal interviewers because special explanations or a certain amount of prodding are needed to induce the respondent to give precise and complete answers. Up to a point, a good mail questionnaire can achieve these results by the careful sequence and phrasing of questions, instructions, and explanations. However, there is a point of complexity beyond which the printed word becomes ineffective, and an interviewer is needed.

The information required is confidential. If a company has a strict rule that its sales or purchasing figures are confidential, no survey will succeed in getting them. There are many types of classified or confidential information. If there is a strong possibility that some of the information requested is classified, a pilot study is certainly advisable so as to establish whether the survey can be done, or certain questions asked.

THE RESPONDENT — THE BUDGET — TIMING

The respondent is not the addressee. It can happen that a wife fills out the questionnaire addressed to her husband or an assistant or secretary completes a form for the boss. This problem can be minimized by specifying in the accompanying letter or on the questionnaire who the respondent should be: the person to whom the mailing was addressed, the head of the household, the president of the company, etc. To check on the size of such "pass-along" respondent groups, one may end the questionnaire with a simple question: "Are you the person to whom the envelope containing this questionnaire was addressed? Yes ☐ No ☐." The problem usually exists in questionnaires sent to home addresses, and in many such cases it makes little or no difference which adult member of the household answers the questionnaire. This is a minor consideration in the case of most surveys, but the researcher should keep it in mind, because on some specific piece of research it may become important.

The available budget is not adequate for a good (mail) survey. "Mail" is in parentheses here because this situation usually means that no reliable survey of any kind can be done. In such a case it is better not to do a poor job, but to save the research budget for another year or two, when there will be enough money to do an acceptable survey. If the available budget would limit the number of mailings, or the incentives used, or the size of the sample, or the amount of checking to such an extent as to impair the reliability of the research, it would be a waste of time and money to go ahead.

The available time is insufficient. If on a nationwide survey the researcher needs the answers in forty-eight hours, the job cannot be done by mail. Timing can be an important factor in deciding which data-gathering technique to use for a research project. In some situations a mail survey may be the fastest or most efficient method for data-gathering within the time available, while in other cases telephone or personal interviewing might do a quicker job.

The above list does not contain one factor which is often considered a shortcoming of mail surveys: the problem of nonrespondents. Many people using research fail to realize that this difficulty exists in connection with *all* types of data-gathering, whether it be personal interviews, telephone interviews, or mail surveys. Usually it is impossible to secure a completed interview from every member of a sample. This common difficulty of all research methods and its particular relevance to mail surveys will be discussed in a subsequent chapter.

REFERENCES

1. Raymond Franzen and Paul F. Lazarsfeld, "Mail Questionnaire as a Research Problem," *Journal of Psychology*, vol. 5, no. 20, p. 317, October, 1945.
2. Franklin B. Evans, "On Interviewer Cheating," *Public Opinion Quarterly*, vol. 25, no. 1, pp. 126, 127, spring, 1961.
3. W. Edwards Deming, "On Errors in Surveys," *American Sociological Review*, vol. 9, no. 4, p. 363, August, 1944.
4. Raymond Franzen and Paul F. Lazarsfeld, *op. cit.*, p. 319.
5. U.S. Department of Commerce, Bureau of the Census, "Planning Notes for 1970 Decennial Census," no. 1, p. 2, Mar. 17, 1966.
6. U.S. Department of Commerce, Bureau of the Census, "Effects of Interviewers and Crew Leaders," ser. ER–60, no. 7, pp. 1–91, 1968.
7. Paul F. Lazarsfeld and Raymond Franzen, "The Validity of Mail Questionnaires in Upper Income Groups," part II, *Time Research Report No. 950*, p. 9, May 15, 1946.
8. U.S. Department of Commerce, *op. cit.*, Mar. 17, 1966.

THREE
Types of Mail Surveys

THE FOLLOWING is a description of some of the principal uses of mail research:

1. In this country, the largest user of the mails for survey purposes is undoubtedly the United States government. The Census of Business, many other censuses and government surveys, and of course the decennial Census of Population, as is indicated in Chapter 1, are now conducted primarily by mail. Anyone conducting any type of research, by mail or otherwise, can benefit by knowing something about both the techniques and the findings of the United States census. The Bureau of the Census, United States Department of Commerce, is most helpful in answering inquiries and maintains libraries of the utmost usefulness to businessmen and researchers.

2. The sciences, and particularly the social sciences, make a great deal of use of mail surveys. They were used during the nineteenth century by Charles Darwin and Sir Francis Galton in England, and by the psychologist G. S. Hall in the United States.[1] Even in instances where an original investigation may have been conducted by

professional interviewers, the follow-ups are frequently conducted by mail. The data for professional and doctoral papers are often gathered by means of mail surveys.

3. Politics, especially in presidential and gubernatorial election years, is a great subject for surveys. Most of these are conducted by personal interview, but many are done through the mails.

4. Business and industry, under constantly increasing pressure for greater efficiency in management, production, and marketing, undoubtedly constitute the largest private users of mail research. Labor relations, materials and brand preferences, packaging, distribution, advertising, and public relations are some of the fields where mail surveys have proved useful.

The following are just a few of the many kinds of surveys used by business and industry which are, or may be, conducted by mail. Similar techniques are often used for surveys conducted by the government or in the field of science.

INDUSTRIAL AND CONSUMER SURVEYS

Industrial surveys are studies conducted among manufacturers, wholesalers, or dealers by suppliers of manufactured products designed for industrial use. These surveys seek to answer such questions as: How useful is the product? How does it compare with other brands of the same product? In what ways is it better? Are there some ways in which it fails to measure up to its competitors? How large is the market for this product? Is it expanding or contracting? What are its prospects for the future? This type of research can readily be done by mail, because most industrial suppliers and manufacturers have lists of customers and prospects which can easily be sampled for industrial mail surveys.

Concept testing by mail can often save time, effort, and money. By testing several concepts of proposed new products, services, sales, or promotion methods, the manufacturer or businessman may be able to eliminate the obvious losers and concentrate on the most acceptable propositions. Before checking the concepts it may not be obvious to the planners that some of the products or services planned will meet with resistance or complete indifference on the part of potential buyers or users, while others will be received enthusiastically. However, this is exactly what a carefully conducted concept test might show. Of course such tests are not always feasible; they are sometimes poorly planned and even when well done may not yield conclusive results.

Nevertheless, many leading firms have proved the value of such tests during years of using them. Often the greatest value of the concept test is a negative one: It may help to avoid a costly blunder. New concepts can be described in words or in pictures, using drawings or photographs.

Product testing is a logical "next step," after a successful concept test, in the chain of consumer surveys. Samples of products are mailed to representative groups of potential purchasers, and either with the product or after it has been used, or both times, a questionnaire is sent to the user.

Other types of consumer surveys are conducted among customers of stores, buyers who return warranty cards, various random samples of the population, etc. Satisfaction with products, reasons for buying, amount spent, how used, volume used, brand loyalty, brand switching, who in the family is the buyer, and who is the user represent some of the fields of investigation on consumer products. Services are researched in the same way: all phases of travel by plane, ship, train, or car; use of credit cards, hotels, and restaurants. Consumers and users can be surveyed by mail about anything they buy or use.

MEDIA STUDIES AND SURVEYS ON ADVERTISING

Media studies represent a very frequently used type of mail survey. Advertisers, their agencies, and the media themselves want to know who is reached by the medium, who reads the message, and, possibly, what the relationship is between the medium and the people it reaches. Publications often survey their subscribers and readers to find out their demographic characteristics, what they own or plan to buy, in what leisure-time activities they engage, their investments, the influence they wield in their businesses and their communities. Business, government, professional, and student groups are surveyed by mail to find out what they read and how thoroughly, what they watch on TV and how often, what they listen to on the radio and for how long.

Advertising efficiency is a frequent subject of mail research. Advertising copy or complete advertisements can be tested either by sending out several versions of the ad with a questionnaire or by sending a questionnaire to people in a controlled area shortly after they have had a chance to see or read the ad. For example, an airline wanted to test the effectiveness of two different newspaper ads. In several test cities the newspapers made a split run of the two ads and furnished the names of subscribers who received each. One day after the ad appeared, a questionnaire was sent to these subscribers, showing a copy of the appropriate advertising with the name of the company and some of the message blocked out. It was possible to establish the percentage of respondents from each section who recognized the ad, remembered the name of the company, and remembered some or all of the message. One of the two ads was easily the winner on all scores.

Another form of advertising research is the readership traffic study. Newspapers mail out a copy of a representative issue to a random sample of subscribers one day after the subscriber has received his regular copy of the same issue. The accompanying letter asks him to use an enclosed red pencil to mark every ad which he has seen in that particular issue and to return it. The resulting analysis—especially if the survey is continuous—can furnish valuable data on the effect of subject matter, size, position, presence or absence of illustration, and other variables upon the effectiveness of advertising appearing in the same paper.

Finally, in some cases advertising penetration and the effects of advertising can be checked by mail surveys aimed at determining, for example, the percentage of people who remembered various slogans or the percentage who were induced by some advertising in a medium to buy a product, or visit a show room, or save an ad, or just to discuss it with someone else. In addition to general questions on these subjects, one can ask for case histories. In a survey conducted for an industrial publication 2,000 questionnaires were mailed out, and 1,200 were completed and returned. One-third of these, or 400, contained case histories giving considerable detail on actions taken by subscribers as a result of reading the advertising. The publication published a report on the statistical findings of this research, but they also Xeroxed the 400 questionnaires with the case histories and used them to impress potential space buyers.

MULTIPLE SURVEYS AND PANELS

Dual- (*or multiple-*) *sample surveys* can be conducted within many of the types of mail research described. Usually such a survey simply involves the use of a control group; sometimes it is a matter of analyzing the problem from different points of view. The survey can be conducted among several groups of people—for example, users of a product, potential users and other nonusers, or subscribers to a publication versus a sample of the United States population.[2]

In an interesting survey of this type a random sample of the subscribers to *Harper's* and *The Atlantic* magazines was selected in each of twelve cities. The same questionnaire was mailed to these 1,500 subscribers and to their next-door (nonsubscriber) neighbors. The 80 percent return to the mailing was then analyzed for many of the comparative characteristics of the two groups surveyed. Among the differences were: Many more tennis players were found in subscriber than in the neighboring households; exactly the reverse situation held true with regard to people interested in hunting, the larger number being found among the nonsubscribers.[3]

If the budget allows the use of a control group or the surveying of a number of different groups of people, the findings can frequently furnish a deeper and more meaningful analysis of the group representing the central or most important universe of the research project.

Panels are often useful for conducting inexpensive mail surveys. Members of a panel agree in advance that they will answer questionnaires, the researcher has to establish the sample only once, and although establishing it is expensive, the costs are more than made up by further use of the panel. The percentage of response will always be high and the questionnaires will be well answered.[4] However, the researcher has to be very careful about a number of pitfalls.[5] Is the person who is willing to become the member of a panel really representative of those who are not? If he was a really representative random-sample type at the beginning, will he be able to keep his pristine randomness after he has answered half a dozen questionnaires, or will he mentally become an actor on a stage, with the self-conscious (and unrepresentative) answers of the professional respondent? The answers to these questions depend on how the panel was picked, how frequently it is surveyed, and how often its members are replaced. The length of time that consumers have been members of a panel often has an effect on their purchasing characteristics.[6] A German researcher refers to these changes in the behavior of panel members as the "Paneleffekt."[7]

Corporate-image studies, recognition surveys, and *"before-and-after" research* are other types of mail surveys often used by large companies. Because the many variations of this kind of survey pose special problems to the researcher, it is discussed more fully in Chapter 23.

The above includes only a sampler of the most commonly used mail survey types; the list could easily be doubled or trebled. Most types of mail surveys can be conducted among people abroad as well as among people living in the United States. International mail surveys will be described in Chapter 24.

"HYBRID" MAIL SURVEYS

Mail surveys can be further subdivided by whether they are conducted entirely by mail (that is, the researcher mails a questionnaire which is completed and returned by the respondent by mail) or combine mail with some other data-gathering procedure. The following are some commonly used "hybrid" approaches:

1. The questionnaire and instructions can be printed as a page of a magazine or newspaper, to be torn out and mailed in by the respondent. In another variation, a regular letter, questionnaire, and reply envelope can be prepared and inserted into a random sample of newsstand copies of a publication, to be mailed back by the respondent. The advantage of this procedure lies in its being able to reach newsstand buyers whose names and addresses are not known. The disadvantage concerns the percentage of response, which is usually low with this method of data-gathering.

2. The questionnaire (with or without separate letter and reply envelope) is distributed to a group of people who are asked by the distributor to mail it to a given address after completion. This often happens in cases where a company or institution agrees to have its employees, executives, or members surveyed but prefers to have the questionnaires distributed by a member of the organization rather than to furnish a mailing list. Occasionally, researchers use the personally distributed, returned-by-mail questionnaire, because it can result in a combination of high response and more carefully filled-out questionnaires. The self-administered questionnaire is filled out at leisure, whenever the respondent has the time to concentrate, think, or look up requested data. The Survey Research Center of the University of Michigan conducted a very interesting experimental research project comparing the accuracy of this data-gathering method with that of personal interviews. The conclusion stated in part: "When one is trying to obtain information for which records may be available or which other members of the respondent's family may have, a self-enumerative procedure yields more accurate information."[8]

3. In connection with product testing, the questionnaire may be attached to a product package, with instructions to the respondent to fill it out and mail it back after trying the product.

4. One can combine several data-gathering procedures for the sake of a high percentage of completion and validation. The researcher can start with a mail survey, mail a follow-up questionnaire to nonrespondents, continue with telephone interviews among nonrespondents to the follow-up mailing, send personal interviewers to the

telephone nonrespondents, and finally, try to get demographic and other available data about the hard core of nonrespondents from credit-checking or similar firms. Another application of this combining method was used in a research project where the data-gathering in general was done by personal interviewers. Wherever a respondent was unable to answer questions relating to other household members not present at the time of the interview, the interviewer left a questionnaire and a stamped reply envelope for each adult about whom additional information was requested.[9]

REFERENCES

1. Christopher Scott, "Research on Mail Surveys," *Journal of the Royal Statistical Society*, vol. 124, part 2, pp. 143–205, read before the Society on Feb. 15, 1961.
2. Arthur J. Morgan, "One Way to Define the Unique Qualities of Audiences," *Media/Scope*, vol. 9, no. 5, pp. 66–76, May, 1965.
3. "The People Next Door," research report of the Harper Atlantic Sales Corp., pp. 1–56, 1962; also "The People Next Door Revisited," a sequel, 1968.
4. Robert C. Nuckols, "Personal Interview versus Mail Panel Survey," *Journal of Marketing Research*, vol. 1, no. 1, pp. 11–16, February, 1964.
5. Paul F. Lazarsfeld, "'Panel' Studies," *Public Opinion Quarterly*, vol. 4, no. 2, March, 1940.
6. Donald G. Morrison, Ronald E. Frank, and William F. Massy, "A Note on Panel Bias," *Journal of Marketing Research*, vol. 3, no. 1, pp. 85–88, February, 1966.
7. Gerhard Merk, "*Wissenschaftliche Marktforschung*," Dunker u. Humblod, Berlin, 1962, p. 72.
8. Charles F. Cannell and Floyd J. Fowler, "Comparison of a Self-enumerative Procedure and a Personal Interview: A Validity Study," *Public Opinion Quarterly*, vol. 27, no. 2, pp. 250–264, summer, 1963.
9. Harry Sharp, "The Mail Questionnaire as a Supplement to the Personal Interview," *American Sociological Review*, no. 20, p. 718, 1955.

FOUR
Survey Design

EVERY RESEARCH MAN must have had the experience of being called to the office of Mr. Big Brass and told that the company needed more information in some area, and "Please let me know this afternoon how long it will take you to make a survey and how much it will cost." As often as not, no one has really thought through the whole problem, and the research man will need all his diplomacy and patience to guide management into a clear definition of the objectives of the proposed research. The following steps are the logical and essential parts of survey design:

1. Outlining the problem
2. Definition of research objectives
3. Investigating existing research on the same problem or with the same objectives
4. Definition of the universe
5. Deciding on the degree of reliability aimed at within a realistic budget

6. Definition of the sample and scope
7. Deciding on the survey method
8. Deciding who will conduct the survey
9. Establishing the techniques that will be needed to achieve the research objectives
10. Outlining the type of tabulation, analysis, and report desired
11. Timing
12. Cost estimate

PROBLEMS — OBJECTIVES — UNIVERSE

Outlining the problem. Researchers can do a much better job if they are familiar with the entire problem, not just with the immediate research objectives. If a company is considering a market study for a group of products, what is the problem that made someone think of the study? Do they want to enter this market? If they are in it now, do they want a bigger share? Are they thinking of a new product? Of changing their product? Knowing the complete background will enable the researcher to raise and answer a whole set of further questions, such as: Will a survey make a real contribution toward solving the problem? If so, to what extent? What is the best time and place for conducting the survey? Are we talking about a single survey or about a research project involving a series of surveys?

Definition of the research objectives. In a market research project, management may have very general problems. A top executive of one of the large United States corporations once stated: "Management should never assign to research a problem as vague as 'How can I get a bigger share of the market at a larger profit?'"[1] Research objectives should be specific and well defined. Such definition can be best formulated by listing a series of questions the researcher should try to answer; for example, Who are the main users of the product? How do they use it? How often? What is the usual quantity used? What are the sources of supply? How often is it bought and in what quantities? How much do they pay for various unit sizes? The first list of objectives should include all desired goals. It is the research man's job to pare the list down to the attainable objectives. There is often some very desirable information which research cannot provide at any cost and this is the time to identify and stop "dream projects." It is also important at this point to discuss with those who will ultimately use the survey results, just *what* use they will make of them. The answer to this question will influence most of the following survey design decisions, because how the findings are to be used will determine the kind of survey results needed and the way they will be obtained and presented.

Investigating existing research on the same problem or with the same objectives. Is there any published or otherwise available research report on the same or related problems or objectives? Perhaps other companies or organizations have been faced with similar problems and published their findings. If so, is there anything in either the procedure or the results which can be utilized or from which a lesson can be learned? In every field where research is used there are associations or organizations that maintain libraries which can be consulted. For example, in the field of marketing research one can consult the library files of the American Marketing Association, the Advertising Research Foundation, the Marketing Communications Research Center, and the International Advertising Association. Of course if the researcher does find a report which seems to include useful information, he should carefully examine who did the work, what the limitations of the study and its findings were, and just how relevant (in timing, subject, scope, etc.) its results are to the present problem.

Definition of the universe. This is often a difficult problem. If we are interested in a political candidate's chances, what is the best group to survey: Registered voters? Potential voters? People who can influence public opinion? Political leaders? Political pundits? If we are interested in a consumer product, who is important, or most important, in influencing its sales: The member of the family who actually uses it? Another member, who usually buys it? The third member who approves the expenditure? The dealers who carry, display, and sell it? The survey can be worthless unless the universe is clearly defined.

RELIABILITY—SAMPLE AND SCOPE

Deciding on the degree of reliability aimed at within a realistic budget. The perfect survey would be a census which collected complete information from every single member of the universe. This is usually impossible. However, within the range of possibilities the researcher may consider various methods and various degrees of reliability. A survey costing $50,000 might be more complete and more reliable than a survey costing $3,000, but the researcher will have wasted most of his money if the additional completeness and reliability do not increase the usefulness of his result. On the other hand, money spent on an unreliable and incomplete project can be a complete waste. This is the point in the planning where the researcher has to think of the amount of information needed and the method, scope, desired stability, and representativeness of the survey. There are minimum requirements for an adequate survey and optimum possible goals for excellent research, and the budget will usually be a major factor in deciding where to compromise between maximum and minimum aims. Compromises can usually be made on many of the survey specifications, but they should never go beyond the minimum objectives to be achieved or the degree of completeness and reliability required by the problem.

Definition of the sample and scope. This is related to a number of the other steps in the survey design, and it is discussed in detail in Chapter 5. The definition of the universe, the stability desired for the ultimate analysis of the data, the survey methods used, and the available budget are all important considerations in deciding on the size and nature of the sample. The sampling methods used for mail surveys are usually much simpler than those used for personal interviews, because it is comparatively simple to select a random sample from a universe consisting of a list of individuals whose names and addresses are available.

TECHNIQUES OF DATA-GATHERING AND DATA-PROCESSING

Deciding on the survey method. The nature of the universe and the research objectives will be the most important factors in making this decision, but it will also be influenced by the budget and by the advantages and limitations of various data-gathering methods. The advantages and limitations of mail surveys are listed in Chapter 2.

Deciding who will conduct the survey. Can the company which needs the research conduct the survey? If not, what should be the criteria for evaluating the competence of various research organizations? Which organization has had the most experience in researching similar problems and using similar methods? Are their costs in line with the degree of their experience and competence?

Establishing the techniques that will be needed to achieve the research objectives. If the decision is to conduct a mail survey with a 65 percent response, what steps will be needed? Do we need an advance postcard, one or two follow-up mailings, any incentive or validation? Can we get all the questions on one questionnaire, or will we need a split mailing, each group receiving a shorter questionnaire with only some of the questions? Very often it is impossible to predict the solutions to some or all of these problems, and the researcher will have to conduct a pilot study before he can complete his planning.

Outlining the type of tabulation, analysis, and report desired. Often it is impossible to work out the technique and costs of a survey or even to construct the questionnaire before knowing in just what form the results will have to be presented. It is very desirable to make up dummy tables at this early stage of the planning. For one thing, the researcher will systematize his own thinking and possibly remember some questions which were overlooked before, or he may find that some questions will have to be asked in a very specific way in order to give the kinds of answers or breaks he needs for his tables. He may also find that he needs cross tabulations, which will affect the size of his sample (see Chapter 5). He may find that the amount of tabulation and calculation required by the projected analysis will result in considerable expenditures, to be reckoned with in his budgeting. He may find that tabulating, calculating, report writing and report-processing operations will raise timing problems. He may decide that he will have to use a statistician and a chartmaker for a more thorough analysis and presentation. It may occur to him that different reports will be needed for different departments of his firm.

TIMING AND COST ESTIMATING

At this point the researcher should set up his timetable. Each operation should be listed in detail, and sufficient time allocated for each. A large percentage of all surveys are poorly done simply because not enough time was allocated for proper completion and then checking of one or more operations. An inadequate (or nonexistent) timetable can also play havoc with the cost estimate if, at the end, inefficient methods or overtime work will have to be used in order to finish the job by a certain date.

The cost estimate should be the last step in the survey design, because it will be affected by all the other considerations. In a way this cost estimate represents a midpoint between a very general idea of the size of the available budget (often referred to as the "ball park"), which has to be established before too much planning can be done, and a firm commitment, which in many cases can be made only after a pilot study.

In general, the good researcher will carefully think through every step of a survey before actually taking one. The greatest help he can have in this planning is a pilot study.

REFERENCES

1. Andrew Heiskell, "The Role of Marketing Research in Today's Business Management," *Marketing and Transportation Paper No. 1*, Bureau of Business and Economic Research, Michigan State University, 1958, pp. 1–21.

FIVE
Mailing Lists and Notes on Sampling

IN ORDER TO DO A MAIL SURVEY, we must have a mailing list. If the survey is a census, the mailing list will contain the name and address of every member of the universe (population), such as an association whose membership is to be surveyed. If the research problem concerns a large universe, it is usually not necessary to survey every member of the population; a relatively small sample of the total may be adequate for the purposes of the study. Sampling procedures will be discussed later in this chapter, but whether or not sampling is used, a mailing list will be needed, if the data-gathering is to be done by mail.

Mailing lists can take many forms. They may consist of handwritten warranty cards, subscriber names on paper tapes taken from the galleys of publications, association membership lists, and so forth. Often they take the form of computer printouts, interpreted punch cards, or addressographed or typed cards. For most research projects it is advisable to have the names and addresses on cards, preferably punch cards.

Card lists have the following advantages:

1. If the list consists of punched cards, it may be possible to in-

clude additional information such as state, sex, demographic data, SIC code (Standard Industrial Classification), and size of business in them. By serializing the mailing cards and keying the questionnaires the researcher can reproduce the mailing data on the questionnaire card. In many cases this may shorten the questionnaire, since respondents need not be asked for data already available from the mailing list.

2. The same operation can be performed even though the information is only printed or typed on the list cards and not punched. In these cases the available information will be transferred to the returned questionnaires and punched like the actual answers. The advantage of the card list for this purpose is the fact that the coder can pull out the card with the matching serial number and copy the data onto the questionnaire. The margin of error will be less than it would be by copying from a large sheet of names and figures.

3. Even if no additional data are available or needed, card lists will facilitate checking counts for total mailing, for geographic distribution, or for any grouping required by the research plan. Blank punch cards are preferable to 3- by 5-in. cards, even if no information has been punched into them, because they can be counted by card sorters in a fraction of the time a hand count would take.

4. Card lists save time and reduce the margin of error in the case of follow-up mailings. It is a good practice to "pull" daily returns of every multiple-mailing survey; this simply means finding the mailing card of every respondent and pulling it from the deck. The card can be identified by the name of the respondent, if it appears on the questionnaire, or by the key number in the case of keyed mailings.

TYPES OF MAILING LISTS

After the researcher has made his decisions on survey design, his toughest job may be to find the proper list. He must start with a complete, or at least representative, list of his universe; it must be a recent, that is, an up-to-date list, and it must be available when he needs it at a cost which he can afford. The following are some of the frequently used types of mailing lists:

1. The most nearly complete listings of the populations of cities and those which yield the best cross sections for samples are contained in the city directories published by R. L. Polk & Co. and others. However, recent editions of these directories are available for only a limited number of cities, and old addresses are not very useful, because of the great mobility of the United States population.

2. Telephone directories represent a wider distribution in the

geographic sense, but also a significant restriction, because the names they include are limited to people with listed telephone numbers and lack correct information on recent movers. There are firms, such as O. E. McIntyre, Inc., which have computerized lists of United States telephone-listed names.

3. Records published by federal, state, and municipal governments often include lists of the names and addresses of people in various groups. For example, the Department of Commerce has a long list of publications which can furnish mailing list sources for many types of research. Voter registration records may be useful where available.

4. Lists and rating books can be purchased from such organizations as Dun & Bradstreet and the Credit Rating Bureau. These can be valuable for surveys among the business and industrial population and for lists of various socioeconomic or occupational groups.

5. Business and trade directories of various kinds, such as Poor's, Thomas's, and various Dun & Bradstreet directories and lists are available. There are directories containing names of companies, such as department-store lists, published by Sheldon and other publishers.

6. Associations, organizations, and clubs often publish lists which can be acquired by the researcher. These can be of use in samples for surveys among professional and other specific, limited, but on occasion, very important groups.

7. Names of subscribers to various publications are sometimes available to the researcher, especially if he happens to work for an important advertiser.

8. Mailing list houses, such as Dunhill, National Business Lists, and W. S. Ponton sell wide varieties of lists, and these are usually kept up to date to some extent. It is good practice to try to get from list houses all available information on the sources and coverage of their lists.

9. Customers and prospects of the sponsoring organization may be sampled for the survey. The sponsor may also persuade other companies which are interested in the results of the survey to contribute their lists of customers or prospects to be sampled. For example the *Oil and Gas Journal* has sponsored biennial surveys among a random sample of the best customers of large corporations which cater to the petroleum industry. These best-customer lists from a number of leading firms (with duplications eliminated) represent an important specific segment of industry, which cannot easily be defined and sampled in any other way. It also comprises a "live" list of people interested in the petroleum industry, as shown by the approximately 80 percent response rate to these surveys.

These are only some of the sources of lists. A detailed catalog of a number of mailing list sources can be found in such publications as the "Directory of Mailing List Houses" published by the B. Klein Company of New York.

The researcher should always aim at acquiring lists which include the names of individuals, and not just the names and addresses of companies or institutions. If we address the mailing to the "Acero Steel Corporation," no individual will feel responsible for answering it. If it is addressed to the purchasing agent or to the president of the company, it is more likely that it will be answered. However, for the best chance of receiving a completed questionnaire we should know the addressee's name and send the questionnaire to "Robert E. Jones, Purchasing Agent, Acero Steel Corporation," etc. Often lists which include the names of individuals are not available. In such cases it may even be worth the time, effort, and money to make a preliminary survey by mail or telephone to determine the names of persons who fill various positions included in the sample design. The Western Union Company has handled a number of such assignments over the telephone.

FRAME BIAS

Unless a census is to be conducted, only a sample of the total population need be surveyed. In these cases the list of names represents the "frame" of the survey; that is, it physically designates every element in the universe. In mail surveys, sample bias (as distinct from sampling error) is often a result of an imperfection of the total list from which the sample was taken. This constitutes frame bias, and it can be one of the most serious flaws in survey design. The following are some of the common causes of such bias:

1. The frame which is being sampled (or, in the case of a census being used in its entirety) is not what it is supposed to be. For example, the frame is a list supposedly comprising registered architects (and *only* registered architects) but actually includes the names of some people who are *not* registered architects.

2. The frame from which the sample is being taken is incomplete and therefore does not represent the universe. In the above example it would not contain the names of *all* registered architects. Usually there is no way of telling how these factors affect the sample; perhaps the largest or the smallest architectural firms are omitted; perhaps the omissions mean that the designers of institutional buildings are underrepresented or overrepresented.

3. The frame (list of names and addresses) is too old. Again all kinds of bias can result: some architects on the list may have died, and some recently registered architects may not yet be included. Others will not receive the questionnaire because they have moved—this may decrease the number of architects who work on specific kinds of projects involving mobility.

4. All or part of the list has been published or sold often for purposes of surveys, promotions, or sales efforts. This will not only reduce the percentage of response, but it may also introduce bias. In our example there may be special groups of architects (such as the most famous ones or the ones building the largest projects) who are approached with particular frequency and who, therefore, will be least willing to answer a questionnaire.

5. Another possibility of error which is often ignored is the duplication of names within the sample. This usually occurs when several lists are merged. In our example of registered architects, the universe may have been established by merging the registration lists of the fifty states. Since an architect can be registered in more than one state, his name may appear several times unless someone has thought of this possibility and eliminated duplications.

These five types of frame bias represent only some of the most common problems. Every survey must be scrutinized at the planning stage to guard against the possibility of such biases.

SAMPLING

A sample is a part of a population selected by some process. There is no reason to survey all people of voting age in the United States in order to conduct a presidential poll, if satisfactory results can be achieved by surveying a sample comprising thousands, rather than the universe which consists of millions of persons. The problem is to define what we call "satisfactory results": exactly how many people are to be included in the "thousands" and how to select them in order to get the desired results. This brings us to the questions of sampling and sampling design.

Statistical sampling may be defined as a process of selecting a segment of the universe to obtain information of ascertainable reliability about the population.

On any survey where information of ascertainable reliability is desired, the errors and variances have to be controlled, measured, and interpreted. For example, if we need a probability sample of all people listed in United States telephone directories and the research plan calls for a relatively small sample which is projectable to the whole universe, we have to start with a plan involving 150 to 300 sampling points, with the statistical knowledge needed to create the sample and precise instructions for using it.

It is beyond the scope of this book to describe such procedures. It is a job for trained statisticians to plan and supervise sample design and sampling operations. While there are many good books on sampling theory (see Appendix), you cannot expect to become a sampling expert just by reading them, just as you cannot become a surgeon by reading a book on anatomy.

Survey sampling has two basic rules: (1) Some acceptable procedures should be used in the selection; and (2) every unit of the universe should have a known chance to be selected.

For mail surveys conducted as part of market research, a very commonly used method is systematic sampling. It usually means using every nth name of the frame. If the list comprises 7,000 names and we want to select a sample of 1,000, the systematic sample will consist of every seventh name on the list. Normally such a sample will represent the universe in every respect: geographic distribution, age, sex, and so on.

One thing to avoid, especially in the case of published lists or of lists purchased from list houses, is to start with the first name and continue with an obvious interval, such as every tenth name or every name starting a page in a directory. There is a chance that others have used the list in the same way and that this may make the sample less responsive or less representative.

To avoid problems of this kind, some researchers prefer the lengthier system of numbering the names in the frame and using a table of random numbers for sample selection. A compromise is to do systematic sampling, starting with a name selected by taking a number from a table of random numbers.

There are many types of mistakes people can make by not following sampling specifications. In one case the sample plan called for a systematic sample of 5,000 from a universe of 50,000. When the researcher checked the sample, he noticed that the state of Wisconsin (and others at the end of the alphabet) were not represented. Upon investigation it turned out that the sampling was done by hand from 3- by 5-in. cards. The clerks doing it decided that it was too boring to count 50,000 cards in order to take every tenth; they just pulled cards by estimating the distance. They were a little off, the cards were in alphabetic order by state, and so they had completed the selection of the 5,000 names when they got to the state of Washington.

The next example brings us to the computer age. On a survey conducted for a mass publication the sampling plan called for two matching systematic samples of 10,000 subscribers. The sampling instructions specified every nth name had to be selected for such a sample. Part of the survey design called for separate analysis for a number of large states and of a number of metropolitan areas. Checking the sample, an alert research man discovered that although the number of names seemed to be correct for each state and metropolitan area, of the two matching random subsamples of the New York Metropolitan Area, one had no addresses from Manhattan and Brooklyn, while the other failed to include any inhabitant of the Bronx or Queens. The resulting investigation showed that all subscriber names were computerized. The programmer had wanted to simplify his job, and so instead of writing a program for two matching samples, he wrote one for a single sample and then divided it improperly.

In general it is good practice to check the sample against some known distribution of the universe. For example, in checking a random sample of the subscribers to a given publication, a tabulation of the state-distribution percentages can be compared with published ABC (Audit Bureau of Circulation) figures.

SAMPLE SIZES

A crucial issue in every mail survey design is the sample size. The sample should be large enough to permit estimates sufficiently precise to serve the research needs, while it should be small enough to fit the available budget.

If we get answers from all members of a known universe, there is no need for sampling, and consequently there is no sampling error. The moment we select a sample, we are introducing sampling error. The advantage of a random (or probability) sample is the fact that this error is measurable. The measurement and control of sampling error is part of the sampling design established by statisticians.

People with little or no experience in statistics or market research often think that there is magic in large numbers. There isn't, and once we decide that we have reduced the sampling error to a level which is acceptable for the purposes of our survey, we can worry about the more dangerous sources of error, such as sample bias or questionnaire bias or unrepresentative returns. The fact that a survey is based on a comparatively small number of questionnaires does not necessarily mean that it is poor; conversely, very large numbers do not guarantee excellence.

Sampling can become more complicated if the sample is to be stratified. We may need a random sample of several groups of a universe because we want to survey each group separately or because we require a disproportionately large representation of a small but important group. Suppose we want to survey the existing market for an industrial product. The market is represented by 10,000 firms who are actual users of this product, but 500 of the 10,000 companies account for 80 percent of the yearly volume used. We may decide to survey all 500 major users and only a relatively small sample of the others. We may, in some cases, end up with a large number of groups (cells), representing various random samples, which must be weighted when showing combined results so that each may be properly represented in the total.

CONSIDERATIONS BASED ON RESPONSE

Up to now we have been discussing a random sample of names and their selection. The difficulty in establishing samples for mail surveys arises from the fact that we cannot expect an answer from every person whose name has appeared in our random selection. This in turn means that the actual number of questionnaires which we will be able to analyze will be less than the number in the original sample and that it will lose some of the "randomness" which makes sampling error mathematically measurable.

Once we start thinking in terms of responses rather than in terms of the original sample or mailout, we have four inevitable considerations:

1. What percentage of response can we expect? The problem of a representative percentage of response and of the nonrespondent bias will be described in Chapter 15. For the purpose of establishing sample size we have to estimate the percentage of response, and we have to assume that it will be a representative response, with the smallest number of nonrespondents the available budget will allow.

2. What subgroups will we have because of the nature of the survey? For example, if the subject of the survey is the leisure-time activities of a given population, there may be a number of questions on boating, to be asked of boat owners. Of a total of 1,000 respondents only 200 are boat owners, and this means that our subsample of boat owners is 200. This subsample was established by the filter question: "Do you own a boat? Yes ☐   No ☐." Subsequent questions on boats were asked only of people who checked "Yes," while nonowners

were filtered out by their negative answers. If we have a number of filter questions in our questionnaire, or even filters within filters, the subgroups may become quite small. For example, we may want to ask a number of questions of the owners of sailboats, who may represent only one-third of the boat owners.

3. What kind of analysis do we plan to make? What will be the smallest group we will need for cross tabulations? We may consider the 1,000 sample which we have discussed as quite adequate, and we may even decide that the 200 boat owners represent a large enough group; but suppose the survey plans call for an analysis by the nine United States census districts and then for an analysis by sex within each of these geographic groups. Now we are no longer talking about 1,000 or 200, but about one-eighteenth of each group, which will obviously represent an inadequate sample and will mean that we must choose between enlarging the sample and giving up the idea of the cross tabulations.

4. What kind of stability do we want for our total tabulation, for the tabulations of each type of answer, and for the smallest cells in our cross tabulations? In the case of a very high response, statisticians can calculate the sampling error fairly closely. Of course this involves more than just consulting tables of sampling tolerances.[1] In the case of most surveys the sample size must be decided after considering the four points just discussed, but we have to remember that all our decisions will be based on a hypothesis. We will have to assume that whatever percentage of response we consider adequate will be representative of the whole sample. If everyone were to answer the survey, the sampling error could be calculated without any trouble. The larger the percentage of nonresponse, the further away we are from the randomness of the original sample, and the less meaningful it will be to "calculate" sampling errors by methods devised for random samples.

For practical purposes we can assume that the response is still a random sample and that we can calculate the chance deviation for each answer or group of answers. What we get this way is an indication of the *negative:* We can be sure that everything found wanting by this method will certainly *not* be adequate for stability. We can only assume that what we *do* consider stable enough will really be stable and that such variables as sample bias, some bias in the letter and questionnaire, or nonrepresentativeness of responses have not corrupted the pristine purity of our random sample beyond redemption. The fact is that surveying by any method is not a pure science. We can approximate the truth by eliminating or at least measuring statistical errors of the sample, but we can never really measure intangibles, such as a man's mood when answering our questions. This is not saying that a well-conducted mail survey is not useful or reliable; it is merely a caveat that in some published surveys the detailed analysis of the sampling error tends to obscure the fact that such error is only one of many considerations to be taken into account in judging mail surveys, or any other surveys. This was expressed in concise terms by Dr. Rex V. Brown: "Usually in market research the total error in practical survey findings is not assessed. Classical confidence intervals are used to explain random sampling fluctuations, but often the intervals are minor sources of error compared with errors of measurement, non-response or frame bias." In his article this author discusses statistical assessments of the total survey error.[2]

REFERENCES

1. W. Edwards Deming, *Some Theory of Sampling*, John Wiley & Sons, Inc., New York, 1950, p. 10.
2. Rex V. Brown, "Evaluation of Total Survey Error," *Journal of Marketing Research*, vol. 4, 117–127, May, 1967.

SIX
Questionnaire Construction
What to Include and How to Get Answers

A GOOD QUESTIONNAIRE appears as easy to compose as does a good poem. The end product should look as if effortlessly written by an inspired child—but it is usually the result of long, painstaking work. The amateur researcher will often "construct" a four-page questionnaire in a few hours. For a professional research house this usually represents a week's work by several experienced people.

The following are the main considerations in questionnaire construction:

1. The questionnaire must include questions on all subjects which are essential to the project; it should contain all the important questions on these subjects, but none which are not purposeful.

2. The questionnaire should appear brief and "easy to complete." Reading it should not destroy this first impression.

3. The reader must be made to feel that he is participating in an important and interesting project.

4. The form should not contain any questions which could bias the answers.

5. It must be designed to elicit clear and precise answers to all questions.

6. Phrasing, structure, and layout must be designed with the problems of tabulating in mind. The saving of time and money in data-processing should be one of the considerations.

COMPLETENESS AND RELEVANCE

Once the returns are in, it is too late to realize that the answers would be more meaningful if we could cross tabulate them by income, occupation, or some other vitally important question which we forgot to include in the questionnaire.

It is helpful to start by making up a list containing all possible subjects which we want to ask about and then paring down this maximum list to the really essential items. Next we can use the same procedure within each subject: list the maximum number of questions which could be asked in connection with that subject and then cross out the ones which are not absolutely relevant or necessary. This compromise between desirable completeness and practical considerations of length must precede all other steps before we can organize the subjects in the best possible sequence, arrange the questions within subjects similarly, phrase the questions, and evaluate the resulting draft by all the criteria discussed in this chapter.

Basically, the subjects to be included in the questionnaire should have been selected at the time the survey design was established. However, now is the time for the questionnaire writer to decide what is absolutely necessary and to think of all possible omissions. Have we included all relevant classification data, such as sex, marital status, family composition, education, line of business or profession, title, and income? If we ask these questions in the form of checklists, are the groupings (such as income brackets) comparable with existing government and other data on the same subjects? Could any further questions clarify the answers to some of the questions already formulated or make them more meaningful? Could any question be omitted because the resulting information will duplicate or overlap data gathered with the help of other questions on the questionnaire? The only questions which deserve space without yielding useful answers are introductory questions or, rarely, questions designed to avoid possible bias, both described later.

We now have the main components which will go into our questionnaire. Only now can we start the actual construction of the form itself. Our aim is to get the maximum amount of reliable and useful data. To achieve this aim, we must be sure that the people who receive the questionnaire will look at it, read it, complete it in the most accurate and unbiased way possible, and then return it.

THE "SHORT AND EASY" LOOK

No matter how good the accompanying letter or how attractive the incentive, a forbidding questionnaire containing too many pages of small type will draw very few replies. We are really talking about two concepts: How the questionnaire *looks* and how it *reads*. When, after having read the letter, the prospective respondent picks up the questionnaire and looks at it, he should take a pencil or pen and start answering. This goal can be achieved if the questionnaire doesn't *appear* too difficult or time-consuming or, on the positive side, if it looks easy to fill out. Having gotten him started, the next step is to keep the respondent going. This can be done if the questions are easy to read, easy to answer, and not too boring. The last point will be discussed later.

"Easy looks" for a questionnaire involve format, layout, and printing.

Size. In general the rule to remember is that the shorter and smaller the questionnaire, the "easier" it looks. Of course this is true only when all else is equal—you will not get better returns by using small type or skimpy margins and crowding too many questions on a small bit of paper. A normally designed questionnaire of monarch size (7 by 10 in.) can generally be expected to produce a higher percentage of returns than one which is letterhead size (8½ by 11 in.) and the letterhead size will get a higher percentage of response than a legal-sized sheet (8½ by 14 in.).

Number of pages. Rule of thumb: The fewer the pages, the higher the percentage of return. Of course this is a general rule, again assuming that all else is equal. The author has received a 75 percent return to a 12-page questionnaire; its subject matter happened to be of great interest to the special group receiving it since it concerned their hobby. Normally, a four- (or maximum six-) page questionnaire that is 8½- by 11-in. can be considered the upper limit in length. There is of course a strong interrelation between size and number of pages. Often a monarch-sized or somewhat smaller four-pager will draw as good a response as an 8½- by 11-in. two-pager. In the experience of the author there is little justification for using the narrow booklet form. A letterhead-sized four-pager will draw better than an eight-page booklet of half that width. This may have something to do with the "psychology" of answering, discussed later in connection with the accompanying letter. A booklet will surely look less personal and more commercial than flat pages.

Illustrations. These should be used *only* when they can help clarify or shorten questions. Figure 1 shows a page from a questionnaire sent out by the Bureau of the Census as an example of the appropriate use of pictures. As purely decorative elements they usually do more harm than good, and it is preferable to save the space and have fewer pages, smaller pages, or to leave more white space on the page. Illustrated questionnaires look too much like advertisements and have a very good chance of being taken for such when the addressee opens the envelope. In such a case the whole mailing may be thrown away as "junk mail" before the letter has had a chance to be read. Some years ago a well-known magazine mailed 5,000 questionnaires on the subject of travel to a sample of its subscribers. It was a four-page questionnaire. The first page had no copy at all: it was a photograph of a happy family romping on the beach. The next three pages, printed on fine, coated stock, contained the questions which were illustrated with amusing little line drawings on various aspects of travel. The mailing resulted in a 15 percent return. This was obviously unsatisfactory. The company drew another random sample of 5,000 subscribers and mailed out a two-page questionnaire, without any photo or illustrations, containing the same questions as the first one. It drew a 51 percent return. On some occasions pictures may be helpful, but their use as ornament is not justified.

PAPER AND PRINTING

Color. Again, because of the resemblance to junk mail, colored stock should be avoided. Occasionally there is a need to differentiate between sample groups, and in these cases the light colors, such as ivory, eye-ease green, light yellow, and light buff are recommended, both because they are easy to read and because they are the least conspicuous.

Paper. The stock used should be pleasant to look at, substantial to handle, thick enough to be printed on both sides without showing through, light enough to fit within the planned weight of the mailing piece, suitable for writing on with pen or pencil, and hardy enough to take some handling in tabulating. Very light, opaque stock should be used for research conducted entirely by air mail and especially for international surveys, where the difference in weight can mean the

② Which one of the following best describes this building? *(The example drawn for each choice may not show your house exactly; it is given only to describe the TYPE of building.)*

1 ☐ Single-family detached house (1, 2, or 3 story) including split-level and ranch type homes..........

2 ☐ Two-family house, over and under duplex..........

3 ☐ Two-family house, side-by-side duplex..........

4 ☐ Row house, end unit.

5 ☐ Row house, inner or center unit.......

6 ☐ Three-family house..........

7 ☐ Other – *Specify* _____

8 ☐ Trailer

9 ☐ Apartment in building with 4 or more apartments

If you marked box 8 or 9, SKIP TO ITEM 12 ON PAGE 4; OTHERWISE CONTINUE WITH ITEM 3.

FIGURE 1 Questionnaire page with illustrations.

difference between 25¢ and 50¢ postage per mailing. Here are a few recommendations:

For letterpress:	20–lb bond
For offset:	60–lb offset
For overseas air mail:	14–lb opaque bond

Method of printing. The questionnaire should look professional but not slick. This means that one should not use mimeographed sheets, but ordinarily there is no need to use the most expensive paper or printing. The choice is usually between letterpress printing and offset printing from Varityped copy or from a typed original.

Typesetting is quite expensive. It is recommended only for very crowded questionnaires, when the extreme sharpness of set type makes a fifty-line page appear somehow less crowded. Some flexibility is gained by using several type sizes. The choice of type is a matter of taste. Of the commonly used type faces Times Roman is the author's preference both for legibility and appearance. The best type size is 10-point for general copy, dropping, if space is needed, to 9-point for checklist lines. Column heads may be in 8-point, and section headings in 8-point bold caps (Fig. 2). The advantages of the Varityper used in conjunction with offset printing is that it saves typesetting and that various type sizes and styles are available.

Possibly the best combination for cost and result is to offset questionnaires from a variable-space, carbon-ribbon typewriter copy (Fig. 3). Column headings may be reduced by photostat and pasted in. The cost is low, and the questionnaire looks very much as though it had been set in type. In the case of a long questionnaire, the typing should be done on a larger sheet which can be reduced to 8½ by 11 in., just as 8½ by 11 in. can be reduced to Monarch size and still be very legible. It is important not to use too small type, as this tends to make the questionnaire look difficult. Caution is recommended in using narrow or unusual typefaces. Too many different type sizes or faces can also make a questionnaire look too "busy" and therefore difficult.

Unlike questionnaires for personal interview, which are usually printed on only one side of the paper for the convenience of the interviewer, *mail* questionnaires more than one page long should always be printed on both sides. A four-page questionnaire should be a folded sheet to be opened and read like a newspaper. A six-page questionnaire can have the same format, with the extra page glued or stapled in. Occasionally the layout may require that a six-page questionnaire be printed on a wide sheet, folded twice, and opened either like an accordion or folded out from the center. In the rare case where the mail

Page 3

ABOUT YOUR COMPANY

1. In what business(es) is your company or division engaged?

   Manufacturing industrial products ☐   Transportation ☐
   Manufacturing consumer products ☐   Service ☐
   Distribution ☐

   What else?_____

2. What was the company's (or division's) sales volume last year?

   Under $1 million ☐ $ 25 to $ 49.9 million ☐ $250 to $499.9 million ☐
   $ 1 to $ 4.9 million ☐ $ 50 to $ 99.9 million ☐ $500 to $999.9 million ☐
   $ 5 to $ 9.9 million ☐ $100 to $249.9 million ☐ $1 billion and over ☐
   $10 to $24.9 million ☐

3. Did your company or division bring out any new products during the past year? Yes ☐   No ☐

   If "Yes," how many?_____

4. Did you test market any product during the past year? Yes ☐   No ☐

   If "Yes," how many?_____

5. In your estimate, about what percentage of last year's sales volume came from products which your company added to its line since 1960? _____%

6. During the last 3 years has your company opened any new factories or branch offices? Yes ☐   No ☐

7. Does your function include any foreign marketing? Yes ☐   No ☐

8. Does your company or division use electronic data processing equipment (computers) for sales or marketing data? Yes ☐   No ☐

   If "Yes," is this work done: _____ In your company? ☐   Outside? ☐   Both? ☐

ABOUT YOU AND YOUR COMPANY

One of the hardest things to establish is the influence exercised by an individual in his company's affairs. This is what we are trying to do with the help of the following questions.

1. Please indicate your spheres of influence by checking one or more of the boxes across for each of the following lines.

	Part of my responsibility is to:			Have some say	Not my concern
	Recommend	Specify	Approve		
Selecting *types* of advertising media*	☐	☐	☐	☐	☐
Selecting *specific* advertising media	☐	☐	☐	☐	☐
Packaging: materials	☐	☐	☐	☐	☐
suppliers	☐	☐	☐	☐	☐
Methods of distribution	☐	☐	☐	☐	☐
Data processing services	☐	☐	☐	☐	☐
Make of company cars to be bought	☐	☐	☐	☐	☐
Car leasing and renting companies	☐	☐	☐	☐	☐
Airline travel policies of sales force	☐	☐	☐	☐	☐
Audio-visual equipment	☐	☐	☐	☐	☐
Types of premiums and incentives	☐	☐	☐	☐	☐
Location of test markets	☐	☐	☐	☐	☐
Location of new plants or branches	☐	☐	☐	☐	☐

*Such as TV, magazines, newspapers, etc.

(Please turn)

FIGURE 2   Typeset questionnaire page.

Sports Illustrated

Confidential survey among our subscribers

In which of the following sports did you participate during the past year? (Please check each box that applies.)

Baseball, softball ☐	Camping, hiking ☐	Paddle tennis ☐	Skiing .... ☐
Basketball ..... ☐	Fishing .... ☐	Pool, billiards ☐	Skin diving, scuba ☐
Boating, yachting ☐	Football ...... ☐	Riding .... ☐	Swimming ...... ☐
Bowling .... ☐	Golf .... ☐	Skating .... ☐	Tennis .... ☐
Calisthenics .... ☐	Hunting .... ☐	Skeet or trap.. ☐	Water skiing .... ☐

What else? _____

I prefer spectator sports ☐

TRAVEL AND SOCIAL ACTIVITIES

1. Did you or other members of your immediate family travel outside the continental U.S. during the past year? (Please omit military travel.) .... Yes ☐   No ☐

    If "Yes," which of these places did you visit?

Alaska .... ☐	Mexico .... ☐
Hawaii .... ☐	Central America ☐
Canada .... ☐	South America .. ☐
Bermuda ...... ☐	Europe .... ☐
Jamaica .... ☐	Africa or Asia .. ☐
Puerto Rico ... ☐	Australia or
Other Caribbean ☐	South Pacific ☐

2. Do you belong to any of the following? (Please check all that apply.)

Country club with golf course ☐	Yacht club .... ☐
Country club without golf club ☐	Skating club ...... ☐
Tennis club .... ☐	Other sports club ☐

3. Which of the following types of beverage do you drink or serve at home? Please write in the brand(s) of each type that you have on hand.

	Drink or serve	Brand(s) on hand		Drink or serve	Brand(s) on hand
Gin	☐	_____	Rum	☐	_____
Bourbon	☐	_____	Cordials, liqueurs	☐	_____
Blended Whiskey..	☐	_____	Cognac, brandy ...	☐	_____
Canadian Whisky..	☐	_____	Beer	☐	_____
Scotch Whisky....	☐	_____	Domestic wine	☐	_____
Vodka	☐	_____	Imported wine	☐	_____

FIGURE 3 Questionnaire page with logo, offset from typed copy.

questionnaire is longer than six pages, it may be collated from four-page sections and stapled in the center.

LAYOUT

One way to emphasize the importance of a good layout is to illustrate the difference between a poor one and a good one (Figs. 4, 5). The layout should give the impression of a neat printed page which is easy to read and easy to fill out. The page should never be overcrowded; it should provide decent margins, white space to separate solidly printed blocks, and the often unavoidable tabular form (multiple columns of boxes) should be kept to a minimum. One of the most unfortunate impressions a questionnaire can make is to remind people of an income tax form.

It must be made clear to the respondent where to *check* the answer and where to *write in* numbers or words. The simple, graphic, way of indicating this is by the use of boxes for check questions and lines (called "rules" in typography) for "open-end" questions. A very important thing to remember in using boxes or lines is to make sure that each *obviously* belongs to one item only. In one unfortunate case, involving 5,000 questionnaires, poor layout necessitated the discarding of the entire response to a question:

What is your age?
Under 25 yrs. ☐ 25 to 34 ☐ 35 to 44 ☐ 45 to 54 ☐ 55 to 64 ☐ 65 or over ☐

The age tabulation results looked strange, and it soon became obvious that respondents were not of one mind about where to check their ages. Some checked the box to the right of an age group while others checked the box to the left. A proper layout would have been:

Under 25 yrs. ☐   35 to 44 ☐   55 to 64.. ☐
25 to 34 .. ☐   45 to 54 ☐   65 or over ☐

It is important that the space for answering (whether indicated by a box or a line) always appear on the same side of questions or of the suggested answers. The right side is preferable because the respondent must read the question and the suggested answers before he can check or otherwise indicate his reply. This makes the right-side position more natural; furthermore, this layout makes the keypunch operator's job easier. Of course check boxes should be vertically aligned as much as possible, both as a help to respondents and to the tabulators and for the better appearance of the questionnaire. A line

Page 3

10 Do you, alone or in conjunction with others, authorize the purchase of the following kinds of insurance for your company? Group__Yes__No Key man__Yes__No Split dollar__Yes__No Deferred compensation__Yes__No Major medical__Yes__No Disability income __Yes__No Workmen's compensation__Yes__No Fire__Yes__No Automotive__Yes__No.

AUTO INSURANCE

1 Do you or members of your household carry automobile insurance?__Yes__No   (If "No," please skip to page 4)

If "Yes," who specified or selected the insurance company? I did ☐ other member of household ☐ My insurance broker ☐ Who else?

2 What is the name of the insurance company(ies) which issued your policy?_____ _____
Don't remember_____

3 From whom do you usually buy your auto insurance?

Agent (salesman) of insurance company _____

Independent agent or broker _____

Bought by mail _____

Bought in conjunction with auto financing _____

Where else? _____

4 Approximately how much did you and members of your household spend on auto insurance and on all cars in 19XX? (Please include: liability, collision, fire and theft, etc., insurance <u>on cars</u>.) About $_____

5 Have you changed auto insurance companies in 19XX? __Yes__No.
If "Yes," why?

__On account of the agent   Lower rates
__Package plan   Any other reason?
_____

(Please turn)

FIGURE 4 Poor layout.

10. Do you, alone or in conjunction with others, authorize the purchase of the following kinds of insurance for your company?

	Yes	No		Yes	No
Group	☐	☐	Major medical	☐	☐
Key man	☐	☐	Disability income	☐	☐
Split dollar	☐	☐	Workmen's compensation	☐	☐
Deferred compensation	☐	☐	Fire	☐	☐
			Automotive	☐	☐

AUTO INSURANCE

1. Do you or members of your household carry automobile insurance? Yes ☐ No ☐

    (If "No," please skip to page 4.)

    If "Yes," who specified or selected the insurance company?

    I did .... ☐   My insurance broker .... ☐
    Other member of household ☐   Who else?_____

2. What is the name of the insurance company(ies) which issued your policy?

    _____ _____   Don't remember ☐

3. From whom do you usually buy your auto insurance?

    Agent (salesman) of an insurance company .... ☐
    Independent agent or broker .... ☐
    Bought by mail .... ☐
    Bought in conjunction with auto financing .... ☐

    Where else?_____

4. Approximately how much did you and members of your household spend on all types of auto insurance and on all cars in 19xx? (Please include: liability, collision, fire and theft, etc., insurance on cars.)

    About ... $_____

5. Have you changed auto insurance companies in 19xx? .... Yes ☐ No ☐

    If "Yes," why?

    On account of the agent ☐   Lower rates ☐   Package plan ☐

    Any other reason?_____

    (Please turn)

FIGURE 5   Good layout.

of dots or "leaders" helps the respondent to put his check in the right box.

The requirements of the survey will often pose special problems in questionnaire appearance. It sometimes happens that specifications simply will not permit the use of an "easy-looking" questionnaire, and then we have to devise a layout which will reduce the "difficult" effect as much as possible. As examples, we show a questionnaire where the requirements called for the use of a scaling system (Fig. 51) and two more where the use of the tabular form was unavoidable (Figs. 2, 6).

The folding of the questionnaire should be such that the respondent sees page 1 first. If possible, the first page should be the shortest, "airiest," easiest-looking page. He may also turn the questionnaire over to look at the last page. For this reason the last page should not be too difficult either—and in no circumstances should the last question bear a high number. Questions are usually numbered, and this is very helpful. But it is hard to impress upon the respondent that he is facing a simple little questionnaire when the last item is question 68. On all but the shortest questionnaires it is advisable to group questions into sections by subject matter and start the numbering with question 1 for each section. Each section should have a heading that is descriptive and, if possible, interesting (Figs. 2, 3).

The primary purpose of each of the above points (small size, few pages, no illustrations, white paper of the right weight and texture, good printing, full utilization of pages, proper layout and sectionalizing) is to ease the respondent into starting to answer, or at least not to deter him from answering. The primary purpose of the following points is to keep him going—or at least not make him throw up his hands and give up before he has completed all the questions.

Of course this goal must be attained without sacrificing the quantity and quality of information which we expect from the answers.

CHECK VERSUS OPEN-END QUESTIONS

In general, it is easier to get answers to check questions than to open-end questions. In a survey on magazine readership, a split mailing was made. Half the questionnaires listed ten magazines, providing boxes where the respondent could *check* those he had read in the past six months. The other half asked the respondent to *write in* the names of the magazines he had read in the same period. The percentage of return was 60 percent for the check version and 50 percent for the open-end version.

Open-end questions are frequently used in mail surveys, but the

U. S. SURVEY OF LEISURE TIME ACTIVITIES

1. Which of the activities listed below do <u>you or any members of your household</u> attend or participate in? (Please check all that apply.)

Golf .... ☐	Skin diving ☐	Art shows or galleries ☐
Horseback riding ☐	Bowling... ☐	Opera or symphony... ☐
Tennis .... ☐	Fishing... ☐	Movies .... ☐
Water skiing .... ☐	Hunting... ☐	Theatre .... ☐
Skiing .... ☐	Gardening ☐	Photography .... ☐

2. To which of the following types of organizations do you or <u>any</u> members of your household belong?

    Social
    Country club (without golf course) ... ☐
    Country club (with golf course) ...... ☐
    Social club .... ☐
    Yacht club .... ☐
    Alumni club .... ☐

    Athletic club .... ☐
    Fraternal (Elks, Masons, etc.) ..... ☐
    Any other? _____

    Community
    Chamber of Commerce .... ☐
    School board .... ☐

    Community (Cont'd)
    Hospital board .... ☐
    Town board .... ☐
    Political organization .... ☐
    Civic organization .... ☐
    Church or religious .... ☐
    Any other? _____

    Business
    Trade organization .... ☐
    Professional group .... ☐
    Service club (Rotary, Kiwanis, etc.) ☐
    Any other? _____

    Do you hold office or act in an official capacity for <u>any</u> of the organizations or groups listed above? .... Yes ☐   No ☐

3. Please indicate: a) which of the following areas you or other household members have visited <u>in the past 5 years</u>, and for each area visited, b) whether plane or ship was used on the trip, and c) the purpose of the trip.

	(a) Visited in past 5 years	(b) Traveled by: Plane / Ship / Both	(c) Purpose Business / Pleasure / Both
Canada	☐	☐ ☐ ☐	☐ ☐ ☐
Mexico	☐	☐ ☐ ☐	☐ ☐ ☐
South America	☐	☐ ☐ ☐	☐ ☐ ☐
Central America	☐	☐ ☐ ☐	☐ ☐ ☐
Bahamas	☐	☐ ☐ ☐	☐ ☐ ☐
Bermuda	☐	☐ ☐ ☐	☐ ☐ ☐
Puerto Rico	☐	☐ ☐ ☐	☐ ☐ ☐
Jamaica	☐	☐ ☐ ☐	☐ ☐ ☐
Virgin Islands	☐	☐ ☐ ☐	☐ ☐ ☐
Hawaii	☐	☐ ☐ ☐	☐ ☐ ☐
Europe	☐	☐ ☐ ☐	☐ ☐ ☐
Africa	☐	☐ ☐ ☐	☐ ☐ ☐
Near or Middle East	☐	☐ ☐ ☐	☐ ☐ ☐
Australia or New Zealand..	☐	☐ ☐ ☐	☐ ☐ ☐
Far East	☐	☐ ☐ ☐	☐ ☐ ☐

FIGURE 6 Questionnaire page with tabular layout.

successful use of this type of questioning will depend on the nature of the question, the interest of the respondent in the subject matter, and the education and literacy of the group surveyed. Obviously it is easier to get college professors to write out meaningful answers about the subjects they teach than to induce sharecroppers to fill out questionnaires with open-end questions on agriculture.

Many questionnaires contain a judicious mix of the two kinds of questions (Fig. 7).

It is often very difficult to decide whether to use the open-end or the check-question form to elicit the desired information. While it is certain that in most cases the check question is more readily answered and much cheaper to tabulate, it can have a number of drawbacks.

Often the researcher has no way of knowing what the answers to his question will be, and therefore he cannot list them. What is worse, he may *think* he knows and be wrong, and in that case he may never find out that he *was* wrong. In a survey conducted in the United States it was decided to ask recent purchasers of a certain make of imported car why they chose it over other makes. The researchers felt that an open-end question might be too difficult to answer and might result in getting only obvious replies such as "cost," "size," and "roadability." The manufacturer had a list of reasonable-sounding replies taken from the results of a survey conducted in Europe. It was decided that it would be risky to assume that the answers of car buyers abroad could be applied to United States drivers, and therefore some test interviewing was needed to help in structuring the question. A small number (25) of depth interviews was conducted with a random selection of recent buyers of the car. The interviewers spent over an hour with each of the owners, who did not know the identity of the sponsor. The interview carried the respondent through his whole history of car ownership, establishing why he bought each successive car owned, what his experiences with it were, and why he bought his next car. The resulting 12 to 15 typed pages per interview yielded a valuable list of reasons for buying the sponsor's make of car. A checklist was made up with the help of these findings. This list included several reasons which simply had never occurred to the manufacturer or the researchers but were mentioned by a number of the respondents. The point of this "case history" is that if the researcher had used only the available or obvious listings, he might never have found out about the existence of the other important reasons which came up. Of course there can be a line after a checklist, such as:

      Other (please specify) _____

Page 3

4. What brand of Scotch do you usually drink? _____

5. Would you tell us why you drink this particular brand?
   _____
   _____

6. How long has this been your brand?

   Less than 1 year ☐   2 years ☐   4 years .... ☐
   1 year .... ☐   3 years ☐   5 or more years ☐

7. Have you switched the brand of Scotch you usually drink in the past two years?
                                                                                          Yes ☐   No ☐

   If "Yes," what brands were involved?

   Switched from _____ to _____

   Why did you switch? _____

8. Do you drink Scotch in restaurants, clubs, bars, etc.? .... Yes ☐   No ☐

   If "Yes," do you specify a particular brand? .... Yes ☐   No ☐

   If you do, what brand did you order on the last occasion?
   _____

BRANDS AND GIFTS

1. Which would you say is the biggest selling brand of Scotch in the U.S.?
   _____

   Which in your opinion is the second best seller? _____

   And which one probably third? .... _____

                                                                                                   (Please turn)

FIGURE 7 Questionnaire page with open-end and check questions.

However, this line is only of limited help in establishing the comparative importance of an answer, because a large percentage of people who would check a reason (or brand, or magazine, etc.) when they are reminded of it through a listing would not remember it or would not bother writing it down as an "other." Incidentally, the next step in the auto research just described was the further testing of the questionnaire with a pilot study. In many cases expensive depth interviews are not required and lists of answers can be established with the help of a pilot mailing containing open-end questions.

The loss of "unlisted" answers is only part of the researcher's problem in considering check questions. Another difficulty concerns the bias which a checklist can introduce. Plain laziness may induce a respondent to check something listed instead of thinking of a more specific (and more correct) answer. He may feel, consciously or subconsciously, that he must check one or more of the items as a matter of prestige or status (ownership of items, use of expensive cosmetics, the reading of prestige publications, etc.), although he might very well be reluctant to write in an untruth himself. Finally, a checklist may confine the respondent's attention to one specific area, while a carefully phrased, unbiased open-end question would start him off with a completely open mind and without the influence of any suggested answer.

GROUPING CHECK ANSWERS

The listing of replies to questions requiring numerical answers usually involves groupings, sometimes referred to as frequency distributions or class intervals. There is one firm rule about such class intervals: They have to be mutually exclusive. When listing age groups, income brackets, price ranges, etc., the same number should never appear in two different groups, as in the following example:

Under 25 yrs ...... ☐
25 to 35 yrs .... ☐
35 to 45 yrs .... ☐
45 to 55 yrs .... ☐
55 yrs and over .... ☐

This listing is quite useless because the answers would not give us the correct number of respondents who fall into any of the age groups, with the exception of the first. We would not know how many 35-year-old respondents checked the second group and how many are included in the third, and we would have the same problem with

45-year-old people and the 55-year-olds. The correct way of listing the same age distribution follows:

> Under 25 yrs ...... ☐
> 25 to 34 yrs .... ☐
> 35 to 44 yrs .... ☐
> 45 to 54 yrs .... ☐
> 55 yrs and over .... ☐

In the case of income groups, it might seem simpler to list breaks such as $5,000 to $15,000 and $15,000 to $25,000 rather than to use a number like $14,999 as shown on Fig. 32. However, to get accuracy in our frequency distributions and average and median income figures, we have to make the questionnaire as precise as possible.

When listing answers for classification data or any other information which is given in the census or other government surveys, it is advisable to use the breaks established by the Department of Commerce or other government bureaus which publish surveys. First, their groupings are usually based on long experience and make good sense and secondly, their use will make the findings comparable with published figures. Various breakdowns for demographic data and other information can be found in such publications as the *Statistical Abstract*, published annually by the Bureau of the Census. To establish groupings (or codes) for occupation questions, the best references are the "Standard Industrial Classification (SIC) Manual" of the Bureau of the Budget, the "Dictionary of Occupational Titles" of the U.S. Department of Labor's Bureau of Employment Security, and the "Alphabetical Index of Occupations and Industries" of the U.S. Department of Commerce. Technological change is quite rapid these days—new occupations, professions, and job titles keep cropping up all the time—therefore it is advisable to consult the very latest edition of any reference book.

Another disadvantage of check questions (other than simple yes—no answers) is the amount of space they use. A list of forty magazines or thirty auto makes may take up much more room than the researcher wants to allot to that question. The eternal problem of questionnaire construction is to choose a course between a long questionnaire and a difficult one. If because of lengthy checklists the questionnaire is ten pages long, the recipient may throw it away before finding out that it is actually easy to answer. If a much shorter questionnaire contains ten open-end questions, the respondent may get tired by the time he is writing his fifth sentence and throw away the time-consuming form. The researcher must consider both aspects in making his decision.

Of course, in many cases the problem does not exist. If the researcher is interested *only* in the number of Fords, Chevrolets, and Plymouths owned by the respondents, he will list only these three makes. He will add an "Other, please specify" line in order to humor the owners of other makes, but he does not have to tabulate them.

PITFALLS TO BE AVOIDED

Asking the wrong questions. The general look, or Gestalt, of the questionnaire might be innocent enough to induce the respondent to take out his pencil, but if he finds that the questions are too involved and too difficult to answer, he will not continue, especially if he feels that the questions do not apply to him. It is not advisable to ask an engineer about the media selection problems of the company or the sales manager about the engineering or chemical processes used by his firm. There is no point in asking housewives about sales figures of their husbands' businesses or the husband about the brand of girdle his wife prefers.

In general the answers to questions concerning the respondent himself will be more reliable than his replies concerning the affairs of other people, including members of his family.

Difficult questions. Even if the question is addressed to the right person, it should not require too much thinking or checking to answer. You cannot ask a librarian to list all books on ten subjects in her library, or an engineer to do a whole calculating job for you, or the sales manager to look up all his sales records for five years back.

Strain on memory. There is no point in asking anyone how much he spent on gas three years ago, because even if he should answer, such replies could not be trusted. In general, when asking about figures, it is a good idea to add the word "about" or "approximately" to the question. Approximation is all one can usually expect anyhow, and if the respondent gets the idea that the answer *must* be exact he may not answer at all, even though he could have given you a pretty close estimate.

In order to get accurate answers, questions should refer to the shortest usable time span. Most people will remember whether or not they listened to the radio last night and, if so, to what broadcasts or stations. Answers will be much less reliable if we ask the same question about listening (or viewing, or reading, or purchasing) of two weeks ago.

Another way of helping the recall of events is to ask about the last trip, the last purchase of a product, the last television show which the respondent watched.

Often importance makes events memorable even though they happened some time ago. People can describe their main vacation trip, remember their largest salary increase, or recall when they were honorably discharged from the marines.

Confidential information. Some business firms have rules against giving out certain information, and some individuals have similar feelings about most of their private affairs. If there is any question of meeting this form of resistance, pilot studies should be made to try various phrasings and to establish the maximum amount of information that one can reasonably expect to receive. In this connection, many people who are unwilling to write in an exact figure in answer to a question are less reluctant to check a box of bracketed information. This is especially true of age and income.

SAVING THE RESPONDENT UNNECESSARY READING

The interviewer will not ask the respondents to answer questions which obviously do not apply to him. Similarly the mail questionnaire should allow the respondent to skip any question, section, or page which is not applicable. It is advisable to start the questionnaire with a section which the respondent can probably answer because it is universally applicable and to end it with another section which can be answered by everyone. The researcher will simplify the task of the respondent on inapplicable sections by using such questions and instructions as the following:

>   Q. 9.   Do you own a private plane? Yes ☐   No ☐
>   (If "No," please skip to Question 14)

This will obviously save the nonowner respondent the trouble of skimming through questions 10 to 13 before finding out where the "private plane" questions end. On the other hand, where we need whole series of filter questions, it might become tedious for the respondent to find too many "skip" instructions. In these cases we can achieve similar results by layout, that is, indenting lines instead of numbering the related questions:

>   Q. 12.   Do you now own a car? .. Yes ☐   No ☐
>   If "Yes," how many? ...._____
>   What makes? _____
>   _____

There are times when a respondent could skip the whole questionnaire because it does not really apply to him. Nevertheless, the researcher is still very much concerned about the return of the questionnaire. For example, in a survey among automobile owners, even the most reliable list may contain the names of some people who disposed of their cars since the list was compiled. In this situation the researcher will try his best to get answers from the nonowners for two reasons. First, it may be of interest to find out how many people in the universe have disposed of their cars without immediately replacing them with another one, and secondly, the percentage of response should not be reduced because of the nonowners. If the whole questionnaire is on the subject of automobile ownership, the first question could be:

> Do you now own a car? .... Yes ☐   No ☐

If the answer is "No," and the researcher is definitely not interested in any data about nonowners, he still has two alternative methods of continuing: He can ask the respondent to return the questionnaire without answering any additional questions, or he can ask him to skip to a general section or question at the end of the questionnaire. The purpose of the second alternative is purely psychological, the respondent may consider it more important to send in his "completed" questionnaire if he can do more than just check one "No" box. Of course in many cases the researcher may really be interested in getting some information about nonowners, for instance, to find out whether they plan to buy a car in the future.

If we want to terminate the mail interview after receiving a negative answer to the first question, it should be done in a way which encourages the respondent to return the questionnaire:

> Do you now own a car? .... Yes ☐   No ☐
> If "Yes," please continue. If you do not now own a car, please make sure to check "No" above and return the questionnaire. Your answer is very important to the accuracy of our research. Thank you.

(The same situation is discussed later from the point of view of bias.)

Unimportant or frivolous questions. One of the main reasons for a respondent to answer a questionnaire is the importance which he attaches to the survey. If the questions look trivial or frivolous, the researcher will lose some of his most intelligent respondents. A questionnaire to engineers must not use grade-school language, and a respondent should not have to answer anything that he might consider obvious or silly or already answered. One has to be very careful about the use of humor. It has its place, but must be used sparingly.

SEVEN
Questionnaire Construction
Interest, Bias, and Precision

SOME OF THE MOST COMMON MISTAKES of questionnaire construction occur because the researcher and the respondent are not interested in the same things. The personal characteristics and ownership data of its subscribers are vitally important to a publication; to the advertising manager they are second only to his circulation figures in importance. He would love to fill a questionnaire with all the questions whose answers he hopes will sell space. At the same time, few things are more boring to Mr. or Mrs. John Doe than answering dozens of questions on demographics (how old is each member of the family, what is the highest level of schooling attained by each, etc.) or on brands of household items, such as pop-up toasters, washing machines, and garden hoses. It is not interesting to answer page after page of such questions, and it does not seem to add up to a very important survey. So why waste time on it?

There are several ways to reconcile these differences in interest. One is careful wording of the letter of transmittal (Chap. 12), the function of which is largely to motivate the respondent to answer. Another is a good introductory question, or set of questions, which will get the respondents started, and nimble sectionalizing and phrasing to help make the subject matter seem more interesting.

TITLE AND INTRODUCTORY QUESTION

In most cases a bridge can be built between the letter of transmittal and the questionnaire by a carefully constructed title. It seems a simple matter to write such titles, but it often takes some hard thinking. The title is not there just to fill up space. It has to earn its keep. It can do so by facilitating a smooth transition from the letter to the questionnaire *plus* serving one or more of the following purposes:

1. Appealing to the respondent's ego ("SURVEY AMONG TOP EXECUTIVES").

2. Emphasizing the subject which will be of interest to the universe surveyed ("STUDY ON IMPORTED CARS").

3. Underlining the importance of the research ("NATIONWIDE SURVEY OF COMPUTER PROGRAMMING").

4. Emphasizing the tie between the researcher and the respondent where such ties exist ("*FORTUNE*—A CONFIDENTIAL SURVEY AMONG OUR SUBSCRIBERS"). It is helpful to use the actual logo of the publication, as in Figure 3.

There are many pitfalls in choosing titles. The choice can misfire if, instead of appealing to *all* respondents, the title discourages some. Title 1 is good *only* if the questionnaire is sent to top executives, and title 2 will work *only* if the questionnaire is directed to owners of imported cars. If this rule is violated, it not only will affect the percentage of response, but will also introduce a bias by getting answers only (or overwhelmingly) from people who have a direct connection with the title. There is one all-important rule for the title: It has to be true. Furthermore, it should be very carefully considered whether or not it might bias some answers. In a readership survey three titles were tested: "SURVEY AMONG EXECUTIVES," "SURVEY AMONG BUSINESS EXECUTIVES," and "SURVEY AMONG KEY EXECUTIVES." The letter and the questionnaire were identical in a split mailing of 600—each of the 3 titles was tested with a random sample of 200. The percentage of response was identical (52 percent). The first question was: "What magazines do you read regularly (3 out of 4 issues)?" The tabulation of this open-end question by the 3 groups showed no significant difference except that mentions of publications with the word "business" in their names were considerably higher when the title of the questionnaire included that word.

The introductory question is always very important, except in cases where the whole subject matter is of great interest to the respondent. A questionnaire on baby care sent to mothers of infants or a questionnaire on Rolls-Royce cars mailed to owners of Rolls-Royces needs no special introduction. On the other hand, the following examples from actual surveys show how introductory questions can be used.

1. A survey among department store buyers drew very poor returns. When the same questionnaire was mailed to a matching sample of buyers, this time with introductory questions on the advisability of congressional action on some pending legislation which was of great interest to these buyers, there was a substantial improvement in the percentage of returns. Respondents completed *all* questions, not only those of the introductory section.

2. A long questionnaire on magazine readership which was mailed to engineers achieved high returns by using the following introductory questions:

> Q. 1. In your opinion, do scientists and other professionals (engineers, physicists, chemists, etc.) have more say in top management decisions of U.S. industry than they had ten years ago?
> Yes, they have more say now .... ☐
> They have less say now .... ☐
> It hasn't changed much .... ☐
>
> Q. 2. Would you say that the amount of voice which engineers and scientists have today in management decisions is:
> Excessive? .... ☐
> Insufficient? .... ☐
> About right? .... ☐

3. A rather uninspiring questionnaire on demographic data and ownership of cameras and appliances was made more attractive by introducing it with the following question:

> I. *Flights of Fancy department.*
> One hypothetical question before we inquire about more specific matters. Just suppose . . .
> You are presented with $2,000 from an anonymous donor who stipulates only that you must spend it within one week.
> *Question:* How would you spend it? _____
>
> II. *Down to Earth department—and to some brief questions about photography.*

4. A questionnaire on advertising which was mailed to business executives of large firms was answered by a very high percentage of the sample (79 percent). These results were partly attributable to the following introduction:

    Q. 1. Do you ever see or hear your own company's advertising? .... Yes ☐ No ☐
        If "Yes," where?
            Television ..☐   Magazines ..☐
            Radio ......☐   Billboards ..☐
            Newspapers ☐   Direct mail ☐
            Other _____
                      (please specify)
    Q. 2. Do you ever notice advertising by your company's competitors?   Yes ☐ No ☐

5. A long questionnaire on home ownership and appliances started as follows:

    What do you like about the location of your home?
        Community activities ☐ Neighbors ....☐
        Cultural facilities ...☐ Schools ....☐
        Sports facilities .....☐ Convenient to
                                  my work ....☐
    What else? _____

The common factor in all the above examples is the personal involvement of the respondent. In two of them, 1 and 2, the introductory question also connected the survey with an issue which was very important to the career or livelihood of the respondent. Incidentally, in these two cases the introductory questions were suggested primarily as "return getters," but in both cases the answers proved to be quite interesting to the sponsoring organization. Of course the best introduction is an interesting question which is connected with the objectives of the research. If this is not possible, one or more "bridge" questions may be needed to guide the respondent into a different subject. Introductory questions are often very valuable in tying in with the letter of transmittal.

AVOIDING JARGON—KEEPING THE RESPONDENT INTERESTED

To keep the respondent interested, it is important to be as brief as possible, to use appropriate language, and to think constantly of the respondent's reactions. Every business and trade has its own vocabulary, and it is hard for each group to remember that the rest of the world is not the liquor industry, or the world of public relations, or the academic field—or even marketing research. John Doe may answer your questionnaire, if he is not referred to as a *respondent* who is asked to give you an *image* of the liquor industry. He may get confused about indicating his purchases of *ethical* brands of drugs or about giving an opinion on the *penetration* of a *message* published in a *medium*. The italicized words may sound common enough to the reader, but they would be Greek to large numbers of people across the land. Always keep in mind that there is no interviewer to translate unusual terms used in a mail questionnaire; it must do the job itself, alone and unassisted.

Sometimes the researcher is interested only in a limited number of all possible answers to a given question. In such cases it may be advisable to think of the respondent's interest as well and to add a line or two to keep him happy. For example, if in a given field the sponsor is interested in three important trade publications, the question should be raised whether listing *only* these three magazines would antagonize the responding engineer who happens to read a fourth one and may not like to appear laggard in keeping up with his profession. The "Other, please specify" lines are often useful for this purpose.

BIAS: THE SPONSOR AND THE SUBJECTS

There are many possible types of bias which the researcher must avoid. Sample distortion can introduce a bias (Chap. 5), and so can a nonrepresentative return (Chap. 15). Further problems can be caused by a faulty letter of transmittal (Chap. 12).

We have already seen how the title of the questionnaire may bias returns, and so can questionnaire construction and specific questions. It is impossible to make general rules to prevent all forms of bias; they are concealed in a variety of disguises. However, here are a few general rules:

In a competitive survey the questionnaire (or letter) should never divulge the *identity of the sponsor* if it happens to be one of the contestants. A questionnaire from General Electric, and so identified, cannot be expected to elicit unbiased answers on the comparative merits of G. E. and Westinghouse appliances. Actually the sponsor is often identifiable without outright mention. For example, if we ask, "Which of the following publications do you prefer for editorial content?" followed by other preference questions and if four publications are listed, including *Life, Look, Reader's Digest,* and the

New York Times, some respondents will assume that the sponsor is the *New York Times* simply because it seems out of place among the mass magazines. This bias is still there even if the *Times* was not in fact the sponsor, and the results are therefore still questionable.

Even in noncompetitive surveys, where we are interested in the respondent's opinion about one corporation or one publication, it is usually advisable to ask the same questions about at least one other similar manufacturer or publication. If a number of opinion questions are asked about the XYZ company, respondents will naturally assume that the survey is being conducted by them or for them. This assumption—whether right or wrong—may bias their answers. If the same questions are asked about two or more companies, there is a better chance of getting objective, unbiased opinions.

If the subject of the questionnaire may appeal to a limited segment of the sample only, care should be taken to get a very high percentage of return, to check nonrespondents if possible, and to fight a possible response bias by means of the wording of the accompanying letter. A good method is to bury the subject of interest in the middle of a longer questionnaire. If we have to ask questions on the ownership of private airplanes from a group of business executives, it is advisable to insert these questions between sections which respondents can answer positively, such as occupation, vacation, and ownership of cars.

BIAS: THE CONTENT AND POSITION OF QUESTIONS

No question should lead (bias) the answers in any direction: not toward the sponsor nor anyone or anything else. It is not reasonable to ask, "In which magazine do you prefer to read about foreign affairs?" when one of the publications listed is *Foreign Affairs.* This brings up the matter of leading questions of the "Are you against sin?" or "Are you for motherhood?" type. You cannot ask the question, "Do you think labor in Hong Kong is cheaper than in the U.S.?" followed by, "Do you think imports from Hong Kong cause unemployment in the U.S.?" followed by, "Would you prefer to buy a flashlight made in Hong Kong or one made by the XYZ Company in Gary, Ind.?" and expect an unbiased answer to the last question. A surprisingly large number of questionnaires contain questions which tend to lead to a biased conclusion. Even certain expressions or emotionally charged words can introduce considerable bias. In a questionnaire on labor relations the answers can be quite different, depending on whether we ask questions about "scabs" or "strike breakers," or refer to "people who continue working at a struck plant."

The lack of a filter question can often bias a respondent's answer. "How many cars do you own?" is a very biased way of starting a questionnaire mailed to the general public on the subject of cars. It is also a poor way of introducing an auto-ownership section within a questionnaire. The proper start is:

    Do you now own a car? .... Yes ☐   No ☐
    (If "No," skip to question X)
    If "Yes," how many cars do you now own? _____

In cases where one still fears possible bias, it might be valuable to insert a sentence on the importance of returning the questionnaire whether or not the respondent owns a car. Without these precautions some nonowners may not return the questionnaire or, even worse, may feel that they have to give a positive answer, such as listing a car they *used* to own.

A bias can be introduced by the *fatigue element* where a number of items are listed in a check question. In the case of short listings, (two or three items) where the respondent can take in the names (of manufacturers, materials, cosmetics, publications, TV programs, etc.) at a glance, the order of names does not seem to cause a significant difference. But where a larger number of items are listed, the ones at the end or ones at the middle of the list may be at a disadvantage. In such cases the items should be rotated (Fig. 8) or at least listed in reverse order on a random half of the questionnaires. Other possible kinds of bias which can be caused by checklists have been discussed in the previous chapter.

A question may *embarrass* the respondent and result in a biased answer or a "No Answer." Occasionally this is unavoidable, and if the information is needed the researcher may have to make his peace with a few missing or biased answers. Age and marital status information could be considered highly confidential by a spinster, but we know from experience that on most surveys this does not occur often enough to bias the results to a serious extent. However, the problem can often be minimized by introducing a section of the questionnaire with a note which emphasizes that the answers will be used only for statistical purposes. Questions which could be considered embarrassing or confidential by some respondents should be placed in the middle or at the end of the questionnaire. Sometimes an introductory sentence can reassure respondents who might feel hurt at being excluded from a status group established by a question: "Some people have the time and interest to belong to various organizations and to

SURVEY OF LEADING ARCHITECTS
on Professional Periodical Literature

1. In how many states are you registered?
   1 state .... ☐
   2 states .... ☐
   3 or more states ☐

2. Please check which of the following architectural publications you receive.

   [The order in which publications are listed has been rotated, so that each name is first on one-fifth of the questionnaires.]

   Architectural Forum .... ☐
   Architectural Record .... ☐
   Progressive Architecture .... ☐
   A I A Journal .... ☐
   Architectural & Engineering News ☐

3 a. For each publication you checked above, please indicate how many of the last four issues you read.

   Check how many of the last 4 issues you read

	4	3	2	1	0
Architectural Forum	☐	☐	☐	☐	☐
Architectural Record	☐	☐	☐	☐	☐
Progressive Architecture	☐	☐	☐	☐	☐
A I A Journal	☐	☐	☐	☐	☐
Architectural & Engineering News	☐	☐	☐	☐	☐

   b. How much of the average issue did you read?

	Under 1/3	1/3 to 2/3	Over 2/3
Architectural Forum	☐	☐	☐
Architectural Record	☐	☐	☐
Progressive Architecture	☐	☐	☐
A I A Journal	☐	☐	☐
Architectural & Engineering News	☐	☐	☐

Please use the reverse side for any comments you may have on these publications.

Many thanks for your help.

FIGURE 8 Short questionnaire with rotation.

become officers in some of them; others do not. In your answers to the following questions please indicate whether or not you happen to belong to the organizations listed and serve as an officer in any of them."

Nobody cherishes the idea of being in a lowest category. For this reason it is advisable to include brackets which are lower than the answers expected. In listing categories for education and yearly family income, it is desirable to include "Grammar school" and "Under $5,000" even if you are sure that all your respondents will be above these categories. Related to this is the fact that nobody likes to admit ignorance or inexperience. It is always good policy to protect the ego of the respondent. "Are you an executive?" is obviously more biasing (by encouraging the top dogs and discouraging bottom dogs) than the more innocuous, "What is your title or position?"

When *examples* are given to instruct the respondent, great care must be taken that the examples themselves do not introduce a bias. "What is your favorite TV program? (e.g., 'The Gunman,' 'Mr. Wong, Detective,' 'Murder Will Out,' 'The Fugitive')" will certainly influence the answers to this open-end question in *one* specific direction.

The order of questions may bias some answers. A section on reading might start with the following two questions:

Have you read any books during the past 12 months?
Yes ☐   No ☐
If "Yes," please list by author and title the books you liked best of those you read in this period.
Author   Title
_____   _____
_____   _____
_____   _____
_____   _____

The answers may vary considerably, depending on whether these two questions are preceded by a section on occupation, travel, or world events. Each of these subjects may place the respondent in an entirely different frame of reference and focus his memory on different kinds of books. If the questionnaire contains several different sections on various subjects, this type of bias can be avoided by placing the sensitive question ahead of the biasing sections. If the whole questionnaire creates a biasing frame of reference in the respondent's mind, the sensitive question may have to be omitted, or the researcher may decide that the survey cannnot be done (a situation described in Chap. 26).

Biases are many and subtle. After the questionnaire is finished, the good researcher will carefully read it with just bias hunting in mind.

Alfred Politz once remarked that it is practically impossible to avoid all bias but that one can usually know about it, estimate it, control it, and even at times use it constructively. If one suspects that teen-age girls will upgrade the brands of cosmetics which they use, one can start with this knowledge, try to measure the degree of upgrading by a validated subsample, and estimate and relate the bias to the whole research. In addition, the knowledge that this tendency exists may furnish new ideas to manufacturers, distributors, and advertising agencies.

CLEAR AND PRECISE ANSWERS

One of the most frustrating experiences a researcher can suffer is to look at a set of tabulations and realize that they are meaningless because some or all respondents misunderstood a question or answered it in such varying ways that they cannot be combined. Questions and instructions must be so clear as to eliminate the possibility of such confusion. One of the main purposes of test interviewing and pilot mailing is to ferret out ambiguous questions and give the researcher a chance to correct them. Here are a few examples:

Any question about size, amount, distance, time lapse, etc., should be asked with reference to a unit of measurement. The answer to the question, "When did you move to your present home?" could be: "In 1961," "Six years ago," "When my wife died," "A short while ago," "Years ago," or "When I was a child."

Here are two good ways of asking this question:

> In what year did you move to your present home?
> In 19_____.   (or)
> How many years ago did you move to your present home? .... _____ years ago.

Here are several additional questions of this nature, with indications of the units wanted:

> How many miles did you drive in the past 12 months?
> _____ miles
> What is the length of your boat? ...... _____ feet
> What is the size of your motor? ...... _____ hp
> How large is your plot of land? _____ square feet,
> or ... _____ acres
> How much did you spend on your last trip? .... $_____

This kind of questioning will help to obtain precise amounts, but each of the above examples can lead us to further problems of ambiguity. The first problem is to establish the correct base; for example, who should answer each of these questions? All respondents? Suppose the respondent has never moved, or does not drive, or has no boat, motor, or plot of land, or never travels? If he completely fails to answer the question, the researcher will not be able to judge whether the question was not applicable to that respondent, whether he did not wish to answer it, or whether he just didn't know the answer.

There are two ways to avoid this type of ambiguity. The best procedure is to introduce each of these questions with an appropriate filter question, such as: "Did you move to a new home in the past 10 years?" "Did you drive a car in the last 12 months?" "Do you own a boat?" The other method is to state the negative after the space left for a positive answer:

How many miles did you drive in the past 12 months?

_____ miles

Did not drive in the past 12 months ☐

This mileage question introduces a new problem: the possibility that a respondent may own more than one car and may also have rented cars during the previous 12 months. Unless we specify the answers we want, some respondents will give only the mileage driven on the car they usually use, others will total the mileage they drove in all their cars, and still others will include the mileage on rented cars. The question should specify exactly what we want; for example, "How many miles did you drive in the past 12 months? Please include the total mileage on *all* cars which you drove, whether owned, leased, or rented." This leads to the next consideration: It is unlikely that any one who drove more than one car can give an exact figure on his yearly mileage. For this reason some respondents may be unwilling to answer the question because they think that an exact figure is required, and so the question should be followed by, "About ____ miles." The words "about" and "approximately" are very often useful in this context. In most surveys an educated guess is preferable to no answer.

Now we turn to our example about boats. We know that we have to ask a filter question on boat ownership. We should also find out how many boats the respondent owns. If he owns more than one, the question on length should be asked about each of his boats, or about his largest boat, or about the boat last purchased; but in any case the question has to be made more specific than it is in our boat example. The same thing is true of motors, plots of land, or any items of which more than one can be owned.

HELPFUL EXAMPLES

Ambiguity can often be eliminated by examples. Take the question "What is your occupation?". To begin with, this is a very poor question because the answer can be "Retailing," "Manager," "Lawyer," "Sales," etc. The following is a very complete way of asking the occupation question. It takes up space, but it yields precise information. (It will also prevent the kind of amusing answer which once appeared on a questionnaire returned from England; Question: "What is your title?" Answer: "Lady of the British Commonwealth.")

> Q. 1. In what type of business, industry or service is your *company or employer* engaged? (Please be specific: e.g., steel manufacturing, education, textile wholesale, state government, hardware retailing, etc.) If you *do not* work for an employer, please give your occupation or profession:
>
> _____
>
> Q. 2. What is your title or position? (e.g., partner, machine operator, sales manager, doctor, letter carrier, etc.)
>
> _____

As has been mentioned, great care should be taken in selecting examples. Question 2 above could be easily biased by using as examples *only* executive titles or *only* unskilled positions.

The "Series name" section of the questionnaire illustrated in Figure 9 shows the use of examples in an automotive question.

RATING VERSUS RANKING

Question 2 in Figure 51 is a good example of a *rating* as distinct from a *ranking* question. Here we are asking the respondents to rate three companies on a specific attribute, using an illustrated rating scale. In a rating question the respondent is not asked to compare the companies (or products, brands, periodicals, etc.) but to rate each of them with the help of a specified measuring system. The advantages of this method over ranking are twofold: (1) The respondent is not forced to make a comparative judgment; he can rate all three companies excellent, or he may indicate that they are all poor on any given criterion; (2) the rating scale can be as wide in range and, therefore, as sensitive as the researcher desires. The comparisons are made after tabulating the replies, by comparing average ratings. The disadvantages of the system consist of its somewhat greater complexity, which necessitates a longer and more space-consuming explanation and the illustration of the scale. In some cases rating may yield too many top-rated or bottom-rated items (companies, etc.) on the same questionnaire, and this may make final comparisons less meaningful.

Ranking questions ask the respondent to rank (array) specified items. In the case of our example in Figure 51, question 2 could have read as follows: "Please rank the following companies for sound management. Write '1' for the company which you think has the soundest management of the three, '2' for the one which comes next, and '3' for the company which has the least sound management." The advantages of the ranking question are its simplicity and the fact that it establishes comparisons in a more direct way. The disadvantages include the danger of forced rankings (some respondents may feel that they must choose even though they have no preference) and the possibility that many people who do not wish to give a choice will not answer or mark "Don't Know." Another shortcoming of the system is the lack of a scale. We cannot tell whether a respondent considers a company he ranked first very good, fair, or just the least bad of a poor lot. Furthermore we won't know whether he considers the company he ranked next nearly as good as the first one or nearly as bad as the last.

Both ranking and rating can be useful. However, it is advisable not to use both systems on the same questionnaire, because the switch from ranking to rating, or vice versa, will tend to confuse the respondents.

LOGICAL ORDER—
DETAILED INSTRUCTIONS

One of the most important rules for clarity is to organize the questions into sections in an orderly and logical manner. This should be true of the *subject*, of the *respondent's relation to the subject*, and of *time*. The first is the simplest: All questions on travel should be in one section, questions on car ownership should be together, etc. Of course there can be a conflict, so that within the travel section it would be logical to keep all air travel together. On the other hand it would also be reasonable to keep questions on domestic versus foreign travel in separate groups, both having questions about air versus surface travel. Often one logical grouping has to be sacrificed for the sake of another, but the guideline should always be clarity and ease of understanding by the respondent. The problems of the respondent's relation to the subject can be illustrated with the following questions:

Q. 1.   Do you own a car?
Q. 2.   Do you or members of your household own a boat?
Q. 3.   Did you take a trip in the past 12 months?
Q. 4.   Did you or members of your household buy any securities in the past 12 months?

The above questions should be grouped by those referring to the respondent only (1 and 3) and those concerning all members of the household (2 and 4). Similarly, if some questions refer to the past year, while others ask about events in the past five years (or the past two weeks), it should be made very clear to the respondent that he will have to switch his frame of reference. Clarity can be achieved by grouping, special explanation, or layout. This is the type of problem which can easily be missed when constructing a questionnaire but invariably turns up in testing.

The best general rule is always to be as specific as possible in phrasing questions and wording column headings above structured answer spaces. We can define "read regularly" as "3 out of 4 issues." We can ask the income question as: "What was your total *family* income before taxes for the last calendar year? (Please include income from all family members and from all sources, such as wages, profits, dividends, rentals, etc.)" If we ask questions about a family, can we make sure that they do not include Aunt Milly, who lives on a goat farm in Montana? We can, by introducing the questionnaire with a statement which defines "family":

> This is a study of a carefully selected sample of U.S. families and individuals, and the homes they live in. The "family" referred to here includes all persons who are related to each other and are living together. A single person, living alone, is a "family."

Can we be sure that respondents will understand a scaling system? We can, by explaining it in detail (Fig. 51).

It is always a struggle to reconcile brevity and simplicity with the need for explaining in detail what we expect from the respondent. The following example shows how detailed instructions and typography can be combined to elicit precise answers. Incidentally, this was part of a four-page questionnaire which was completed by a high percentage of the sample, proving that detailed instructions do not necessarily deter people from answering.

> Now to sum up your household's air travel: Altogether, how many separate times were you and other household members airline passengers during the past 12 months? **Count one time for each time an individual was a passenger. If you made one round trip by yourself, using air both ways, this is 2 times. If you and one other member made one round trip using air both ways, and a third member of the household made one trip using air one way only, this is 5 times. If you are very frequent air travelers, please give us your best approximation.**
>
> Total number of separate times you and other household members were airline passengers during the past 12 months:
> On flights that began *and* ended within the U.S. ——
> On all other flights .... ——

QUESTIONNAIRE CONSTRUCTION AND TABULATING

The primary considerations in constructing the questionnaire have to do with the points already discussed. However, once the researcher is satisfied that his questionnaire is unbiased, precise, interesting, and "easy" enough to be answered, he should look it over from the point of view of data-processing. Is there any possible change in layout, structuring or wording which would make the data-processing operations more accurate, less costly, or both, without impairing the quality of the questionnaire? The answer is usually "Yes."

Precoding is the easiest way to make the punching operations fast and accurate. It is advisable to have precoding (printed numerical codes) on most questionnaires used for personal interviews. In the author's experience it is not usually advantageous to precode mailed questionnaires. No matter how well we explain to the respondent the purpose of precoding and that he need not pay attention to it, the fact remains that the appearance of the precoded questionnaire is different: There is more printing on it and less open space. It has to look heavier and more difficult than the same questionnaire without the precoding. Furthermore in ranking, rating, and choice questions, the codes themselves may have a slight subliminal influence. Finally, with proper layout we can achieve results very similar to precoding, and this "proper" layout will help the respondent as much as it will the keypunch operator. We have already discussed the importance of leaving space for all answers on the right side of the copy and of lining up check boxes. A good keypunch operator is able to punch directly from a well-laid-out questionnaire containing check questions, without any coding or precoding, with a very small margin of error (under 0.5 percent) and at a reasonable speed. Experience shows that the keypunch operator can accurately "take in" a column of a maximum of 6 boxes, but that errors increase sharply beyond that number. As a consequence, answers to check questions should be printed in groups of 4, 5 or 6, with white spaces between the groups (see Fig. 6). Each segment of 6 (or fewer) boxes will occupy a separate column on the punched card, with the next segment below it representing the next column. This simple visual separation will help both the respondent and the keypunch operator.

Proper layout and structuring of the questionnaire can effect substantial savings in editing, coding, punching, and machine tabulation. At the same time this can also increase the clarity and accuracy of the results. If, for example, we were to ask separate questions on the make, series name, model year, etc., of each automobile now owned, we would force the respondent to repeat the makes each time, add to the works of editors, coders, and keypunch operators, and end up with a complicated program for tabulations. A well-thought-out auto section, as illustrated in Figure 9, will result in more accurate answers, less work for the respondent, and substantial savings of time and money in data-processing. On some large surveys thousands of dollars may be saved by improving questionnaire design.

BUILT-IN CONTROLS—COURTESY

After satisfying himself that all possible relevant questions have been asked and all possible pitfalls avoided, the researcher may want to consider one last addition to his questionnaire: a question or series of questions which can be added to serve as a control on the accuracy of the findings. Are there any known data about the universe, such as demographic characteristics, consumption figures, or census information, which could be used to check on the accuracy of the findings, or on such phases of the research as the soundness of the sample and the data-gathering and data-processing operations? If we are conducting a survey on the uses of a specific type of steel among a representative sample of the manufacturers who use this product and if the total yearly sales of the product are known, the questionnaire could contain a question on the amount of purchases for a given year. If all phases of the research have been handled correctly, the total purchases projected from the results of the survey should be reasonably close to the known data.

There is another kind of "built-in" safety guard. If we suspect that some respondents go on checking boxes to appear knowledgeable or just for the fun of checking, we may add some nonexistent companies, brands, or products to a checklist to determine the percentage of these "overeager beavers" and possibly to eliminate their questionnaires from the survey.

AUTOMOBILE AND TRAVEL

1. Do you (or any members of your household) own a car now? .... Yes ☐   No ☐
   If "Yes," how many? .... _____

   Please indicate the make, series name and model year of each car now owned and check how and when it was bought.

MAKE	SERIES NAME (NEW YORKER, F-85, FALCON, ETC.)	MODEL YEAR	HOW BOUGHT NEW / USED	WHEN BOUGHT MONTH / YEAR
_____	_____	_____	☐ ☐	_____ _____
_____	_____	_____	☐ ☐	_____ _____
_____	_____	_____	☐ ☐	_____ _____

2. Did you or any other members of your household lease a car during the past 12 months?
   Yes ☐   No ☐

3. Do you plan to buy a new car within the next 12 months? .... Yes ☐   No ☐

FIGURE 9   Layout for interconnected questions.

The tone of the questionnaire should always be as polite as precision of language and brevity will permit. In any case, the last page should always end with a "Thank you" note. A "Please turn" note at the end of the next to the last page will assure that the respondent will not miss the last page.

If verbatim comments can be useful, the following note will usually elicit a number of them without adding to the length of the questionnaire:

> No more questions—thank you for your cooperation. We would appreciate any comments or suggestions you may care to make about any subject mentioned in the questionnaire. You may use a separate sheet and return it with the completed form.

Once the questionnaire is written, it is always good practice to run off a few (or a few dozen) copies and to have the researcher or a personal interviewer hand them to people whose characteristics are similar to those of the members of the sample. (There is not much point in checking a questionnaire designed for young mothers among engineers.) These people are requested to fill out the questionnaire and are afterward asked about any difficulties they may have encountered. Their suggestions and criticism may be very helpful in improving the questionnaire.

The final testing of the questionnaire takes place in the course of the pilot study (Chap. 9).

EIGHT
Cost Estimating and Scheduling

THERE ARE THREE CONSIDERATIONS which are important in estimating survey costs:

1. No item which adds to cost should be omitted.
2. The cost of each item should be figured as closely as possible.
3. Timing, insofar as it affects cost, should be carefully considered.

The first step is to establish a list of items which will cost money. This can include salaries, machine time, supplies, postage, premiums. The list is long and can vary widely for different surveys. Figure 10 shows a workable estimating form for mail surveys.

The item which is most often forgotten or underestimated is "executive time." Even if the survey is being done by an outside research organization, the initial discussions, periodic checks, final reading and discussion of the findings, and finally, top-level analysis and reporting will mean valuable executive time spent by the sponsoring organization. Of course these executive-time costs increase sharply if the research is conducted by the sponsoring company itself. Very few

ESTIMATE SHEET Date:_____

Job description:_____

Job number:_____ Person responsible:_____

Number mailed: Test .... _____
                Main Mailing .... _____
                Follow-up mailing _____
                Others: description and quantity (advance and reminder postcards, third mailing, wire and telephone validation, etc.)_____

Printing and mailing costs:

	Test	Main mailing	Other: ____
Stock, typesetting, printing questionnaire	$_____	$_____	$_____
Personalizing or keying questionnaire (if needed)	$_____	$_____	$_____
Stationery	$_____	$_____	$_____
Mailing operations (addressing envelopes, processing and personalizing letters and cards, processing and stamping reply envelopes, preparing premiums, inserting, stuffing, stamping, mailing, etc.)	$_____	$_____	$_____
Postage (both ways)...............	$_____	$_____	$_____
Premium-incentive	$_____	$_____	$_____

Total printing and mailing $_____

Cost of materials and services (such as directories for sampling, translations, test or validation by wire, telephone or personal interviews, purchase of lists, charting, binders, etc.)

Description	Cost
_____	$_____
_____	$_____
_____	$_____
Total materials and services	$_____

(Continued on next page)

FIGURE 10

ESTIMATE SHEET (Continued)

Operations other than printing, mailing, materials & services.	Estimated hours	$ Rate per hour	$ Amount
Survey planning	_____	_____	_____
Preparing estimate	_____	_____	_____
Sample design	_____	_____	_____
Clerical list preparation (sample selection, numbering, etc.)	_____	_____	_____
Processing mailing lists (computer printout, typing cards, etc.)	_____	_____	_____
Open envelopes, pull keyed cards	_____	_____	_____
Test tabs: tabulating...............	_____	_____	_____
recapping	_____	_____	_____
Code setups: preparing	_____	_____	_____
typing	_____	_____	_____
Control and procedure setups	_____	_____	_____
Programming, preparing run sheets	_____	_____	_____
Coding, editing	_____	_____	_____
Other clerical (handtabs, posting, proofreading, etc.).................	_____	_____	_____
Checking and job supervision	_____	_____	_____
<u>Machine time</u> (including card cleaning, marginal runs, cross tabs, corrections, etc.)			
Keypunch & verifier..................	_____	_____	_____
Counter-sorter	_____	_____	_____
Computer	_____	_____	_____
Other machines (collator, reproducer, etc.)	_____	_____	_____
_____	_____	_____	_____
Bursting, binding, collating	_____	_____	_____
Recapping	_____	_____	_____
Percentaging (other than computer)	_____	_____	_____
Other calculating (averages, medians, projections, etc.)	_____	_____	_____
Typing............................	_____	_____	_____
Reproducing setups and tables (Xerox, copyflex, etc.)	_____	_____	_____
Checking final tables	_____	_____	_____
Report writing and analysis...........	_____	_____	_____
Printing or processing final report	_____	_____	_____
Job cleanup (boxing, labeling cards, filing, wrapping work sheets, etc.)	_____	_____	_____
Executive time not included above	_____	_____	_____
General overhead	_____	_____	_____
Total cost of all items		$_____	

FIGURE 10 *(continued)*

surveys will have all the items listed; for instance, the use of computers may eliminate such cost factors as the use of other machines and percentaging and other calculations, while increasing certain other costs, such as programming and making changes and corrections.

The "printing and mailing costs" section as shown in Figure 10 is already a recapitulation; it would be too lengthy to show an hourly rate and amount sheet for these items because the listings would vary greatly with the printing and mailing methods used. Unless the printing and mailing operations are farmed out, a specific and detailed cost estimate should be designed for these operations.

ESTIMATE SHEET FOR
EDITING -- CODING – PUNCHING – TEST TABULATIONS

Date _____

Job description _____

Job number _____ Person Responsible _____

Number of questionnaires: to be tabulated _____ test-tabbed _____

Page & Quest. Number	Description	No. ops. editing & coding	No. cols. single punch	multi-punch	Test-tab hours tabs	recaps

Total operations and columns: _____ _____ _____

Questionnaires punched per hour: _____

Total hours: ...... _____ _____ _____ _____
 (ed. & code) (punch) (t. tab) (t.recap)

FIGURE 11

The time needed for test tabulating, editing, and coding the questionnaires, and for punching and verifying tabulating cards, has to be calculated question by question, using a dummy questionnaire if the actual one is not yet available. The estimating form for this procedure can be a long (8½- by 13-in.) sheet, with rules for each question and headings like those shown on Figure 11. The editing and coding operations will take more or less time depending on the expertness and speed of the editors and coders, but the *number* of operations needed will depend on the nature of the questions and the answers in the judgment of the estimator. One way of estimating these operations is to arrive at a norm, which the estimator knows from experience. For example, the simplest type of coding, such as coding the makes of refrigerators, may take 1 hour for 200 questionnaires, based on the time spent on this work by the average coder using a one-column code (11 makes plus miscellaneous). We can now decide that one operation equals the time it will take to code 200 questionnaires for the simplest code and that it also equals one hour. If, instead of coding 11 makes, we want to use several columns and code 53 makes, the coding of the same question may take twice as long and the estimator will list 2 operations (the coding of 100 questionnaires per hour). On an open-end reason question, the estimator may decide that 4 or 5 operations are needed, because long sentences will have to be read by the coders who may then have to use multiple codes for multiple answers. As the measurement always remains 200 questionnaires per operation hour, the time estimate of the editing and coding operations will be quite simple: After listing all questions with the estimated number of operations for each, the number of operations will be totaled and multiplied by the number of questionnaires divided by 200. For example, if 1,200 questionnaires are to be coded and the total number of editing and coding operations is 20, the calculation is as follows:

$$\text{Editing and coding} = 20 \times \frac{1,200}{200} = 20 \times 6 = 120 \text{ hrs}$$

The total number of columns and multiple-punch columns will enable a keypunch supervisor to estimate the hourly rate of production. Both accuracy and production will vary with the operator, the way the questionnaire is laid out, and the legibility and systematic order of codes.

Machine tabulating time depends entirely on the data-processing equipment used and must be estimated by the supervisors or operators of the machines. If the estimator's firm has its own data-processing department, it is a good idea to consult its personnel on tabulating estimates, even if the estimator is quite familiar with these operations.

INDIVIDUAL ITEM COSTS — TIMING AS IT EFFECTS COST

The cost of each item should be estimated with great care. Whenever possible, use actual past experience; it is the best guide. When no past records are available, the estimator can often do some production-time testing on various phases of the survey. Perhaps a small part of a complicated sampling operation can be completed to measure the time involved. Printing and mailing costs may be available from other jobs involving the same-sized questionnaire and similar procedures; perhaps the estimator can recall similar tabulating problems. Often parts of the estimating can be postponed until the pilot (test) mailing is completed and the results of the pilot can be used as a model for testing the timing of various operations. The estimator has to try to use as little guesswork and as much previous or present experience as possible in order to arrive at the closest possible estimate of expenditures in time and money.

Timing should be carefully considered insofar as it affects cost. There are two time elements to reckon with:

1. *When* the survey is to be done. If the estimate is being prepared for a survey which will be conducted a year from now, can the estimator be sure that the costs of postage, printing, and salaries, etc., will still be the same?

2. The *time available* for completing the survey. If there is a rush to get the job done, it may have to be done the quickest way, which is usually not the most efficient and therefore not the most economical way of doing it. If a very large crew has to work on editing and coding, more time will elapse in training them, more supervisory time will be needed, and there will be less opportunity to find the best people for the job. Overtime pay can run into very serious expense.

As the job proceeds, it is a good idea to keep track of expenditures and compare them with the estimated figures from time to time.

When the job is finished, the researcher should fill out another estimate sheet (Figs. 10, 11) with the actual expense figures and compare these line by line with the estimated amounts. This procedure will help him give an estimate based on actual experience, if the job should ever be repeated. If costs are found to have run higher than the estimate, the sponsor should perhaps be warned against assuming that the job can be repeated at the same cost.

SCHEDULING

Many a researcher has come to grief on the hidden shoals of timing. A mail survey can be an intricate maze of interlocking operations, in each of which something may go wrong. In order to establish a realistic target date for completing a mail survey, a schedule must be established. This will enable the researcher to plan and control the flow of work and its timing. The following are some of the requirements which must be taken into consideration in constructing a schedule:

1. Sufficient time should be alloted for each operation. Presumably this has been already done when completing the estimating sheets. Adequate timing should take into consideration the time needed to instruct operators, to complete the work, check it, correct errors, and allow a period of grace for the unexpected, time-consuming problems that are bound to bedevil some phases of most major jobs. Of course one cannot foresee major disasters, such as strikes or mistakes or misunderstandings which may call for the repeating of several days' work, but such contingencies are always within the realm of possibility. Both for this reason and for cost considerations, it is best to set up a schedule which does not include any overtime work. The use of overtime is then available as a safety valve in emergencies.

2. The schedule should translate the number of hours needed for each operation, as specified by the estimating sheet, into man days. This will enable the heads of various departments to allocate adequate personnel and provide the necessary machine time for each phase of the work.

3. The schedule should specify starting and completion dates for the various operations. This is perhaps the most difficult part of scheduling and takes considerable experience. The timing of several operations has to be synchronized. There are overlapping operations, such as coding and punching. While some questionnaires are still being coded, others are being punched or verified. The problem is how to avoid the bottlenecks that can result from allocating too much or too little operator or machine time to one particular phase of the work. In a busy organization the time of each operator, supervisor, and machine has to be scheduled weeks or even months in advance. If we want to allocate people and machines to a particular phase of a job which will have to be done four months hence, we must know whether or not the required men and machines will be available at that time.

4. Once the number of man hours and machine hours have been established, and starting and completion dates specified, the schedule itself should function as an automatic control over the flow of work. Figure 12 shows a filled-out schedule sheet. The head of every depart-

JOB SCHEDULE

Job description *Automotive Survey*

Job number *6432*   Person responsible *Harry Jones*

Operations	Number of: Hours	Number of: Man-days	Dates From	Dates To	Initials of person in charge
Preliminary work: conferences, survey design, sampling plan, etc.	50	7	1/15	1/22	A.G.
Sampling, mailing list construction	140	20	1/22	2/6	C.D.
Questionnaire and letter construction	55	8	1/22	2/8	E.F.
Processing and mailing*	180	26	2/8	2/19	G.H
Opening and pulling	21	3	2/21	4/8	A.B.
Test tabs, code construction, instructions for editing and coding	60	9	2/28	3/11	A.B.
Editing and coding	630	90	3/7	4/9	L.M.
Punching, verifying	126	18	3/18	4/10	O.P
Programming, specs for consistency checks and runs	40	6	3/18	4/9	J.K.
Consistency checks and corrections	28	4	4/11	4/15	R.S.
Tabulating (runs)	13	2	4/16	4/17	R.S.
Bursting, binding, cleanup	3	½	4/18	4/18	R.S.
Calculating (not done with tabs)	—	—	—	—	—
Recaps	—	—	—	—	—
Checking tabs and recaps	20	3	4/19	4/22	A.B.
Writing report, analysis	49	7	4/19	4/29	P.E.
Typing and processing	22	3	4/29	5/1	G.N.

Delivery date *MAY 3*

Data gathering schedule

	First wave	Second wave	Other: REMINDER POSTCARD	Other: —
Mailing date	2/19	3/14	2/22	—
Closing date	3/11	4/8	—	—

*For first mailing. Processing of other waves must be scheduled between their mailing date and the closing date of the previous wave.

FIGURE 12

ment concerned with the automatic survey should receive a copy of the schedule sheet. If Mr. Martin, the head of the coding department, has not received the codes and coding instructions by March 7 when he is supposed to start coding operations, he is going to ask Miss Brown for this material, knowing that she was supposed to have it ready on that day. On the other hand, if Martin fails to deliver some coded questionnaires to the keypunch department by March 18, he will have Mr. Perry of that department in his hair, and so forth. Of course the heads of the coding and keypunch departments will have to implement the schedule by deciding on the number of questionnaires which each needs and can finish every day.

Adherence to the schedule makes it likely that the job will be delivered by the May 3 deadline; it even provides two "safety days" for straightening out last-minute problems. Of course while the schedule's timing is realistic, it also makes sure that no time is wasted. The time-consuming operations of editing, coding, and punching are kept up to date with the returns, so that coding can be finished one day after the closing date, and punching the day after that.

NINE
Pilot Studies

UNLESS THE RESEARCHER is quite sure of the proper procedure to use, it is advisable to start every major research project with a pilot survey. (Other terms for this are "pilot study," "pilot mailing," and "test mailing.") Pilot studies can be divided into several distinct categories by the purpose they serve.

1. Testing the quality of the mailing list
2. Checking the percentage of returns
3. Checking the effectiveness (in producing higher percentage of returns) of various segments of the data-gathering process, such as postcards, advance letters, incentives, and various types of follow-up efforts
4. Checking the occurrence of bias resulting from the wording of cards, letters, and questionnaires
5. Checking on how well questions are understood and answered
6. Checking the usefulness of information received
7. Checking or even establishing a cost estimate

BASIC PRINCIPLES

Before discussing in some detail each of these pilot study purposes, it is important to list a few basic principles which are essential to all of them:

1. Each pilot study has to be conducted among a random sample of the universe surveyed. Obviously a biased sample (as regards geographic division, sex, age, or any other criterion) would be as wrong for the test as for the main mailing.

2. The number of questionnaires to be mailed in a test study should be large enough (that is, sufficiently stable) to make the results meaningful for the purpose of the test. For example, 200, or even 100, questionnaires mailed out in a test may furnish enough information on some of the qualifications of the mailing list or on the approximate percentage of returns. A pilot study of this size, however, might be completely inadequate to foretell how the answers to basic questions will fall.

3. We must not try to measure more than one variable at a time. For example, if we want to measure the effectiveness of using an advance postcard (Chap. 10) and of using a 25¢ incentive, there is not much point in sending out a pilot mailing of 400, with 200 containing the quarter incentive and preceded by the postcard and the other 200 without either of these elements. We would not know from the returns whether any difference in the percentage or nature of the response was caused by the postcard, the money incentive, or the combined effect of both. The proper procedure is to divide the 400 test names into 4 random groups or cells of 100 each:

   a. Neither postcard, nor incentive
   b. Postcard, no incentive
   c. Incentive, no postcard
   d. Both postcard and incentive

Of course the questionnaire groups must be coded by color or key number to distinguish the returns. This way it will become clear what the reason for any difference in the percentage of returns was. In some cases there may be a dozen such groups or cells in the pilot survey. The essential consideration is that each cell should test only one variable, while all other elements of the mailing remain constant. Each of these cells must be a separate random sample of the universe and has to be based on a mailing large enough to result in a meaningful measurement of the specific element it is testing.

Bearing in mind these general rules, we can return to a discussion of the categories of pilot studies as defined by their purpose.

PURPOSES OF PILOT STUDIES

1. Testing the quality of the mailing list. Unless we have a good idea of the quality of the mailing list because we have used it before or know enough about the sources from which we compiled or bought it, we cannot predict how good it will be for our purpose until it is tested. For example, the list may be old, or it may have been used for a large number of promotional mailings or surveys. In one case the "undeliverable" mailings may be too high (because people have died, moved, etc.), while in the other case the nonresponse may be excessive. The list may not represent what it was supposed to: a list of supposed recent purchasers of Volvo cars may include a group of Volkswagen buyers. Occasionally pilot studies reveal that the mailing list does not represent a random sample of the universe.

2. Checking the percentage of return is the most common reason for sending out pilot mailings. The feasibility of conducting a proposed mail survey cannot be ascertained without knowing that people in the sample are willing to complete and return the questionnaire. Unless the researcher has had some experience with similar types of research, it is advisable to be cautious and make sure that he is actually conducting a survey, not just sending out a mailing.

3. Checking the effectiveness of various "return boosters." Unless the researcher is sure that he can achieve a high percentage of response without any special effort, he may want to test the effectiveness of advance or reminder postcards or letters, various incentives enclosed with the questionnaire or offered to respondents, the "pulling power" of several alternative accompanying letters, a shorter or longer questionnaire, and various types of follow-up. One seldom has to worry about *all* these variables, but quite often one or two of them may well be tested.

4. Checking the occurrence of bias. Avoiding, or at least minimizing, bias is a major problem in many types of mail surveys. A discussion of this problem will be found in several of the chapters of this book. The pilot study, especially when it is based on a reasonably large number (several hundred) questionnaires, may indicate the presence of bias arising from any number of sources: mailing list, letter, card, incentive, questionnaire, time of the year, etc.

5. Checking how well questions are understood and answered. In Chapter 7 we discuss the importance of using precise, clear questions in an attempt to elicit equally precise, clear answers. However, even the most experienced researcher can miss the inherent ambiguity of some question insofar as a specific group of respondents is concerned. By carefully scanning or by tabulating the pilot returns it is usually

possible to ferret out such soft spots and obtain more precise answers, sometimes by changing just one or two words in a question.

6. Checking the usefulness of the information is important on all mail surveys. We may find that the respondents simply do not know the answers to some of our questions or that they are not willing to divulge them. Some surveys are conducted in order to prove a point which the sponsor considers valid, such as the leading position of a brand or a publication. The test study may indicate that the results would show the sponsor's preconceived ideas to be wrong and that, if the planned survey had no other purpose, he should not waste any more money on it.

7. Checking the cost estimate. It is often impossible to give a close estimate of the costs of a mail survey without knowing how many questionnaires have to be mailed out and what kind of incentives and follow-ups have to be used in order to secure the required number of questionnaires and the planned percentage of returns. Furthermore, the completeness and precision of answers received may make a substantial difference in the time and cost involved in editing and coding.

PILOT STUDIES ARE WORTH DOING

Pilot studies are sometimes omitted because of time and cost considerations. This is often false economy. A little advance planning can reduce both the time and the cost needed for testing.

In most situations no follow-up mailing is needed for the pilot study because the additional percentage of response resulting from a follow-up mailing can be approximately predicted from the percentage of response to the first mailing (Figs. 54–57). In many situations it is also possible to gain all the required information from the pilot study by counting the responses from the various test cells, by careful inspection of the returns, and by a quick tabulation of the answers to a few important questions. By using air mail both ways a large enough percentage of the returns will come in within two weeks to enable the researcher to draw his conclusions. If the result of the pilot study does not call for any major changes in the questionnaire, the total time loss due to such a pilot study need not be more than fifteen or sixteen days even though the test was nationwide.

In most cases, provided the questionnaire has been carefully constructed, the results of the test will not indicate the need for any major change. If the main mailing follows the pilot mailing by two to three weeks, the returns from the pilot test can usually be included in the main survey. If the original survey design called for mailing 4,000 questionnaires and the test consisted of 400 then the careful researcher will start with two random samples, containing 400 and 4,000 names respectively. However, if he finds that he did a good job to begin with and that the questionnaire does not have to be changed, he can pull a random 400 from his sample of 4,000 and mail 3,600, the missing 400 being made up by using the pilot study as an integral part of the main survey. In cost accounting this means that his only additional expenditure for the pilot study consisted of processing and mailing the 400 and the 3,600 questionnaires separately and the planning and evaluating of the test mailing. In a major survey costing thousands of dollars such a pilot study may cost a few hundred dollars.

It is obvious that pilot studies can guide the researcher and considerably improve the quality of his research. It may not be so obvious that he may also save money. A pilot survey may prove the percentage of returns to be higher than expected and that therefore a smaller number of questionnaires can be mailed. It may show that by using the right incentive the number mailed can be drastically reduced. Or it may prove that the survey cannot possibly produce the desired results (either quantitatively or qualitatively), in which case the forewarned researcher will have saved the lion's share of the budget allocation by *not* doing the rest of the survey.

TEN
Advance Notice of the Questionnaire

MANY TESTS HAVE SHOWN that the percentage of returns can be increased by an advance notice. The following are some of the types of advance notice which have proved successful.

The simplest and least expensive way of announcing a survey is to send out advance postcards. It is more effective when the sender or his organization is known to the recipient. For example, a test conducted among subscribers to a well-known magazine showed that an advance postcard, containing a one-line personalization and the facsimile signature of the research director of the publication, increased single-mailing response from 50 to 58 percent. Both the card and the questionnaire were mailed by the magazine to its subscribers. The same advance card and the same questionnaire were mailed to another random sample of subscribers to the same publication, but this time the name of a research organization was used on the postcard, letterhead, and envelopes, and the recipients had no way of knowing that the magazine was the sponsor of the survey. This time the additional response among the recipients of the advance postcard was only 3 percent instead of the 8 percent differential resulting from the advance card sent in the name of the publication.

It is difficult to generalize on the effectiveness of advance cards, because it varies on different surveys. Logically the card should be more effective when sent to a home address, because it has a better chance to get directly to the addressee than it does when it must get past a secretary, but it has often proved to be of great help even on mailings to business addresses. Of course it should be used only when it can be sent to an individual whose name is known ("Mr. Smith," and not "General Manager"). It should be timed to arrive two to five days before the questionnaire.

The easiest form to use is the standard government postcard. The copy will depend on the nature of the survey, but it has to be short, polite, and to the point. Figure 13 is an example.

Dear Mr. Smythe:

    We are asking your help in a nationwide research project.

    In a few days you will receive our simple questionnaire. It will take but a short time to fill out -- and your answers will be of the greatest importance to the success of our survey.

    We would appreciate your cooperation.

                       James B. Jones
                  James B. Jones, Director
              Professional Mail Surveys Company

FIGURE 13 Advance postcard.

The effect of the postcard can be increased by a reference to it on the outgoing envelope which contains the questionnaire. This can be a single line printed in red on the lower left part of the envelope:

THIS IS THE SURVEY WE WROTE YOU ABOUT.

This reference is most useful when the sender is an organization, institution, or publication which has used the same mailing list in the past for promotion, renewal notices, billing, and so on. The reference on the envelope will make it clear to the recipient that the envelope does not contain "unpleasant" mail, such as bills and renewal notices or junk mail.

THE ADVANCE LETTER

An advance letter serves approximately the same purpose as the postcard and generally the same rules apply to it. Several researchers have tested the effectiveness of advance letters and found them helpful.[1] It is usually used in the following situations:

1. When the sample consists of persons too important to be sent a postcard, for example, senators and chairmen of the board. In such cases it is important that the highest-ranking member of the sender's organization sign the letter.

2. The message is too long for a card. This should not be true in most cases. Figure 14 illustrates a special situation which warrants a longer letter: The sponsor, a manufacturer, advises its dealers that a forthcoming survey will be conducted by an outside organization in order to guarantee anonymity to respondents and thereby encourage frank replies.

3. The contents of the survey, or even the fact that it is being done, is confidential.

4. When there is reason to believe, or a pilot study has actually proved that an advance letter is much more effective in a particular instance than an advance postcard, and therefore it justifies the additional expense.

OTHER METHODS OF GIVING ADVANCE NOTICE

Telephone introduction of a mail questionnaire is a rather expensive method for giving advance notice. Obviously this method would not be used in the case of a short questionnaire, but it has been found effective when an important research project involving a lengthy questionnaire required a special effort. In one case the preliminary telephone call resulted in 47.8 percent replies within ten days as against 28 percent without phone calls.[2] Another published test showed that the percentage of replies increased from 20.5 to 68.2 percent with the help of a prior phone call.[3]

Notice of the survey in a publication can be very helpful when the sample is drawn from among its subscribers or from the membership of the association or organization which publishes it. The notice in Figure 15 appeared in *Barron's* magazine a few days before a random sample of its subscribers received the questionnaires.

THE A.B.C. CORP.

Camping and Hunting Equipment
"The Top o' the Line"

175 Mercedes Road
Long Lake, Illinois 60710

April 7, 19--

Dear Mr. Smythe,

As one of our valued dealers, we would like your opinion with regard to a proposed advertising campaign. A.B.C. dealers would participate in this campaign by underwriting part of the cost.

In a few days you will receive a questionnaire about this plan in the mail. Please have the person responsible for advertising at your company fill out the form. It will take only a few minutes of his time to answer it.

In order to keep all replies confidential, we have engaged an independent market research organization, Professional Mail Surveys Co. of New York, to administer the survey. They will process the questionnaires and report only the statistical totals to us.

Because the individual reply of every dealer is important, we would appreciate it if you would make sure that the questionnaire receives prompt attention when it arrives.

Cordially yours,
The A.B.C. Corp.

J. Herbert Strong

J. Herbert Strong,
Marketing Research Manager

JHS/lp

FIGURE 14 Advance letter.

Notice to Subscribers

Every week Barron's provides facts for you. Now we would like to get some facts from you.

Selected at random from our subscriber rolls, many of you will receive questionnaires in the next few days. We need information for a composite profile of our subscribers as readers of Barron's. We would like to know something about you as a business man, as an investor and as a homeowner. We would also like to know something about your buying preferences and your travel for business and pleasure.

If you are among those who receive a questionnaire in the mail, we will be most grateful if you take the time to fill out the form. Although your answers will be used to form statistical tables, rest assured you are far more than a statistic to us, and we deeply appreciate your cooperation.

Research Department

BARRON'S

FIGURE 15 Advance notice of survey.

REFERENCES

1. Eugene H. Heaton, Jr., "Increasing Mail Questionnaire Returns with a Preliminary Letter," *Journal of Advertising Research*, vol. 5, no. 4, pp. 36–39, December, 1965; also, James E. Stafford, "Influence of Preliminary Contact on Mail Returns," *Journal of Marketing Research*, vol. 3, no. 4, pp. 410–411, November, 1966; also, Neil M. Ford, "The Advance Letter in Mail Surveys," *Journal of Marketing Research*, vol. 4, no. 2, pp. 202–204, May, 1967.
2. F. B. Waisanen, "A Note on the Response to a Mailed Questionnaire," *Public Opinion Quarterly*, vol. 18, no. 2, pp. 210–212, summer, 1954.
3. James E. Stafford, *op. cit.*

ELEVEN
Incentives

THE USE OF AN APPROPRIATE INCENTIVE will usually increase the response rate, which, in turn, will make the results of the survey more reliable. Incentives are needed whenever the subject matter of the questionnaire is not of sufficient interest, or the prestige of the sender not impressive enough, to induce a high proportion of the sample to complete and return the questionnaire.

The following considerations are important in selecting the incentive for a survey:

1. It has to be effective in increasing the percentage of response.
2. The incentive must do this without biasing distribution of the returns in any way.
3. Its cost must fit the available research budget.
4. It should be small and light enough to be mailed easily and inexpensively.

There are two ways of using incentives: Either they are mailed out with the questionnaire, or they are promised as a gift to those answering the questionnaire and mailed to them after they have sent in their answers.

It is more effective to send out the incentive with the questionnaire, but unless the incentive is very inexpensive and the percentage of returns quite high, this is the more costly procedure. Nevertheless, this method is recommended for surveys conducted in the United States, where most researchers use the kinds of incentives which are interesting enough to capture the attention of the addressee, but not valuable enough to constitute "payment."

In international surveys where currency, which is the most commonly used incentive for domestic surveys, cannot easily be used, the situation is quite different and will be discussed in Chapter 24.

Many different kinds of incentives have been used in an effort to induce mail survey recipients to answer questionnaires. Among them are trading stamps, unused postage stamps, packets of stamps for collectors, tie clips, pennies (both United States and foreign), books, pencils, and pens. Many tests have been made to check the effectiveness of various incentives and a number of these have been published.[1]

In general, money seems to be the most effective and least biasing incentive, the easiest to obtain and mail, and the most useful to *all* recipients. This last point is extremely important from the point of view of bias. If the researcher uses foreign postage stamps as an incentive, he may end up with a sample slanted toward stamp collectors or fathers of stamp collectors. If he promises a classical record he may get an entirely different distribution of his respondents in age and education than if he had promised a rock-and-roll record. With the use of any incentive the question must be raised whether it is about equally desirable to all members of the sample or whether it will have more attraction for one particular segment.

When using incentives in general, and money in particular, it must always be borne in mind that the incentive is not supposed to be a payment or even a reward, but only an attention getter and a token of appreciation. In this day and age nobody would feel that he is well paid with a quarter or even a dollar bill for answering a questionnaire. People's time is worth more, or at least they want to think it is. The sample letter in Figure 16 shows how the desired effect can be achieved.

Dimes, quarters, and dollar bills are the incentives most often used in the United States. In most surveys such incentives will substantially increase the percentage of response, but the researcher must know which premium to use and how to use it. With a 25¢ coin incentive one can sometimes increase the response by half or more. R. A. Robinson has described a test in which the control group (no incentive) returned 15 percent of the questionnaires, while the test group (25¢

coin inducement) completed and returned 70 percent of the questionnaires mailed.[2] This is an extraordinary increase; a coin incentive is not usually that effective. Nevertheless in a great many cases the use of a money premium is the best way to achieve a high percentage of response.

WHY MONEY IS AN EFFECTIVE INCENTIVE

Money is an attention getter, especially if it is neatly and attractively presented. Experienced researchers always use new (uncirculated) money: shiny coins or crisp bills. The coin may be enclosed in a cellophane envelope, which will make it more attractive in appearance and also keep it from sliding around in the out-going envelope. In most cases it is not the value of the enclosed coin or bill which achieves the desired effect, but its attention-getting ability. A dime has some effect, but is somewhat puny compared with a quarter. Paper money is more dramatic than a coin, but in some cases it does not seem to have made much difference whether the incentive was $1 or a $5 bill.

We can report an interesting aspect of a research project conducted among doctors without trying to attach any particular statistical, medical, or sociological significance to the findings. A large drug company sponsored a survey among 4,000 doctors, 400 in each of 10 specialties such as pediatrics, internal medicine, and surgery. The survey plan called for a 60 percent response rate. A pilot study showed that the use of a new 25¢ coin incentive would achieve the required response rate in 9 of the groups of 10 specialties. Doctors in the tenth group, the psychiatrists, were not responsive enough to the 25¢ incentive, but yielded the required percentage of response when a crisp, new $1 bill was enclosed with the questionnaire instead of the quarter. Perhaps the subject matter of the questionnaire (drug samples) was of less interest to psychiatrists than to other doctors, and therefore a more effective attention getter was needed.

Money poses a problem to the recipient. What does he do with that shiny quarter? Put it in his pocket without answering? To most people this seems a bit dishonest. Throw it away? That would be plain silly. Return it without completing the questionnaire? This is almost as much trouble as returning the completed questionnaire. This psychology works on secretaries too: The young lady who might ordinarily try to screen her boss from what she considers a time-wasting questionnaire may still feel obliged to show him a mailing which contains a coin or dollar bill. After all, it's *his* money!

MONEY INCENTIVES AND BIAS: EXECUTIVE RESPONSE

Money causes little if any bias. One might think that poor people, having more need for money, would be more moved to answer by a money incentive than wealthy people. This, however, does not seem to be true.

A publication wanted to conduct a survey on the newspaper and magazine reading habits of the top executives of the largest corporations of the United States. The research plan called for a random sampling of the top executives of United States firms having a net worth of $1 million or more. The research man suggested testing two different incentives. Top management agreed that this was a good idea but wanted to know what kinds of incentives would be tested. Upon being told that the researcher wanted to test the effectiveness of a dime against a quarter, management was quite dubious as to whether it made sense to send a dime to the chairman of the board of a large automobile manufacturer or to mail a quarter to the president of a giant bank. However, management agreed to make the test. The same mailing was sent to three random samples of 666 executives, the only difference being the incentive and the reference to it in the postscript of the accompanying letter. To one of the three random samples no premium was mailed, and the letter had no postscript. The executives in the second sample received a new dime in a cellophane envelope, while the members of the third sample got an unused quarter. The questionnaire was a one-page, one-side sheet with open-end questions on newspaper and magazine reading and preference. The percentage of returns was as follows:

With the 25¢ coin incentive:	63%
With the 10¢ coin incentive:	54%
With no incentive:	40%

This test showed that powerful, affluent business executives are susceptible to coin premiums. The next example proves that these incentives do not appear to bias the demographic distribution of a sample in any predictable way.

MONEY INCENTIVES AND BIAS: CLASSIFICATION DATA TESTS

On a readership survey, questionnaires were mailed to 5,000 people —most of whom were in business or professional occupations. Of this number a random 1,000 received a 25¢ coin. On a single mailing, 58 percent returns were received from the premium mailing and 35 percent returns from the nonpremium mailing. Here are some classification data tables for the two groups:

	Percentage of respondents	
	With premium	Without premium
Age:		
Under 25	3	3
25–44	54	55
45–64	33	33
65 and over	10	9
Marital status:		
Married	88	88
Single	12	12
Yearly family income:		
Under $5,000	16	19
$ 5,000–$ 9,999	46	48
$10,000–$14,999	19	17
$15,000 and over	19	16

These tables show remarkable consistency in the age and marital-status tables. The differences in the income percentages, though too small to affect the results of the survey, are in the opposite direction from what we might have expected: The average income of premium respondents was somewhat higher than that of nonpremium repliers. I cannot offer any explanation for this unless it is that while the wealthier citizens apparently appreciate the value of a quarter, at the same time they don't like to accept something for nothing.

On a survey conducted for a publication, 3,752 questionnaires were mailed to builders who had attended the National Association of Home Builders convention. In the first mailing, half received quarters, the other half did not. The premium mailing drew replies from 56 percent, the other received replies from 34 percent. Analysis by classification data of this first mailing showed only small differences between the two groups:

	Percentage of respondents	
	With premium	Without premium
Education:		
Grade school	5	4
High school	29	26
College	66	70
Number of homes built by respondent's firm during the past year:		
1– 9	19	19
10–49	48	47
50–99	16	15
100 or more	17	19

OTHER ADVANTAGES OF MONEY INCENTIVES

Money is small and light. In the case of two-page or four-page questionnaires the inclusion of a dime or a $1 bill does not add to the postage. The 25¢ coin will not increase the postage of the two-page questionnaire or of the Monarch-size four-page questionnaire on average weight paper. But it will double the out-going postage on the 8½- by 11-in. four-pager.

The researcher has flexibility in using money incentives. He can use it in the main mailing and in one or more follow-up mailings. He can use it only in the first mailing or only in one of the follow-up mailings. He can increase the amount of the incentive in successive mailings.

The following is a test of the pulling power of a quarter versus a dollar bill in a specific universe. A survey was conducted among executives of advertising agencies to test the penetration of various publicity messages and slogans aimed at this particular group. A test mailing was sent to each of three random samples of 200 executives. Each group received the same one-page, two-side questionnaire with the usual letter and reply envelope. The first group received no premium, the second group got a new 25¢ coin, and the third group received a new $1 bill. On the second mailing the researcher sent a $1 bill to those who had received no premium the first time, and no premium to those who had received one before.

The following table shows the results of this test.

	Group 1	Group 2	Group 3
First mailing (Nov. 16)			
Premium	None	25¢	$1
Returns (% of total mailing)	23%	40%	54%
Second mailing (Dec. 7)			
Premium	$1	None	None
Returns	27%	3%	6%
Total returns	50%	43%	60%

Of course the percentage of response can be improved by using incentives in both mailings. This will also be discussed in Chapter 14, which deals with techniques of follow-up mailings.

People with no research experience often feel that it is wasteful to give away money. It can be easily shown that by using money incentives the researcher can often save money. The first saving is simply the fact that, because of the higher response rate, the sponsor paid for a reliable survey instead of wasting his money on a poor one. Next, there can be actual savings on a per-questionnaire basis, even though the total cost of the research is somewhat higher.[3] Finally, sometimes when the percentage of replies is much higher with the use of an incentive, the number mailed can be reduced to such an extent that there is an actual saving in terms of total research cost.[4] There is evidence that the use of money incentives results not only in higher response, but also in more completely filled out questionnaires.[5]

The Appendix shows the mail-out and return figures for 413 different surveys, representing over 700,000 mailings. Most of the surveys included incentives.

REFERENCES

1. Robert D. Brennan, "Trading Stamps as an Incentive in Mail Surveys," *Journal of Marketing*, vol. 22, no. 1, pp. 306–307, January, 1958; also, Andrew E. Kimball, "Increasing the Rate of Return in Mail Surveys," *Journal of Marketing*, vol. 25, no. 6, pp. 63–64, October, 1961; also, William M. Kephart and Marvin Bressler, "Increasing the Responses to Mail Questionnaires: A Research Study," *Public Opinion Quarterly*, vol. 22, no. 2, pp. 123–132, summer, 1958; also, John J. Watson, "Improving the Response Rate in Mail Research," *Journal of Advertising Research*, vol. 5, no. 2, pp. 48–50, June, 1965.
2. R. A. Robinson, "How to Boost Returns from Mail Surveys," *Printers' Ink*, vol. 237, no. 6, p. 36, June 6, 1952.
3. Lester R. Frankel, "How Incentives and Subsamples Affect the Precision of Mail Surveys," *Journal of Advertising Research*, vol. 1, no. 1, pp. 1–5, September, 1960.
4. R. A. Robinson and Philip Agisim, "Making Mail Surveys More Reliable," *Journal of Marketing*, vol. 15, no. 4, pp. 415–424, April, 1951.
5. Thomas R. Wotruba, "Monetary Inducements and Mail Questionnaire Response," *Journal of Marketing Research*, vol. 3, no. 4, pp. 398–400, November, 1966.

Note: Parts of this chapter were contained in articles the author wrote for *Printers' Ink* (now known as *Marketing/Communications*.)

TWELVE
The Accompanying Letter

THE ACCOMPANYING LETTER, or letter of transmittal, represents an all-important step in the effort to get back a high percentage of the questionnaires mailed. Before the addressee opens the envelope, he or she can have no idea of the contents. I am assuming now that the researcher did a good job and that the shape, addressing, stamping, and color of the envelope and the first look at its contents will *not* give the recipient the impression that he is dealing with junk mail which can be thrown away without being read. He may notice practically at the same time, an interesting and easy-looking questionnaire, a premium (incentive), a stamped reply envelope, and a letter. If he reads the letter, the first hurdle has been passed.

What will induce a busy housewife or an important executive to read your letter? There are a number of things which can attract his or her attention: It looks interesting; it can give an answer to the puzzling question "Why should anyone send me a quarter?"; it looks important, and beyond all other consideration, it appears short, therefore the reader will not have to waste much time to find out what the whole thing is about.

The next hurdle comes *after* the reading: Will the letter fulfill its purpose, which is to induce the reader to complete and return the enclosed questionnaire? The answer depends to a large extent on the contents of the letter, and that is why the accompanying letter is so important and why it very seldom happens that a good letter is written in a hurry. Usually it is the result of a series of painstaking rewritings and thorough discussion.

The following list shows the most important thoughts good letters should convey and the most important considerations in their construction:

1. Personal communication.
2. Asking a favor.
3. Importance of the research project and its purpose.
4. Importance of the recipient.
5. Importance of the replies in general.
6. Importance of the replies where the reader is not qualified to answer most questions.
7. How the recipient may benefit from this research.
8. Completing the questionnaire will take only a short time.
9. The questionnaire can be answered easily.
10. A stamped reply envelope is enclosed.
11. How recipient was selected.
12. Answers are anonymous or confidential.
13. Offer to send report on results of survey.
14. Note of urgency.
15. Appreciation of sender.
16. Importance of sender.
17. Importance of the sender's organization.
18. Description and purpose of incentive.
19. Avoiding bias.
20. Style.
21. Format and appearance.
22. Brevity.

Each of these considerations merits detailed discussion, but first let us look at a sample letter embodying most of them (Fig. 16).

Of course it rarely happens that all twenty-two elements mentioned above are needed or can be used. Since brevity is very important, we do not want to use a single sentence which does not earn its keep by serving a definite purpose. In Figure 17 we show a short letter which was actually used on a very successful mail survey.

PROFESSIONAL MAIL SURVEYS COMPANY —— 17

7432 East Court Avenue

Elveron, California 90101

213 991-5550

(Date)

1 —— Dear Mr. Smythe:

2 —— Will you do us a favor?

3 —— We are conducting a nationwide survey among executives and managers in the metalworking industries. The purpose of this research is to find out the opinion of yourself and other experts on the advantages and disadvantages of using three new steel products. Your —— 1
5 —— answers will enable steel manufacturers to be aware of the requirements of the users and the opinions of non-users of these items
3 —— and this in turn will help them to design the products you need.
— 6   — 7

5 —— Your name appeared in a scientifically selected random sample. —— 11
6 —— Your answers are very important to the accuracy of our research, whether or not your company is a user of one or more of the products described.

9 —— It will take only a short time to answer the simple questions on the enclosed questionnaire and to return it in the stamped reply envelope. —— 10

12 ——
Of course all answers are confidential and will be used only in combination with those of other metalworking executives and managers —— 4
3 —— from all over the U.S.

13 —— If you are interested in receiving a report on the findings of this research, just write your name and address at the end of this questionnaire, or if you prefer, request the results of the Survey on Steel Products in a separate letter. We will be glad to send you a complimentary report when ready.
12

14 —— Please return the completed questionnaire at your earliest convenience. Thank you for your help.
15

Sincerely,

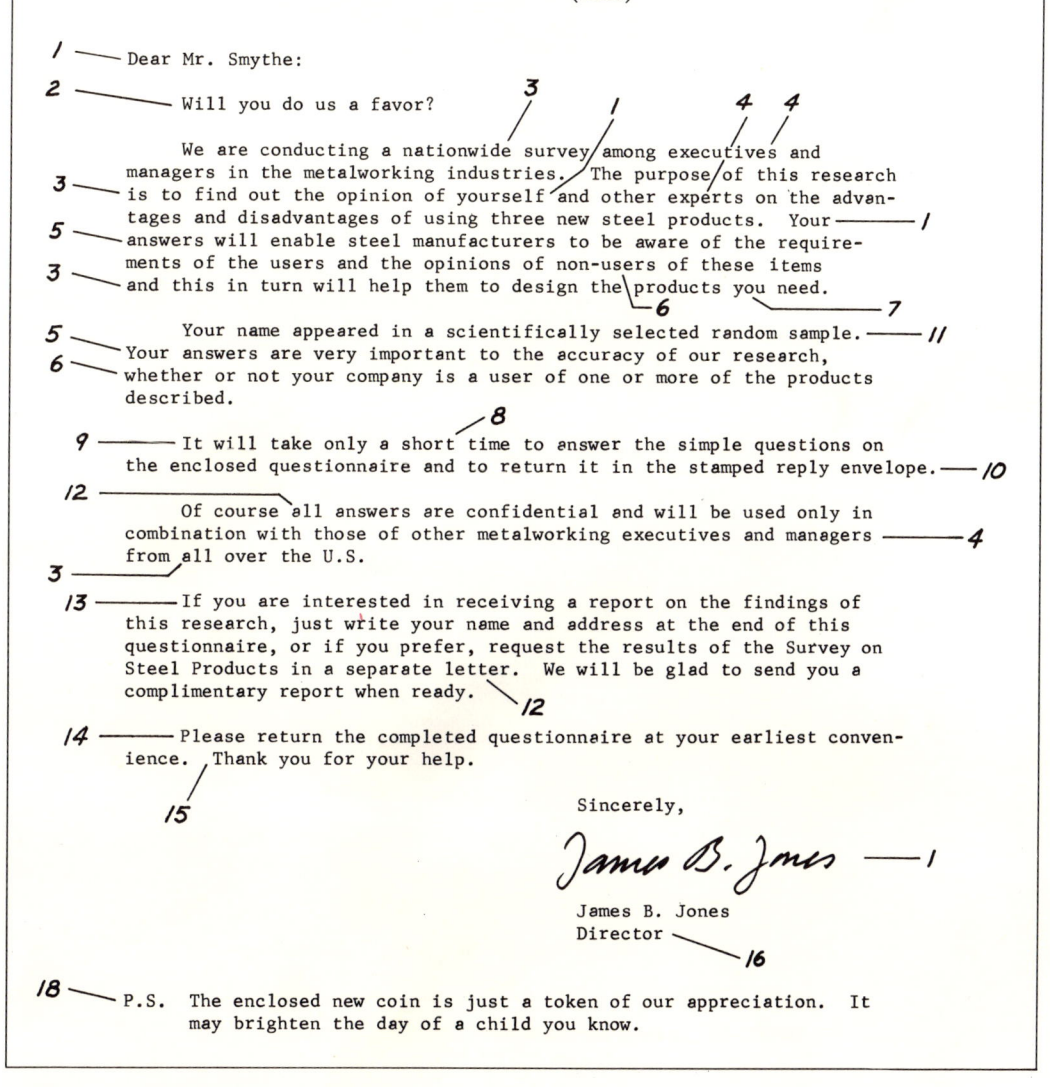

James B. Jones —— 1

James B. Jones
Director
—— 16

18 —— P.S. The enclosed new coin is just a token of our appreciation. It may brighten the day of a child you know.

FIGURE 16 Accompanying letter. (Numbers refer to corresponding subchapters in Chapter 12.)

PROFESSIONAL MAIL SURVEYS COMPANY

7432 East Court Avenue

Elveron, California 90101

213 991-5550

(Date)

Dear Mr. Clark:

    We are conducting a survey to gather information on the leisure time activities of American families.

    It will take but a few moments of your time to answer the simple questions on the enclosed form and you might find it a pleasant experience.

    Your answers will be kept confidential and used only in combination with others to get a composite picture. They are essential to the accuracy of our research. We enclose a stamped reply envelope for your convenience.

    Thank you for your valuable assistance.

Sincerely,

Earl P. West

Dr. Earl P. West

P.S. The enclosed crisp dollar bill is just a token of our appreciation.

FIGURE 17 Accompanying letter.

Now let us consider each of the twenty-two points on our list.

1. PERSONAL COMMUNICATION

It cannot be repeated too often that the best and usually the only way to get a high percentage of response on mail surveys is to create the feeling of personal communication between researcher and respondent. The letter should look like a personal communication, starting with the recipient's name typed in to match the body of the letter and ending with the sender's signature printed in blue. The addressee should get the impression that the letter he is holding in his hand was addressed to him by an individual who personally signed it, and this impression must be established *before* he has had a chance to read a single word of the message. After reading it, he will know exactly what it is all about, who wrote it and why, but we need every possible inducement to make a busy person *read* the letter. The slightest suggestion that this may be a form letter, a sales message, or some kind of junk mail may mean that the entire mailing piece will wind up in the waste basket without ever having been read.

Addressing the recipient by name (personalizing) will always make the letter look more personal than a "Dear Sir" salutation. However, tests showed little or no difference in returns whether a one-line personalization ("Dear Mr. Jones") or a full fill-in (containing the name and address, followed by "Dear Mr. Jones") was used in a survey of businessmen. It is very important that the personalization should be accurate, otherwise it may have exactly the opposite effect from the one intended. Correct spelling of the name, correct use of military ranks and of titles, such as "Senator," "The Rev. Mr.," "Dr.," are very important. It also helps if we are sure of the sex of the recipient, and this may be difficult, because some names on a list may have only initials instead of first names, and some names are used by both sexes.

There is evidence that in some cases the personalization of the letter will increase the percentage of returns only very slightly,[1] not at all,[2] or may even decrease the response rate. The researcher whose study indicated this negative effect of personalization on the employees of an industrial firm tested a personalized and individually typed accompanying letter against a mimeographed form letter. He thought that a possible reason for the negative effect of the personalized letters may have been that ". . . when used in surveys of employees they cause respondents to reflect that anonymity, even though assured, is not really certain because the letters are addressed to them personally."[3] Nevertheless, a number of tests conducted by the author have indicated that personalization of the letter will generally increase the response by several percentage points.

Another personal touch is using the second person ("you," "yourself") in the copy of the letter, instead of talking in the third person about those receiving the questionnaire (Fig. 16).

There are situations where we do not know the name of the person who should receive the questionnaire. In some of these cases an effort can still be made to direct the questionnaire to a person in the sample, and paradoxically, a sort of personal relationship can be established by explaining to this person why the letter was not personalized.

From time to time the *Wall Street Journal* conducts a survey among its subscribers. Some copies of this publication are addressed just to companies, and in these cases the names of the individuals receiving them are unknown. The letter accompanying this particular group of questionnaires starts as follows:

> Please direct this letter to the attention of the person who receives the daily copy of the *Wall Street Journal*
>
> Dear Reader:
> We wanted to start this letter with your name, but we don't know it since your subscription lists only your company's name.

2. ASKING A FAVOR

It pays to be polite. A split mailing test among businessmen showed that the "Will you do us a favor?" line increased returns by 2 to 3 percent. This is a small percentage and it may not work in all circumstances, but there can be very few cases where it can cause damage. It is not essential, of course, and may be omitted where the nature of the survey calls for the shortest possible letter (such as shown in Fig. 17).

"Asking a favor" can be more effective if it can be made more specific by putting it on a reciprocal basis. The following is a quotation from the letter of transmittal of quite a successful survey of businessmen:

> We hope that you will give us the same friendly kind of advice you might some day want from other American businessmen.

3. IMPORTANCE OF THE RESEARCH PROJECT AND ITS PURPOSE

This example illustrates a situation which is unusual in one sense: Usually one should avoid emphasizing the commercial or businesss aspect of the survey. It might interest the reader of your letter to participate in an important research project. If the letter explains that the main purpose of the survey is to make a product more profitable or to help in selling advertising space for a TV station, the reaction can easily be "Someone will make a lot of money with the help of my answers—what do I get out of it?" Obviously such reasoning is not very conducive to completing the questionnaire. For the same reason it is poor practice to write: "We have been commissioned by a large manufacturer to conduct this survey." Unless the sponsor's name adds prestige to the letter and can be used without introducing bias, it is better to omit it and write about the importance of the research and how it can help the respondent, his company, industry, or profession.

The importance of the project can be indicated by describing the nationwide or industrywide scope of the project. Another, and possibly the best method, whenever it is applicable, is to emphasize the benefits the research project may bring to a profession, an industry, or a group of people. Of course it is essential that all such claims should be true and sound reasonable. It would not be reasonable to say that the respondent will be able to buy a cheaper car as a result of a survey about metals—it is believable that it will enable producers to have better information about the requirements of industrial respondents and that this might induce them to produce more appropriate basic products.

The logical approach is to explain the purpose of the survey to the addressee, and the usual place to do so is in the beginning of the letter. It should be done in a few words and, if possible, connected with a hint about the importance of the project. On the other hand, there are cases where it is not advisable to mention the purpose of the survey at all. For instance, if we feel that the subject of the survey is not pleasant to the respondents, we may decide to say nothing about it in the letter and try to sandwich the less palatable questions in the questionnaire between more pleasant ones. In some cases we may feel that describing the purpose of the survey would bias answers, and in others the purpose may be too vague or involved to be readily explained. Finally, we may decide that such explanation is not important enough to warrant adding to the length of the letter. In all such cases the description of the purpose of the research can be omitted. The description of the survey, which usually begins the letter, will than be replaced by a description of the group among whose members it is being conducted (Fig. 18).

PROFESSIONAL MAIL SURVEYS COMPANY

7432 East Court Avenue

Elveron, California 90101

213 991-5550

(Date)

Dear Mr. Smith:

    We are conducting a nationwide survey among key purchasing men.

    It will take only a few moments of your time to check the simple questions on the enclosed sheet and return it in the stamped reply envelope.

    Your answers are very important to the accuracy of our survey. Of course all replies are confidential and will be used only in combination with answers from other key purchasing men from all over the U.S.

    Thank you for your help.

Sincerely yours,

James B. Jones

James B. Jones
Director

P.S. The enclosed bright coin is just a token of our appreciation.

FIGURE 18 Accompanying letter.

4. IMPORTANCE OF THE RECIPIENT

Everybody likes to feel important, to know that he is a member of an important group, and to realize that he is participating in an important project. On the other hand, few people like to be flattered if they feel the flattery is insincere or has an ulterior motive. Once more, truthfulness must be the guideline. A good writer may dramatize the truth or show it in the most flattering light, but will never go beyond it. Of course there is a very fine line between politeness and flattery. Administrative and managerial employees of United States business firms do not object to being referred to as "executives and managers" or even "executives," but once on a similar survey made in Switzerland scores of blank questionnaires were returned, noting that the recipient was only an assistant director or department manager and was therefore ineligible to answer a questionnaire aimed at higher echelons. The Swiss may be excessively modest or take things too literally, but every reader has a "line of demarcation" about flattery. There is no sense in addressing the subscribers to a mass publication as "key men of America," even though a number of them may be just that. It is also not reasonable to talk in your letter about "an important executive like yourself" or to address executives as "captains of industry." Meaningless statements should also be avoided, such as "We are conducting a survey among important people." The letter writer has to find the highest possible title, rank, or description which will still fit the lowest-ranking person in the research sample. Of course one can use more than one title, for example, "We are sending this questionnaire to executives, managers, and professional men."

Rule of thumb: When writing a letter, try to give the reader the impression that he is very important to you (he is!), but once you have finished your letter, reread it to make sure that it does not ring false and that the tone is not obsequious.

5. IMPORTANCE OF THE REPLIES IN GENERAL

The reader of your communication should feel that it is very important to you that he should answer and return the completed questionnaire. This can be simply stated, as in the letter in Figure 17. It can be stated more specifically, as follows:

> Since your name was drawn as one of a scientifically selected random sample representing the whole industry, your reply is essential to the accuracy of the survey.

The importance of the answers can also be emphasized by mentioning the limited size of the sample:

> This questionnaire is being sent to a small number of St. Louis registered voters, selected by a chance method. For this reason your replies are extremely important to the success of our poll.

As shown in the letter in Figure 16, another way of underlining the importance of the response is by connecting it with the ultimate usefulness of the survey.

6. IMPORTANCE OF THE REPLIES WHERE THE READER IS NOT QUALIFIED TO ANSWER MOST QUESTIONS

The recipient should be asked to return the questionnaire even if he is not qualified to answer most questions. This is necessary for two reasons: first, because we want a high percentage of response, and secondly, because in many cases nonresponse will introduce a bias. A good example for this situation is an automobile survey. In conducting such a survey among the subscribers to a publication, the letter included the following paragraph:

> <u>Your answers are of the greatest importance to the success of this study whether you own a car or not.</u>

After one follow-up mailing, 74 percent of a random sample of 10,000 subscribers had returned the four-page questionnaire. Without the quoted paragraph, many respondents who did not own a car would have failed to answer the questionnaire, assuming that it did not apply to them. With the help of the underscored request the proper percentage of nonowners sent in their answers. This was ascertained by checking the results of this research against figures from another, different type of survey conducted among members of the same universe. The "Please answer, whether ... or not ..." request is very important in all surveys where the researcher has reason to believe that the questionnaire would be of very little interest to nonowners, nonusers, nontravelers, or any other "negative" groups.

7. HOW THE RECIPIENT MAY BENEFIT FROM THIS RESEARCH

The usual way of making this appeal is by a reference to the benefits which the results of the survey may bring to the respondent as a member of a group. As a result of a survey on the editorial contents of a publication, the editors will try to make a magazine more interesting to its readers; a survey on auto accessories may result in some improvements which are of importance to drivers (including the respondent), and so on. In some cases the importance of the research project can be connected with benefits to very large groups, such as the people of a state, whole industry, the users of a group of products; in other instances it is possible to pinpoint the benefits to some group or institution closely connected with the respondent. In either case (as discussed under "Importance of the research project") the statement has to be both true and believable.

8. IT WILL TAKE ONLY A SHORT TIME

It is quite important to make this statement, even when the questionnaire is short. Once again it is essential to be truthful. When mailing a six-page questionnaire which may take forty-five minutes to complete, one cannot make the "short time" statement. In such cases it might be possible to point out that not all sections of the questionnaire will necessarily apply to the respondent or that he may find the questions interesting to answer.

9. THE QUESTIONNAIRE CAN BE ANSWERED EASILY

Even a short questionnaire may take a lot of thought to answer, or it may seem so to a person who has never answered one. The reference to simple questions easily answered is helpful in getting people to answer—provided it is true.

10. A STAMPED REPLY ENVELOPE IS ENCLOSED

This is a simple, but psychologically important, statement. It reminds the reader that it will not cost him any money or effort to return the questionnaire and that not only the envelope, but also a perfectly good stamp will be wasted if he fails to do so.

11. HOW RECIPIENT WAS SELECTED

Many readers of the letter will wonder why *they* happened to receive the questionnaire rather than their next-door neighbor. Whenever it can be done simply and the length of the letter permits, the researcher may want to answer this question by indicating that a chance (random) method was used in selecting the individual participants of the survey.

12. ANSWERS ARE ANONYMOUS OR CONFIDENTIAL

Most people are reluctant to answer some questions when they can be personally identified, and some people dislike to answer practically any question under these circumstances. A woman's age, an executive's income, opinions on controversial issues, religious or political affiliations are a few examples of the subjects which may be held as confidential and which respondents might be reluctant to discuss if aware they can be identified. It is very difficult to make cut-and-dried rules about the desirability of anonymous response, because the situation changes with the subject matter, respondent group, and sponsorship of the survey. In general one can say that assurance of anonymity is likely to help the response rate. If the questionnaire is keyed in any way, ethical researchers will not use the word "anonymous" and will not even imply it by saying "There is no need to sign your name." As a matter of fact in many cases it appears to be more reassuring to the reader to be told that replies will be handled confidentially and will be used only in statistical tables or only in combination with the answers of other respondents. The word "confidential" often fits the personal relationship which the letter is trying to establish better than the word "anonymous." On a survey among the passengers of an airline a test was made on the use of the two words. The short questionnaire was identical in mailings to both test groups; the questions concerned the number of flights taken in the past 12 months, the respondent's sex, age, and magazine reading. The letters were identical except that one test group used the word "anonymous" and the other the word "confidential." All mailings included a new 25¢ incentive and a stamped reply envelope. The number mailed in each test group was 250, and answers were accepted for a period of three weeks. The two groups were selected at random. The mailing using the word "confidential" had 181 answers, or 72.4 percent, while the one with the word "anonymous" resulted in a 65.6 percent response.

Of course there are some cases where emphasizing anonymity may increase returns of a questionnaire on a particularly touchy subject, while in some situations it can be helpful to write to the recipient of an unkeyed questionnaire: "There is no need to sign your name unless you wish to do so." Emphasizing the confidential or anonymous nature of the survey is very desirable, when (especially in the case of consumer surveys) people may suspect a possible follow-up by a salesman.

13. OFFER TO SEND A REPORT

An offer to send a report on the results of the survey can be helpful, if the subject matter of the research is of interest to people who receive the questionnaire. On a recent survey conducted for the National Geographic Society it was found (by using a split mailing) that the offer of a report on the results of the survey increased the returns of a four-page questionnaire from 39.5 to 47.5 percent in the first mailing. Because of the importance of anonymity to some respondents, it is good practice to afford them the opportunity of requesting the report in a separate letter (Fig. 16). The report offer can be made more interesting by pointing out that the respondent may want to compare his own answers with those of the others who answered. Depending on space requirements and the nature of the survey, this offer can be accompanied by a detachable coupon on the letter or on the questionnaire, or by a separate postcard to facilitate the respondent's request for a copy of the report.

14. A NOTE OF URGENCY

A note of urgency, such as requesting an immediate answer or giving a deadline is recommended only if the survey will have to be closed in the short space of two or three weeks. In other circumstances it may cut down the percentage of returns because people who are too busy to answer at once or have been away on a trip might feel that it is too late to answer. Also it is more advisable to use a note of urgency in requesting answers to a short questionnaire than to a long one; in the latter case the respondent may resent being pushed.

15. APPRECIATION OF THE SENDER

Politeness is good policy; furthermore, the "Thank you for your help" note at the end of the letter, and again at the end of the questionnaire, may move the reader by reminding him that in failing to answer he is refusing to help someone.

16. IMPORTANCE OF THE SENDER

The recipient of the letter is much more likely to cooperate if the writer is known and respected by him. A letter from a favorite professor asking his students or ex-students to complete a questionnaire might not need any further inducement. But most mail surveys are not conducted by a researcher personally known to many people in the sample; therefore the importance of the sender has to be indicated, if possible, by title, rank, or occasionally by graduate degree. The subscribers to a publication will be more impressed by a letter signed by the editor or the publisher than by one signed by the circulation manager, whose name is less likely to be known to the respondent. If the research is believably important, businessmen will be more impressed by a letter from the chairman of the board of a company than from its research analyst. A "Dr." in front of the signer's name will be helpful in some surveys. (Unless the writer is a physician it is better to use "Ph.D." when addressing doctors: They may very well look up the "Dr." in a medical directory and assume fraud if they cannot find him.) Once more, the ethical researcher will not use nonexistent titles, ranks, or degrees.

17. IMPORTANCE OF THE SENDER'S ORGANIZATION

The rule here is similar to the one just discussed about the person signing the letter: The closer the contact between the addressee and the organization or firm whose name appears on the stationery, the greater the motivation for answering. Of course the "contact" has to be a friendly one. For example, it is not suprising that a company can get better than an 80 percent response to a long questionnaire mailed out on its own stationery to its own dealers or that a prestige publication such as *Fortune* gets a high percentage of response from its own subscribers.

The use of the name of the organization sponsoring the survey will nearly always help in getting higher returns provided it is known to the addressee, has prestige, and has no unpleasant associations for him. Before, however, deciding to use the name on the stationery, it has to be carefully weighed whether or not the name of the sponsor may introduce any bias. For example if the management of the Rush Motor Company sends a questionnaire to its own dealers on its own stationery, it would not be reasonable to ask them to criticize the company's sales policies: the answers would be certainly biased. Similarly, a questionnaire from *Timely Digest* to its subscribers should not include questions on its own merits as compared with those of other publications. In such cases the stationery of a research company or a blind (fictional) company should be used. In the majority of cases, surveys will be mailed out in the names of organizations not known to the persons receiving them. It may help somewhat if the name of the firm or organization sounds important, but in general, incentives and all the other points mentioned in this chapter will have to make up for the lack of familiarity and prestige.

18. DESCRIPTION AND PURPOSE OF THE INCENTIVE

The use and nature of incentives is discussed in Chapter 11. The points to remember in writing the letter are as follows:

1. The reference to the incentive should take into consideration the kind of people you are addressing (as discussed later in this chapter under "Style"). One might hesitate to suggest in a letter addressed to owners of Rolls-Royce cars that they should send the "enclosed dollar bill" to a charitable institution, for fear the suggestion would appear ridiculous to people whose contributions are usually very much larger.

2. No matter what kind of people we are writing to, it is always poor practice to talk down to them. "You can use the enclosed quarter to buy a cup of coffee (or a glass of beer)" belongs in this category: it might antagonize some people.

3. It is often helpful to make the reference to the incentive stand out by making it a postscript (Figs. 16, 17).

19. AVOIDING BIAS

When the letter is finished, it is essential to reread it, scrutinizing every sentence for any possible bias it may introduce. We have already seen that the subject of the survey and the sender's stationery may introduce bias, as can the choice of the wrong type of incentive. But there are many other possibilities of bias, and some of them may be caused by the accompanying letter. Will the letter influence the respondent to overstate or understate anything in his answers? For example, will he state that he is making more money than he actually does, because he wants to shine to his alma mater conducting the survey among alumni; or will he understate his income because he suspects from the tone or contents of the letter that the Bureau of Internal Revenue or his landlord is checking up on him? Will his answers be different because of a lingering thought that the whole survey is part of some sales effort or that it will help some organization or cause that he dislikes? If we are interested in opinions and attitudes, is there anything in the letter which might put the reader into a frame of mind which can color his answers? If it has been decided not to use the name of the sponsoring organization because it would introduce bias, have we made sure that the letter (or the questionnaire) does not give away the omitted name?

20. STYLE

It goes without saying that the letter should be written in good, clear, and precise English. A point often forgotten is that in writing the letter one must also take the nature of the sample into consideration. If the survey is conducted among physicians, the letter should be written in a different style from one addressed to the mothers of newborn babies. For instance, a word like "prognosis" can be used when addressing the former, but not the latter. Furthermore, the subject of the survey may also determine the style of the letter. For instance, even when addressing the same group of physicians, we might take a different approach and tone when conducting a survey on diabetic agents from the one we would use when asking about leisure time activities such as sports and travel. The writer has to use his judgment about when to be very polite, or very friendly, or enthusiastic, or matter of fact.

21. APPEARANCE AND FORMAT

As mentioned at the beginning of this chapter, in order to be sure that your letter will be read, it must look like a personal communication. It should not look like a form letter; if possible, it should not be mimeographed or printed in a type face obviously different from typewriter type. It should not be part of a questionnaire, it should have a matching personalization, a date, and blue plate signature. It should look neat, have short paragraphs, and a reasonably wide margin. Except in very special cases it is not necessary to use fancy (engraved, etc.) stationery.

To have the letter and the questionnaire on the same page poses a problem even in the case of a short questionnaire containing only two or three questions. For one thing, the letter will not look like a personal letter, and furthermore it cannot be personalized, or the questionnaire will no longer be anonymous when returned.

The following test represents an interesting illustration of the advantage of the separate letter. A short questionnaire was mailed to 600 businessmen who were known to be interested in advertising and advertising media, specifically business and industrial publications.

Respondents were asked to read the list of ten publishers of such publications and to indicate which of them they considered "tops" in a number of areas, such as editorial content, research, and help to advertisers. The sample was divided into two random halves; one group received a separate questionnaire and letter, while the mailing to the other group included a letter and questionnaire printed on the two sides of the same page. All mailings contained a new 25¢ incentive and a stamped reply envelope, and all letters had a matching one-line personalization and blue plate signature; in fact the two mailings were identical in every respect except the one characteristic which was tested. One month after the mailing date 54.7 percent completed returns had been received from the "separate letter" group, and 50.3 percent from the "letter on back of questionnaire" group. People in this second group (whose answers thus were not anonymous) also sent back six blank questionnaires with comments such as "I cannot give an objective answer; two of the publishers are my clients," "Since I am in the publishing business, I don't feel it appropriate to answer," and "I must disqualify myself."

22. BREVITY

The brevity of the letter is really the most important aspect of its appearance, and merits special attention. Very few surveys are vitally important to the people who are supposed to answer them. Many of these people will be busy and therefore reluctant to read a long letter. While the letter has to include all the points which the researcher considers essential for his particular survey, its length should be kept to an absolute minimum. The majority of mail surveys do not need more than the space of a monarch-sized letter to request the recipient's cooperation. Occasionally the message is long enough to fill an 8½- by 11-in. letterhead, but more than that is seldom needed. Any detailed instructions should be incorporated in the questionnaire rather than in the letter. When your letter is finished, look at it with the eyes of the recipient: Does it look like quick, effortless reading? If not, it should be rewritten.

REFERENCES

1. John J. Watson, "Improving the Response Rate on Mail Research," *Journal of Advertising Research*, vol. 5, no. 2, pp. 48–50, June, 1965.
2. Andrew E. Kimball, "Increasing the Rate of Return in Mail Surveys," *Journal of Marketing*, vol. 25, no. 6, pp. 63–64, October, 1961.
3. Raymond Simon, "Responses to Personal and Form Letters in Mail Surveys," *Journal of Advertising Research*, vol. 7, no. 1, pp. 28–30, March, 1967.

THIRTEEN
Mailing Procedures

BEFORE ASSEMBLING THE MAILING PIECE and actually putting all the elements in the outer envelope ("stuffing"), the researcher has to make sure that they have all been properly processed and are ready for the final operation.

THE OUTER ENVELOPE

The appearance of the outside envelope is important because it is the first thing which the addressee will see. It should create the impression that it contains a personal communication which ought to be read. In Chapter 12 we discussed the importance of the name of the sender organization. The name of the sender should appear neatly printed in the corner of the envelope. Good-quality white paper, proper addressing, and first-class postage (preferably stamped, rather than metered) are all necessary in order to avoid any suggestion that the contents of the envelope could possibly be junk mail.

The addressing should be done by typewriter. The use of labels, addressograph, and computer addressing indicate that the addressing was mass produced. It also makes it look like all the other promotional, advertising, fund soliciting, and junk mail which the addressee is accustomed to receiving. This may adversely influence the recipient's attitude when opening the envelope and reduce the chances of response.

It is worthwhile to make a special effort, such as screening all mailing lists, to make sure that the names and addresses are correct and as complete as possible. Dignitaries, clergymen, physicians, etc., should be addressed in the customary way. Full names rather than initials should be used whenever possible, and of course great care should be used to spell names correctly. Addresses should be as complete as possible; zip codes can save time.

The size of the envelope must be considered in connection with the contents and with the weight of the mailing piece. For example, if the research design calls for a four-page, monarch-sized questionnaire, a monarch-sized accompanying letter, 25¢ incentive, and a monarch reply envelope, then it would seem natural to use a number 10 outgoing envelope, which is the next larger size in common use. This, however, is not the best solution for two reasons. The contents do not fill out the outgoing envelope, which means that if the coin is in a cellophane folder not attached to the letter (an avoidable additional operation) it will rattle, slide around, and possibly break through the envelope. Also the weight will be dangerously close to double postage (over one ounce), and a slightly heavier stock could cause additional postage expense. The answer is to use an in-between size, sometimes called empire (4⅛- by 8¼-in.), which is not often kept in stock but can be ordered. In other words, time must be taken for the advance planning of even so simple an ingredient of a mail survey as the outgoing envelope. As previously noted, stamped letters look more personal than metered mail, and first-class mail should be used both ways.[1]

THE QUESTIONNAIRE

The questionnaire and its construction have been described in Chapters 6 and 7. Here we are concerned with its keying and folding.

The researcher may want to identify groups of respondents or individual respondents. Identifying a relatively small number of groups is quite simple. For example, if the survey is done among lawyers, doctors, and engineers, and all three groups receive the same questionnaire, then we can easily identify the replies if the "Thank you" note on the bottom of the last page of the questionnaire is printed in a different position (left, center, right) for each of the three groups. The same results could be achieved without additional expense by using a different color paper for each group's questionnaire.

If we are dealing with a large number of groups, the researcher will usually identify the individual respondent. There are several reasons other than group identification for this procedure. If we plan any follow-up mailing or any type of validation, we have to know who answered and who did not. The mailing list might include data (such as size of company, specialty of physician, sex, age) which can be useful in analyzing the survey. If we can match the responses with the mailing list, we do not have to make the questionnaire longer and more difficult by asking questions whose answers we already know. Finally, we may wish to survey the same respondents or a subgroup of respondents at some later date, and the comparison of individual answers may be important for our analysis.

The surest way of identifying the respondent is to type the individual addressee's name on each questionnaire. This is expensive and in many cases may annoy the recipient. One can ask the respondent to sign the questionnaire. This, however, might reduce the percentage of response, and not all respondents will sign their names. The usual practice is to key questionnaires with individual numbers.

Keying simply means giving a consecutive number to every name on the mailing list and numbering the questionnaires the same way. If the mailing operations, specifically the stuffing, have been done with the proper care, respondents can then be easily identified by the key number.

Keying can be open or concealed. In either case the researcher should never claim that the questionnaires are anonymous. The keys can be on the reply envelope as room number or written under the flap. However, this requires the additional operation of manually transfering the key onto the questionnaire. Small keys and keys written with invisible ink are often used. It is an elementary rule of ethical practice that whether open or concealed, keying should be used only for statistical purposes.

There is a way of following up nonrespondents while maintaining and even stressing anonymity: A postcard can be mailed out along with the questionnaire, the card containing a simple statement indicating that the respondent has returned the questionnaire in a separate envelope. The accompanying letter explains that no reminders or follow-up mailings will be sent to people who sign and return the card. Few people will return the card without sending back the completed questionnaire; similarly, few will mail back the questionnaire without returning the card. Furthermore, the card may help achieve a higher rate of response because of the implicit "threat" of continued follow-up mailings in case of nonresponse.[2]

The folding of the questionnaire should be carefully planned. First of all the questionnaire should be folded to fit the reply envelope. It is very annoying to the recipient, who has just done us the favor of completing the questionnaire, to find that it does not easily fit the reply envelope; if it had been folded right in the first place it would do so naturally. Next, we have to make sure that after the questionnaire has been folded the title of the first page is on top (masthead up): it should be the first thing read by the recipient. Finally, in the case of keyed questionnaires, the key must be located on one of the two outside segments of the folded questionnaire, to make it easier for the stuffing clerk to match the numbers on the questionnaire with those on the mailout (list) cards.

LETTER, INCENTIVE, AND REPLY ENVELOPE

The accompanying letter has been discussed in Chapter 12. It must be properly printed or processed, personalized, and folded.

If the incentive is a coin, it can be taped to the accompanying letter, placed in a cardboard coinholder, or slipped into a cellophane envelope so as to fit snugly.

The reply envelope must be small enough to fit inside the outer envelope and large enough to contain the questionnaire. It is better to place a stamp on it than to use a business reply envelope.[3] First, the psychological reason: Nobody likes to throw away money. Unused stamps represent money; business reply envelopes do not. Furthermore, business reply envelopes make the whole package look less like personal mail and more like junk mail. Finally, if we expect a high percentage of returns, the use of business reply envelopes may not represent significant savings. For another small emphasis on the personal contact, the reply envelope should be preaddressed to the individual who signed the letter, rather than to his company, which seems less personal.

A CASE HISTORY: PAST PRACTICE AND CHANGES

The most important consideration in getting a high response to mail surveys must be the integration of all possible elements which can help to achieve this goal. The following case history may illustrate this point.

The American Bankers Association had conducted a yearly survey among its more than 13,000 member banks on advertising expenditures and various aspects of marketing. A one-page, one-sided questionnaire was mailed on the association's stationery, addressed to the person in charge of marketing or advertising operations at each of the member banks. In some cases the name of this person was known, in others it was not. The mailing was sent out in an envelope with a pasted-on computer-made label, the accompanying letter was printed in one color, no personalization was used on the letter, but a label pasted on the questionnaire identified the bank. The reply envelope was addressed to the association and was not stamped. It seemed like a reasonable assumption that the prestige of the association would induce many members to answer, that the personal touch was not an essential factor to a banker when receiving a letter from the association, and that providing and placing a stamp on the reply envelope would present no problem to an officer of a bank. The response rate was 34 percent after one follow-up mailing.

In a subsequent survey on the same subject, the association decided that it needed more information from its members on advertising and marketing policies, and this requirement increased the size of the questionnaire to four pages. It was also decided to make all possible effort to receive a high percentage of response to this longer questionnaire but at the same time to experiment with a shorter questionnaire containing only the most important, key questions. It was also planned to test several mailing procedures, while using changed techniques on all mailings.[4] The changes introduced in *all* mailings were as follows:

1. The outgoing envelope was addressed to an individual whose name was known. This person was not always the individual in charge of advertising operation, but to cover such cases, the letter requested the recipient to turn the mailing piece over to the proper person. The purpose of this change was to establish a personal contact.

2. The letter was written in a more personal tone.

3. The letter emphasized that the member's answers were equally important whether or not his bank happened to use the advertising and marketing operations which were the subjects of the survey.

4. The letter stressed that the information would be kept confidential.

5. The questionnaire was printed on white stock, instead of the buff-colored stock used in previous surveys.

6. More attention was paid to making the questions clear, precise, and simple.

7. Great care was taken in laying out the questionnaire to make it "look easy."

8. The reply envelopes were addressed by name to the advertising manager of the marketing department, whose signature appeared on the outgoing letter. Reply envelopes in previous surveys had been addressed to the association, and it was hoped that the change would once more emphasize the personal touch.

The universe was the same as on previous surveys. The subject matter and the nature of the questions were very similar. The combined effect of the above changes was a 60 percent response instead of the 34 percent received on the previous projects.

TESTING IMPROVED METHODS

In the same research project further changes were tested to find the most effective procedure. The survey was mailed out in six random groups as follows:

Test 1 (the control group) was nearest in procedure to previous mailings, although it included all the changes already described. The outgoing envelope had a computer-made label, the letter was printed in one color and was not personalized, the reply envelope was not stamped, and the four-page questionnaire bore a label containing the name and address of the bank. No incentive was used on any of the mailings, except for the offer of a report on the survey findings, and all groups received one follow-up mailing to nonrespondents. The control group consisted of a random sample of 553 members, and 60 percent completed and returned the questionnaire.

Test 2 also contained the same four-page questionnaire with the identifying label, but the letter had a one-line matching personalization and blue plate signature, the address was typed on the envelope instead of appearing on a label, and the reply envelope bore a first-class stamp. This test was mailed to a random sample of 3,858 members and achieved a 71 percent response.

Test 3 was similar to test 2, except that instead of an identifying label, the questionnaire bore a key number. Mailing: 551; replies received: 72 percent.

The next three tests (4, 5, and 6) included the short, one-page one-sided questionnaire, omitting some of the questions on the longer questionnaire. Test 4 was mailed in a computer-labeled envelope, the letter was printed in one color and was not personalized, and the reply envelope was not stamped. The short questionnaire bore the identifying label with the name and address of the bank. Mailing: 7,451; response: 69 percent.

Test 5 was identical with test 4 except for the use of a key instead of the identifying label. Mailing: 497; response: 72 percent.

Test 6 was identical with test 2, except that it used a short questionnaire. Mailing: 495; response: 80 percent.

The obvious conclusion we can draw from these results is that the highest response can be reached by coordinating all elements to achieve an easy-looking questionnaire mailed in a personal manner and promising to keep the information confidential. It is usually impossible to use all ingredients of such an ideal mix for a given survey, but it is the combination of a number of these elements which helps, rather than any isolated factor.

THE SEQUENCE OF MAILING OPERATIONS

The nature and sequence of mailing operations may vary according to the size of the mailing and the degree of automation used. Here is one possible plan for preparing keyed mailings:

1. Prepare instructions for printing, keying, and mailing (Figs. 19, 20).
2. Print questionnaires.
3. Key questionnaires.
4. Type or process list cards.
5. Key list cards (numbering).
6. Process accompanying letters.
7. Process blue facsimile (plate) signature on letters.
8. Address envelopes from list cards making sure to keep them in sequence.
9. Personalize letters and place each letter under the flap of its envelope, observing the sequence.
10. Process the address onto the reply envelope.
11. Stamp the reply envelope.
12. Place the incentive coin in a cellophane envelope or tape it to the letter.
13. Fold the letter and stuff the envelopes with the four items (letter, questionnaire, incentive, and reply envelope), checking every tenth outgoing envelope and its contents to make sure that the name on the outgoing envelope matches that on the personalized letter

PRINTING INSTRUCTIONS

Job # _____   Date: _____

Job name: _____

Person in charge: _____

Description: Questionnaire ☐   Number of pages
               Letterhead ☐   1 side   ☐
               Envelope ☐   2 sides   ☐
               Card ☐   4 pages   ☐
               Other: _____   Other: _____

Size (overall): _____ x _____   Quantity: _____

Printing method: Letterpress ☐   Offset ☐   Ribbon press ☐
                   Other _____

Paper: Type Bond ☐   Offset ☐   Other _____
       Color: White ☐   Other _____
       Weight: 60# (offset) ☐   50# ☐   24# (bond) ☐   20# ☐   16# ☐
       Other _____

Ink Color: Black ☐   Other _____

Keying: Not keyed ☐
         Keying instructions: _____
         _____

Folding: None ☐   2-fold, masthead up ☐   3-fold, masthead up ☐
          Other _____

First proof or Van Dyke needed on: _____

Printing completion date: _____

Special directions: _____
_____

FIGURE 19

MAILING INSTRUCTIONS

Job # _____   Date: _____   Keying: Yes ☐   No ☐

Job name: _____

Person in charge: _____

Mailing date: _____   Postcard: Advance ☐   Reminder ☐
                                  Fill-in: Yes ☐   No ☐

First line of letter: _____

Letterhead: _____   Fill-in: None ☐   1-line ☐   Full ☐

Outgoing envelope: _____

Reply envelope: Size _____   Copy: _____
                                           _____
                                           _____
                                           _____

Quantity: _____   Postage: _____

Mailing list: Source _____   Description: _____

Questionnaire: Title or first line _____

Premium: _____

Special directions _____
_____
_____
_____
_____

FIGURE 20

```
                          MAILOUT CHECKLIST


To fill out:

Job #_____          Mailing date_____
Name of checker_____
Reply envelope:  Size_____ Copy_____
                                          _____
                                          _____


Number mailed:_____
Description of sub-samples (if any) requiring special handling:_____
_____

To check:
                                  Total         Sub-samples
                                              a    b    c    d

Letter
   Stationery ......................  ☐       ☐    ☐    ☐    ☐
   Fill in (vs. envelope) ..........  ☐       ☐    ☐    ☐    ☐
   Signature .......................  ☐       ☐    ☐    ☐    ☐
   Copy ............................  ☐       ☐    ☐    ☐    ☐

Questionnaire
   Copy ............................  ☐       ☐    ☐    ☐    ☐
   Key (vs. mailing card) ..........  ☐       ☐    ☐    ☐    ☐

Reply envelope
   Name and address ................  ☐       ☐    ☐    ☐    ☐
   Size ............................  ☐       ☐    ☐    ☐    ☐
   Stamps ..........................  ☐       ☐    ☐    ☐    ☐
   Key (if any) ....................  ☐       ☐    ☐    ☐    ☐

Other enclosure
   Incentive .......................  ☐       ☐    ☐    ☐    ☐
   Other ...........................  ☐       ☐    ☐    ☐    ☐
```

FIGURE 21

and that the name on the envelope *and* the key number on the questionnaire match the same name and key on the list card.

14. Check by supervisor.

15. Seal and stamp. This is usually one mechanical operation. The number of stamps used is a check on the total count.

16. Mail. It is advisable to get a receipt from the post office bearing the date of mailing and the number of pieces mailed. The post office checks the number of identical pieces mailed by weight.

The checking by a supervisor (14) is an essential part of the operation. The supervisor should not be an employee of the mailing house or a member of the mailing department: He should be the researcher himself or his assistant. If anything goes wrong with the mailing, it may be impossible to save the survey. Only the researcher and his staff know the importance of each item, of each word, or each operation in the survey, and some of these may seem to be unimportant and negligible to people in the mailing department. When the supervisor checks the completed but unsealed mailing "packages," he must have a copy of the instruction sheet (Fig. 20) in front of him. To make sure that he himself did not overlook anything that can be checked, he can have a "mailout checklist" (Fig. 21), which will also serve as a record of the mailing. The supervisor should check a number of mailing pieces selected at random. The number to be checked will depend on the size and complexity of the mailing.

REFERENCES

1. R. A. Robinson, "How to Boost Returns from Mail Surveys," *Printers' Ink*, vol. 237, no. 6, pp. 35–37, June 6, 1952.
2. Kenneth Bradt, "The Usefulness of a Postcard Technique in a Mail Questionnaire Study," *Public Opinion Quarterly*, vol. 19, no. 2, pp. 218–222, summer, 1955.
3. Andrew E. Kimball, "Increasing the Rate of Return in Mail Surveys," *Journal of Marketing*, vol. 25, no. 6, pp. 63–64, October, 1961.
4. Lawrence N. Van Doren, "Advertising: Banks up the Ante by a Big 5% in 1968," *Banking*, vol. 60, no. 10, pp. 71–76, April, 1968.

FOURTEEN
Follow-up Mailings

THE PRIMARY PURPOSE of follow-up mailings is to reduce the percentage of nonrespondents and thereby make the survey more representative. No matter how high a percentage of response is achieved by the first mailing, a follow-up mailing will nearly always produce some more returns. In general, and from the researcher's point of view, every sample consists of three types of individuals:

1. Eager beavers, who love to answer practically anything
2. Just people, who are more or less uninterested in answering questionnaires, but who can be induced to do so by an interesting subject, a well constructed questionnaire, the importance of the sender or his survey, an attractive incentive, and/or repeated prodding
3. Born nonrespondents who hate to be bothered by interviewers or mail surveys and who seldom if ever answer anything

Follow-up mailings are aimed chiefly at group 2. The researcher's hope is to attack the inertia of the members of this (largest) segment of the sample and to get as many of them as possible to complete and return the questionnaire. In addition he will also reach some of the eager beavers who happened to be out of town or who for some other reason did not have a chance to answer, and he may even find a few perennial nonrespondents in a rare responsive mood.

A secondary purpose of follow-up mailings, especially if there are two or more, can be to establish a curve of the responses to key questions on successive waves of mailings. This may enable the researcher to draw some conclusions about the nature of the nonrespondents. For example, if successive waves yield returns which show successively lower education and income patterns, it can reasonably be assumed that this tendency will continue among *most* other nonrespondents—most, but not all, because the small group of die-hard nonrespondents (group 3) may possibly include some professors and some millionaires, causing the downward curve to take an upward turn toward the end. Of course the higher the percentage of return, the less important this consideration becomes.

The follow-up mailing must get the highest possible number of returns from nonrespondents to the first mailing, without becoming a nuisance to people who have already answered the questionnaire. The researcher must also avoid tabulating more than one questionnaire from the same person or from the same home. In some cases an "eager beaver" type of respondent will fail to read the follow-up letter carefully and will answer the questionnaire a second time. More often another member of the family will answer a questionnaire which has already been completed and returned by someone else in the family. For these reasons it is desirable to key the first-mailing questionnaires and to send a follow-up mailing only to nonrespondents. Whenever there is a reasonably high return to the first wave, this procedure is also more economical.

THE REMINDER POSTCARD

A reminder postcard is often effective. It is usually sent out three to five days after the first mailing and is mailed to the entire sample. This is just a reminder and not a real "follow-up" or "second wave." Figure 22 shows an example.

Once again, the use of the respondent's name in the salutation and the blue facsimile signature are helpful in making the communication more personal.

THE SECOND WAVE

This follow-up mailing will contain another copy of the questionnaire and a reply envelope identical with those used in the first mailing. The accompanying letter will be different, and the researcher must decide whether or not to use an incentive, and if so, whether to use the same one as before or a different one.

If the questionnaires of the main mailing were keyed, and if enough time is available, the second wave can be mailed to nonrespondents when the returns from the first wave start petering out. In the United States on nationwide mailings this usually happens in two to three weeks, as shown in "The speed of response" section of the Appendix.

Dear Mrs. Eres:

Recently we mailed you a questionnaire asking for your participation in an important survey.

If you have already returned the questionnaire, please consider this card a "Thank you" for your valuable help.

If you have not had a chance to do so as yet, may we ask you to return the completed form now? Your participation is vital to the success of our study.

Sincerely yours,

James B. Jones

James B. Jones, Director
Professional Mail Surveys Company

FIGURE 22 Reminder postcard.

Ninety percent of all the returns that are going to come in in response to a survey mailing will come in within two weeks after the mailing.[1] Nevertheless, if time permits, the follow-up mailing should be sent out three to four weeks after the main mailing, because it has a better chance of reaching people who have been on a trip or who have had a particularly busy period. It is also economical because the second mailing will be sent to a smaller number of nonrespondents. The practical procedure is to open the incoming mail each day and to pull the list card of every respondent. This will result in the immediate availability of a mailing list of nonrespondents on the day the researcher decides to close the first mailing.

If for any reason the researcher has decided against keying or otherwise identifying the questionnaires, the second wave will be sent to the total sample. In this case timing can be more flexibile. Sometimes it may make little or no difference in the effectiveness of the second wave whether it is mailed a few days or a few weeks after the first mailing. As indicated before, this kind of second wave has some drawbacks, although it has been used with success by researchers.[2]

If the available time is very short, the survey may have to be closed within two or three weeks after the main mailing. In this case any follow-up mailing will have to be done a few days after the first mailing. It may then become questionable whether the available money should be spent on a follow-up mailing or on increasing the incentive used for the main mailing. One possibility is to use a bigger incentive and a reminder postcard.

LETTER AND INCENTIVES

The accompanying letter for the follow-up mailing may include, possibly in a shortened version, most of the elements of the first letter. But there are two additional thoughts it must contain. The writer should express his appreciation to the addressee in case he has completed and returned the first questionnaire and ask him to do so in case he has not. There are very good reasons for mentioning this subject in the letter. In the first place, even with a keyed mailing, it is unavoidable that a few people should receive a second questionnaire, even though they answered the first one, because their reply may arrive during the short interval between the closing of the first mailing and the delivery of the second. These respondents must be told that they do not have to answer again and that we are thankful for their help. On the other hand the researcher will not want to emphasize that he knows the identity of nonrespondents. The sample letter in Figure 23 shows how this delicate point can be handled.

It is often quite hard to decide what incentive, if any, should be used for the follow-up mailings. In general it is a fact that using an incentive in the follow-up mailings increases returns and that a dollar bill will have more effect than a coin. If no incentive was used in the main mailing, the follow-up mailing using an incentive may result in a larger return than the first mailing. On the other hand, a follow-up mailing with no incentive after a main mailing with an incentive may draw very little response. The same is true of a follow-up incentive which is smaller than the first one. This is once more a matter of statistical and/or executive decision, weighing the comparative requirements of high percentage of response versus available budget. The Appendix shows the percentage of response to over 400 mail surveys, some analyzed by incentives used.

In the case of a survey where the sample is large enough and the percentage of returns from the first mailing reasonably high, one may send the follow-up mailing to every second nonrespondent and give each answer a weight of 2. This is a generally accepted procedure and can result in considerable savings. The weighting can be simplified by

PROFESSIONAL MAIL SURVEYS COMPANY

7432 East Court Avenue

Elveron, California 90101

213 991-5550

(Date)

Dear Mr. Smythe:

    Recently we sent you a short questionnaire asking what trade magazines you read, and which one is most helpful to you. As we sent out only a limited number of these, your answer is very important to the accuracy of our survey of executives and key operating people.

    It will take only a moment to fill out and return the form in the stamped envelope enclosed. If you've already done so, many thanks. If you have not yet had a chance to answer, we should be most grateful if you would do so now. Your answers will be held in strict confidence, of course.

                           Cordially yours,

                           James B. Jones

                           James B. Jones
                           Director

P.S. Possibly our original request went astray in the mails. Therefore we enclose another form, together with a token of our appreciation which may please some child you know.

FIGURE 23 Follow-up letter (second wave).

punching two cards for each questionnaire returned on the follow-up mailing.

THE THIRD WAVE

The third wave is supposed to squeeze a few more percentage points worth of answers out of the sample, and the research man must think hard how best to do it.

1. He will wish to emphasize the great importance of receiving an answer from every person in the sample.

2. He may feel that an incentive which is the same as, or larger than, the one in the second wave will help.

3. It might be helpful to emphasize urgency by giving a closing date for the survey, by using special-delivery postage, or both.

4. If a high percentage of response has already been received, the researcher may feel that it is good psychology to mention this fact.

5. In the case of some surveys the length of the questionnaire might be a deterrent to a significant segment of the sample, or they may resist answering because the questionnaire contains one or more questions which are difficult to answer or which ask for confidential information.

In such cases the research design may call for sending out a shorter version of the questionnaire which, while not containing all questions, can help increase the representativeness of answers in some key areas. Another possibility is to mail the original questionnaire again, with a postscript in the letter as shown in Figure 24.

A series of tests were conducted on a survey about insurance mailed to members of a large society. The subject was of no particular interest to the members of the society, and answering the four-page questionnaire was fairly time-consuming. After one follow-up mailing and no inducements other than the letterhead of the society and the offer of the survey report, the response rate was 61 percent. At this point it was decided to send out a split-sample third mailing to test the effectiveness of (1) special-delivery return postage and (2) a request for at least a partial answer. Each of four random groups of nonrespondents consisted of 244 members. The following table shows the results of this test:

	Percentage of returns; each based on 244
Special-delivery reply envelope and postscript as on Fig. 24	29.4
Special delivery reply envelope, no postscript	24.3
Postscript, but no special delivery reply envelope	17.2
Neither special delivery nor postscript	13.5

PROFESSIONAL MAIL SURVEYS COMPANY

7432 East Court Avenue

Elveron, California 90101

213 991-5550

(Date)

Dear Mr. Smythe:

 We mailed the enclosed form to you as a member of a scientifically selected sample of families from all over the U.S. The overwhelming majority have been kind enough to help us with this important project by sending in their answers. If you were one of them, this is our way of saying, "Thank you."

 In case you were away or too busy to complete the questionnaire before, may we ask you to do so now? We are trying to get as near to a "perfect survey" as possible. This would mean getting a reply from everyone who received a questionnaire.

 I'll appreciate your earliest reply, and am enclosing a self-addressed SPECIAL DELIVERY envelope to facilitate this. Of course answers will be used only for constructing statistical tables. Many thanks for your help in this survey.

Sincerely yours,

Professional Mail Surveys Co.

James B. Jones

James B. Jones,
Director

P.S. If you feel that some questions do not apply to you, please answer only those which do. We need your questionnaire even if not completely filled out.

FIGURE 24 Follow-up letter (third wave).

Of the 114 respondents who received the "partial reply" postscript, only a few skipped one or more questions. The test indicates that the combined use of the two procedures tested can more than double the third mailing response. In the case of the "optimum" effectiveness of the four variations of third mailing tests, the total response rate of the insurance survey was increased from 61 to over 72 percent. Most of this increase results from the use of the special delivery reply envelope.

6. If at the time of any of the follow-up mailings the researcher feels that the addressees may resent the successive waves of reminders and that a point of no return is approaching, he may decide that the forthcoming mailing will be his last effort, and he will state this fact in his letter. This procedure is also useful if successive mailings contain progressively more valuable incentives and if the researcher suspects that a few people in the sample may not be answering just to see what will come next. In such cases the following short closing paragraph may be helpful:

"This is our last note, since we have to start preparing our report. Once again, thank you for your help."

Figure 24 shows a sample of a third-wave letter.

FURTHER EFFORTS TO INCREASE RESPONSE

The fourth and successive waves may be sent out by mail or by wire, or they may consist of telephone or personal interviews. They may attempt to have more people answer the whole questionnaire or some parts of it, and they may be designed to contact all nonrespondents or a random sample of this group. Of course in the case of verbal interviews the questions will have to be rephrased to some extent, and a proper introduction must be worked out. Because of the cost in time and money and diminishing returns, very few mail surveys use more than three waves. Where they are used, the primary reason for making this further effort is usually not to gain the small increase in returns, but rather to probe the nature of the nonrespondents.

Some recipients of a questionnaire may have the suspicion that the "research" is really a sales gimmick and will be followed by the visit of a salesman. The subject matter of some questionnaires may awaken such suspicions, and there are unscrupulous salesmen and sales organizations which use the pretext of a "survey" as a door opener. If the nature of the questionnaire could possibly arouse suspicion, the accompanying letters should emphasize that the purpose of the research is to gather statistical information, and not to sell anything. A number of research firms find it useful to include a leaflet from the National Better Business Bureau in one of the follow-up mailings. The note is entitled "Memo to the Public" and states:

> The sole purpose of the organization which uses this leaflet is to secure information on a matter of interest to business and the public.
>
> The organization will not try to sell you anything, will not ask for any money and will not ask you to sign an agreement to buy anything. Should you be asked to buy anything by anyone using this leaflet you will know that its use is unauthorized.

REFERENCES

1. R. A. Robinson, "How to Boost Returns from Mail Surveys," *Printers' Ink*, vol. 237, no. 6, pp. 35–37, June 6, 1952; also, William E. Cox, Jr., "Response Patterns to Mail Surveys," *Journal of Marketing Research*, vol. 3, no. 4, pp. 392–397, November, 1966; also, Appendix, "The Speed of Response."
2. John J. Watson, "Improving the Response Rate on Mail Research," *Journal of Advertising Research*, vol. 5, no. 2, pp. 48–50, June, 1965.

FIFTEEN
The Nonresponse Problem

IT IS PRACTICALLY IMPOSSIBLE to get answers from every single person in a large sample selected at random. In some instances this nonresponse is caused by the imperfection of the frame. Some people may have died between the time the sample was established and the time of actual data-gathering; others may have moved without leaving a forwarding address. However, when we speak of a "nonresponse problem," we usually refer to people who can be reached with proper and, if necessary, repeated effort and who could answer our questions if they wanted to. They may have been ill at the time of the first approach, or away on a trip, or just too busy to answer. There is also a hard core of "born nonrespondents," who simply refuse to answer questions at all. These problems exist, no matter what data-gathering technique the researcher employs.

Each technique has its own methods for reducing the percentage of nonresponse. In other than mail surveys, repeated call-backs by the interviewer (in person or by telephone); in mail surveys, follow-up mailings, incentives, following up one technique by using another (such as telephone interviews among people who failed to respond to mailings)—are all parts of this effort. And though such methods can reduce the percentage of nonresponse, they cannot altogether eliminate it.

In the case of low response, the first question the researcher has to answer is whether the problem is serious enough to warrant further steps and, if so, how such steps would fit in with the survey design and the available budget. In an interviewed survey, how many call-backs can the interviewer make? Can he make substitutions after several futile calls? If so, how should these be selected? In the case of a mail survey should another mailout with increased incentives be sent to nonrespondents? What about the nonrespondent bias: does one exist? Can it be reduced or eliminated? If so, is this worth the effort? Many such questions can be raised and answered differently for different surveys. However, there are several general considerations which we can discuss:

1. The effort required to get a high rate of response, regardless of the data-gathering techniques used
2. Representativeness; nonresponse and the problems it raises
3. The nonrespondents
4. What to do about nonrespondents
5. Conclusions

PROBLEMS OF ACHIEVING A HIGH RESPONSE RATE

It is nearly impossible to achieve a 100 percent response, and this is true no matter what data-gathering methods are used. In all survey work it takes careful planning, repeated efforts, and considerable costs to come anywhere near a 100 percent or even a 90 percent response rate.

There are exceptional cases when favorable circumstances (great interest in the subject matter of the questionnaire, very high prestige of the organization conducting the survey, etc.), combined with careful planning and repeated efforts, result in unusually high rates of response. In such cases even lengthy questionnaires may not be deterrents. For example, a study of the Blue Cross Plan sponsored by the Health Information Foundation consisted of two different questionnaires mailed to each of eighty-five Blue Cross Plan groups. One questionnaire required from one hour to an hour and a half to fill out, and the other required from twenty minutes to half an hour. The first one was to be filled out by the enrollment director of each plan, and the other by the executive director. It was a very carefully conducted survey. An advance letter was followed by the questionnaire and letter of transmittal offering a report of the final results to respondents. This in turn was followed by a second questionnaire and letter mailed to nonrespondents. These mailings resulted in a 90 percent response. The remaining 10 percent received telegrams or telephone calls, and the survey closed with a 100 percent response to both questionnaires.[1]

As an example of the endurance test between researcher and nonrespondent we can cite a survey conducted among 624 contributors to the National Committee for an Effective Congress.[2] The questionnaire was preceded by two advance letters. The main mailing, sent by special delivery, contained the 25-page questionnaire, a letter, a reply envelope, and a postcard for use in requesting a copy of the report. After the main mailing there was a follow-up mailing, then a second follow-up mailing containing a handwritten postscript; the third follow-up used a shorter questionnaire, the fourth contained the same short questionnaire printed on different colored paper, and the final mailing consisted of a double postcard with 13 key questions. The result was an 85 percent response: 63.5 percent returned the long questionnaires, 19.5 percent the short forms, and 2 percent the postcards. Once more respondent involvement made feasible the use of a long questionnaire, but the high percentage of response would have been impossible without the effort and expenditure required by the many waves of mailings, plus a last one to send out the promised reports.

In commercial mail surveys the questionnaire is usually limited to four pages, but it still takes either a close relationship with the sponsoring organization or several mailings with incentives to achieve a better than 80 percent response. For example, subscribers to the *Christian Science Monitor* received long four-page questionnaires in two surveys.[3] The accompanying letters were processed on *Monitor* stationery, and each questionnaire was mailed to a random sample of 1,500 subscribers. No incentive was used; one follow-up mailing was sent to nonrespondents. One survey closed with an 81.9 percent response; the other with 80.8 percent as a result of the close connection between this publication and its readers. In the case of a survey among the subscribers of another publication, the mailings were sent out in the name of the marketing research company conducting the survey. In this research an advance postcard was followed by a four-page questionnaire containing a new dollar bill incentive. Nonrespondents received one follow-up mailing with another dollar bill incentive. The total response was 80.9 percent.[4]

COMPLETION RATE IN PERSONAL INTERVIEWING

A high rate of completion is no easier to achieve by personal interviewing than by mail. Good mail surveys have high percentage rates of completion, and so do good personal interview studies: in both cases the degree of achievement is commensurate with the amount of effort and money invested.

The research methods committee of the American Marketing Association found that "Even with several attempts at contact it is seldom possible (for personal interviewers) to reach and interview 90 percent, usually not more than 85 percent, often as little as 75 or 80 percent."[5]

In a very thorough media survey conducted by Alfred Politz Research, Inc.,[6] unusually great effort was made to achieve a high completion rate. Each interviewer was instructed to make up to eight calls, if necessary, and there were special occasions when twelve calls were made to reach one respondent. Most interviewer visits were made in the evening, but if any particular respondent preferred to be interviewed at another time or place, then the interviewer returned to him at the time and place specified by that particular respondent. The probability sample for this research consisted of 8,060 names. The completed interviews for the basic phase of the survey numbered 7,141, or 88.6 percent of the sample. Very few research projects can afford to utilize the time of trained personal interviewers at this prodigious rate.

In another carefully planned research project W. R. Simmons & Associates, Inc., conducted 12,867 personal interviews based on a national probability sample. Interviews were obtained from 80.5 percent of the total eligible designated respondents. The technical appendix of the report of this survey describes how this high percentage of response was achieved:

> A great many interviews were obtained only by virtue of the fact that interviewers made personal visits on at least six different evenings in order to contact respondents not easily found at home. Many respondents (particularly in upper-income areas) were interviewed only after appointments had been arranged by telephone. When necessary, interviewers obtained such appointments through the intercession of other members of the household or neighbors.[7]

What all the above examples illustrate is the simple fact that regardless of the subject matter of the survey, or who conducts it, or what method of data-gathering is used, a high percentage of response *cannot* be achieved without spending effort, time, and money. However, mail surveys, like other data-gathering methods, can result in better than 80 percent response if proper care is given to the planning and execution of the survey and if the sponsor is willing to spend the time and money needed to get this high rate of response. Often sponsors of mail surveys are more conscious of the budget than of the need for high response. The result is usually a poor survey.

THE PROBLEMS OF NONRESPONSE

The random sample selected for any research must be representative of the universe; the completed questionnaires must be representative of the sample; *ergo*, the respondents represent the universe. Any flaw in this chain of argument threatens the validity of the whole research. The most common flaw is nonresponse of a size or nature which makes the answers nonrepresentative of the total sample and thus of the total universe.

The best-laid plans of research men often go astray because of unrepresentative response. The greatest danger in this situation is the fact that the researcher may not even be conscious of it and therefore may draw misleading conclusions from biased data. The best sampling plan can become worthless because of nonrespondent bias.

Let us take an extreme hypothetical case: After a mailing to what was presumably a probability sample of the United States population, the tabulation of demographic data shows that only elderly, male corporation presidents answered the questionnaire. The researcher would know at once that his results are worthless. Next, let us suppose that among the respondents the group just described is represented three times as strongly as it proportionately should be. This may not be readily noticeable, but it may very well bias the response to some key questions. Unless we have a 100 percent response, we can never be sure that some such distortion does not occur. What we can and should do is to diminish the chance of nonrepresentativeness to the degree required by the survey design.

"Representative response," as commonly used, means that the distribution of answers reflects similar results to those which would have been achieved with a 100 percent response. It usually also means that the distribution of the respondents by any criterion is close to that of the mailout (the original sample). Differences between the two in demographic data, ownership, attitudes, or anything else may distort the results of the survey.

If we conduct a mail survey among a sample of the United States population, there is a good chance that the least literate part of our sample will be least willing or least able to answer and that the responses will have too high a representation of the upper socioeconomic groups. We would have less reason for concern about this particular bias when surveying the subscribers to *Fortune* magazine or *Harper's*.

When surveying the United States population as a whole, a questionnaire on TV viewing has a better chance for a representative response than does a questionnaire on Greek archaeology; one subject represents the everyday interest of most members of the universe, while the other is of interest only to a small segment.

AN EXAMPLE OF DISTORTED RESULTS

Both the accompanying letter and the questionnaire have to be constructed with an eye to minimizing nonrespondent bias. However, we can never be sure of the extent to which we have succeeded. We can minimize bias due to nonresponse by aiming for the highest possible percentage of response. The importance of this is demonstrated in the following table, which shows the answers to a car-ownership question. Let's say the hypothetical questionnaire was mailed to 1,000 people whose car-owning data were known, which means that we knew the percentage of car ownership of nonrespondents as well as of the respondents.

Now let's imagine that 100, or 10 percent of the sample, returned the questionnaire.

	Known data	*Respondents*
Base	1,000	100
Own a car	420	60
Do not own a car	580	40

For some reason, too large a proportion of car owners answered the questionnaire. If the researcher based his analysis on the assumption that 60 percent of the universe owned cars, he would be quite wrong. Stability has nothing to do with this. The results would still be wrong if we analyzed 1,000 returns on a 10,000 mailing.

Now let us consider the other side of the coin. Suppose in another, similar survey 900 of the 1,000 people in the sample returned the completed questionnaire and that, because of some freak chance or bias, *all* car owners were among the respondents.

	Known data	Respondents	
Base	1,000	900	100%
Own a car	420	420	47%
Do not own a car	580	480	53%

In this case the nonrespondents are to an extreme (and unlikely) degree different from the respondents. Nevertheless, the ownership figure shown by the respondents is only 5 percent off from the truth, while in the first example, because of the small response rate, a comparatively smaller distortion caused a complete reversal in the ownership pattern.

The rule we have to follow is quite simple: No mail survey can be considered reliable unless it has a high percentage of return, or unless some kind of verification proves that the response actually received is representative of the entire sample.

A HIGH PERCENTAGE OF RESPONSE

What is a "high" percentage of response? This is a much debated question and the answer must depend on the degree of reliability which the researcher wants to build into his survey design. It has much to do with the nature of the universe, the sample and the questionnaire, how the results are to be used, and whether the researcher is looking for general patterns and approximations or accurate projections and detailed analyses.

The Advertising Research Foundation recommends an 80 percent or better response on mail surveys, which brings the rate of nonresponse in line with the rate of substitution in well-conducted personal interview studies. In both this country and abroad numerous mail surveys achieve better than 80 percent returns every year, while some succeed in getting even 90 percent or better response. For most purposes it may not be essential to reach this high degree of representativeness. The last few percentage points of an 80 percent response are by far the most costly to achieve, and often the researcher will feel that for his purposes the additional representativeness gained is not worth the cost increase.

While it is impossible to generalize about what constitutes an adequate return rate, it is also unwise to side-step the question or to hedge on it. In this author's opinion a minimum standard can be established, which sets at least a negative limit: *No mail survey can be considered reliable unless it has a minimum of 50 percent response, or unless it demonstrates with some form of verification that the nonrespondents are similar to the respondents.* Of course this does not mean that a 51 percent response is necessarily adequate or representative. Actually no level of response is automatically "sufficient"; the acceptability of the response has to be judged in each case by the nature of the survey and the goals and standards which the researcher sets or should set for a particular piece of research.

OCCASIONAL USEFULNESS OF LOW-RESPONSE SURVEYS

Occasionally the findings from a survey with a low response rate can be useful, as in the case when no information is available about a universe and when the replies are clearly labeled and used for what they are. For example, in a survey of the top political leaders and opinion makers of Latin American republics, answers were received from 32 percent of the sample. While it cannot be claimed that such a response represents the sample surveyed, it does show the current opinion of nearly one-third of these important people. This may be valuable information, as long as we are aware that the opinions of the other two-thirds of the universe may be quite different.

For another example let us consider a publication with 60 percent subscription sales and 40 percent newsstand sales. A survey conducted among subscribers resulted in a 75 percent response. The identical questionnaire distributed as an insert in copies sold at newsstands drew a 31 percent response. In a situation like this the best procedure is to verify the newsstand response in some areas with personal interviews among newsstand purchasers of the publication. However, even without such verification the newsstand returns can fill two important functions:

1. We can see whether or not they are radically different from the subscriber answers. For instance, if in general the newsstand readers who responded belong to lower socioeconomic groups than the subscriber-respondents, the researcher may decide to show even this low percentage of newsstand response in parallel columns with the subscriber answers, in order to call attention to the difference between one subsample and a sizeable segment of the other.

2. The 31 percent response from the newsstand buyers, plus the 75 percent answers from subscribers represent 57 percent of the total circulation of the publication (31 percent of 40 percent, plus 75 percent of 60 percent). The weighted results are usually closer to the true facts of the total circulation than tabulations based on subscribers only.

The example just described also illustrates the fact that a 50 percent or better response, while it may serve as a minimum requirement, does not guarantee a representative survey. It is the job of the sample designer to take into consideration such subuniverses as subscribers and newsstand buyers, large firms and small firms. The returns may be representative in one subsample, but not in others. The more homogeneous the sample (that is, the fewer conceivable different subgroups it contains) the less we have to worry about obtaining a very high percentage of response.[8]

THE NONRESPONDENTS

Many researchers have tested the nature of nonresponse and come to the conclusion that two factors, education and interest in (or familiarity with) the topic under investigation, are among the most important influences in the return of mail questionnaires.[9] It is certainly true that a greater effort is needed to coax response out of uneducated and uninterested people than from their opposites. However, with proper follow-ups we will get nearer and nearer to the hard core of "refusers," who will simply not answer anything or anybody, or who cannot do so for any number of reasons.

Researchers R. A. Robinson and Philip Agisim received an 80.2 percent response to a mail survey on men's wear conducted among the subscribers of a publication.[10] With a special effort they increased the percentage of return to 93 percent, and then analyzed the answers of the 369 men whose replies represented the 12.8 percent difference and the effect these answers had on the total response. They found that the answers of the "hard to get" group were similar to the replies of the 80.2 percent who replied to the previous effort and that adding the new figures caused little or no significant change in the results of the survey. The follow-up questionnaire asked the respondents to tell them "in the interest of research," why they had failed to answer the original questionnaires sent to them. The answers of the 369 non-respondents may or may not represent the truth (on the conscious or subconscious level), but it is interesting to read them:

Reasons given by non-respondents for not replying to original questionnaire.

Mislaid it	22.4%
Overlooked answering	20.8
Already filled out and returned questionnaire	14.8
Too busy at the time	10.0
Away from home	10.0
Never received it	8.8
Not interested in subject	4.2
Don't answer questionnaires	3.0
Ill when received	2.1
Enjoyed questionnaire and kept it	1.2
All others, No Answer	2.7
(Base: 369 non-respondents)	100.0%

The researchers point out that "For the most part the nonreplying group of this study was made up of people whose reasons for not replying were the result of physical causes, neglect, loss, etc. There are no indications that non-responders were to any significant degree of a different *type* than responders."

This is true with three qualifications: (1) It applies to nonrespondents who decided to answer a follow-up mailing, and does not apply to the 7 percent who never answered; (2) it applies to nonrespondents who failed to answer a questionnaire which was completed by 80 percent of the sample; and finally, (3) some respondents in this group may have rationalized their reasons for not answering. It is likely that the 7 percent final nonrespondents included a high proportion of people who do not answer *any* questionnaire, while in another mailing which received only 30 percent response, there was a higher proportion of nonrespondents who did not answer because the subject did not interest them. Nevertheless, this tabulation does give some of the main reasons why people fail to answer a questionnaire, or at least why they believe they do not answer.

Nonrespondents basically fall into just two categories: Those who refuse to answer and those who cannot be located; all others are really potential respondents, and it is only a matter of time and effort to get them to answer. Some refusers can be converted to respondents in most surveys, given correct planning and sufficient money and time. People who cannot be located usually represent more of a problem in personal interviews than in mail surveys, because if people are away from home, the mail will be there when they get back; and if they have moved, it is usually forwarded to them. On some surveys people who cannot be located may bias the results because they represent a segment of the sample which has the characteristics of greater mobility than the rest of the sample and consists of different types of individuals or families.[11]

WHAT CAN BE DONE ABOUT NONRESPONDENTS

It should be part of the survey design to decide how high a percentage of nonresponse can be tolerated and what, if anything, should be done about it. The researcher can choose from among several procedures:

He can take a chance on assuming that the nonresponse will not be different in any significant way from the responses received or that it is so small that even if it is different it could not affect the results. In either of these two cases he will just ignore the problem. Of course such a decision should be based on something more than guesswork, such as previous experience with the same universe or known facts which are relevant.

He may decide to disregard the nonrespondents because his survey design called for selective returns to begin with. For example, "If we send out a questionnaire on skiing equipment and if only skiers answer it, we will, nevertheless, get exactly the kind of information (as to type of equipment, not proportion who ski) for which we are looking."[12] In such cases the survey is just an expensive (but perhaps the only possible) way of getting in touch with the small subgroup we are interested in. There are other examples of this effect of nonrespondent bias.[13]

WEIGHTING THE NONRESPONSE

The research man may feel that while the returns to the first mailing are not representative of the sample, the last wave or a combination of the last waves of returns are representative of all nonrespondents to the first mailing. In this case he will weight the final nonresponse by the replies to the follow-up mailing(s). For example, in a survey conducted among 5,000 subscribers to the *National Geographic* magazine and among a control group of 5,000 representing a random sample of people listed in United States telephone directories two mailings were sent out. There were some significant differences between the replies to the two waves and based on previous experience, it was decided to weight all nonrespondents by the results of the second wave.[14]

Another method would be to establish trends from the results of several waves and weight the nonresponse by continuing these trends. For example, if after analyzing four waves of returns on an income question we find that the average income is lower for each successive wave, we may decide that the income of the nonrespondent group is the lowest. Again, this is not a decision which one can reach automatically. The hard-core nonrespondents may include a few secretive millionaires. There may very well be a point where the direction of the curve changes. Another example: While it is often true that nonrespondents include a higher proportion of poorly educated people than respondents, it is also true that in most market research surveys conducted among subscribers to rather sophisticated publications such as the *New Yorker* magazine, there will be a higher percentage of refused or blank questionnaires than among subscribers to publications which appeal to less sophisticated audiences. It takes a good combination of research experience and statistical knowledge to plot a trend by extrapolating from waves of returns.

The survey design may call for verification by analyzing a random sample of nonrespondents and, if necessary, by weighting all nonresponse according to the results of this procedure.

Because the problem of nonresponse is common to all data-gathering techniques, a number of reliable statistical methods have been worked out for eliminating or at least reducing the bias which it may create in any type of survey. For example, the Politz-Simmons method classifies respondents according to the chance of finding them at home and then weighting the responses accordingly.[15] Hansen and Hurwitz have developed a double sampling procedure which offers a formula for determining the number of mail questionnaires to be sent out and the number of personal interviews to take, in following up nonresponses to the mail questionnaire, in order to attain the required precision at minimum cost.[16] The Swedish researcher, Tore Dalenius, has worked out a special design of the Hansen-Hurwitz scheme aimed at the "hard to contact" segment of the sample.[17] Rex V. Brown has developed a technique called "credence decomposition," which relies on splitting out the various sources of error, including nonresponses, to which a research estimate may be subject.[18]

CONCLUSION

There is a problem of nonresponse in all survey methods. There are many ways of reducing the bias which nonresponse may create. By far, the best way of doing so, whenever the timing and budget factors allow, is to reduce the percentage of nonresponse to the lowest possible level.

The one rule which is true for all survey methods is that if the job is well planned and well executed, the percentage of nonresponse will be small. For example, a cost-of-living survey in Sweden, conducted by personal interviews, ended with a 35 percent nonresponse. By giving extensive training to interviewers before repeating the survey, the researchers were able to reduce nonresponse to 8 percent.[19] One of the purposes of this book is to indicate the most effective mail survey procedures for achieving high response rates.

There is no magic wand which can be waved to guarantee a high percentage response; it can be achieved only through careful planning in all phases of a mail survey. This aspect of mail research is discussed in detail in the chapters describing each of the following:

1. Questionnaire construction (Chaps. 6, 7)
2. Pilot studies (Chap. 9)
3. Advance notice of the survey (Chap. 10)
4. Incentive (Chap. 11)
5. The accompanying letter (Chap. 12)
6. Mailing procedures (Chap. 13)
7. Reminders, follow-up mailings, and follow-ups by other data-gathering techniques (Chap. 14)

REFERENCES

1. Sol Levine and Gerald Gordon, "Maximizing Returns on Mail Questionnaires," *Public Opinion Quarterly*, vol. 22, no. 4, pp. 568–575, winter, 1959.
2. Stanley D. Bachrack and Harry M. Scoble, "Mail Questionnaire Efficiency: Controlled Reduction of Nonresponse," *Public Opinion Quarterly*, vol. 31, no. 2, pp. 265–271, summer, 1967.
3. "Profile of the Subscribers to *The Christian Science Monitor*" (research report), Boston, May, 1967.
4. Lester R. Frankel, "How Incentives and Subsamples Affect the Precision of Mail Surveys," *Journal of Advertising Research*, vol. 1, no. 1, pp. 1–5, September, 1960.
5. Reuben Cohen, Samuel Richmond, J. Stevens Stock, and Thomas T. Semon, "Sampling in Marketing Research," Marketing Research Techniques (ser.), no. 3, *American Marketing Association*, p. 9, 1958.
6. Alfred Politz, "A Study of Four Media" (research report conducted for *Life*), pp. 146–147, 1953.
7. "Selective Markets and the Media Reaching Them: 1968 Magazine Audience Report, Vol. I," W. R. Simmons & Associates Research, Inc., Appendix p. 7, 1968.
8. Raymond Franzen and Paul F. Lazarsfeld, "Mail Questionnaire as a Research Problem," *Journal of Psychology*, vol. 5, no. 20, pp. 293–320, October, 1945.
9. Edward A. Suchman and Boyd McCandless, "Who Answers Questionnaires?" *Journal of Applied Psychology*, vol. 24, no. 6, pp. 758–767, December, 1940; also, John A. Clausen and Robert N. Ford, "Controlling Bias in Mail Questionnaires," *Journal of the American Statistical Association*, vol. 42, no. 240, pp. 497–511, December, 1947; also, Marjorie N. Donald, "Implications of Nonresponse for the Interpretation of Mail Questionnaire Data," *Public Opinion Quarterly*, vol. 24, no. 1, pp. 99–114, spring, 1960.
10. R. A. Robinson and Philip Agisim, "Making Mail Surveys More Reliable," *Journal of Marketing*, vol. 15, no. 4, pp. 415–424, April, 1951.
11. Charles S. Mayer and Robert W. Pratt, Jr., "A Note on Nonresponse in a Mail Survey," *Public Opinion Quarterly*, vol. 30, no. 4, winter, 1966–1967.
12. Raymond Franzen and Paul F. Lazarsfeld, *op cit.*, p. 296.
13. Richard F. Larson and William R. Catton, Jr., "Can the Mail-back Bias Contribute to a Study's Validity?" *American Sociological Review*, vol 24, no. 2, pp. 243–245, April, 1959.
14. "Travel patterns: National Geographic Households Compared with U.S. Telephone Households" (research report), *National Geographic Magazine*, New York, 1964.
15. Alfred Politz and Willard R. Simmons, "An Attempt to Get the Not-at-homes into the Sample without Call-backs," *Journal of the American Statistical Association*, vol. 44, no. 245, pp. 9–31, March, 1949; also, W. Edwards Deming, "On a Prob-

ability Mechanism to Attain an Economic Balance between the Resultant Error of Response and the Bias of Nonresponse," *Journal of the American Statistical Association*, vol. 48, no. 264, pp. 743–772, December, 1953.
16. Morris H. Hansen and William N. Hurwitz, "The Problem of Nonresponse in Sample Surveys," *Journal of the American Statistical Association*, vol. 41, no. 236, pp. 517–529, December, 1946; also, Morris H. Hansen, W. N. Hurwitz, and W. G. Madow, *Sample Survey Methods and Theory*, John Wiley & Son, New York, 1953, vol. I, pp. 473–474.
17. Tore Dalenius, "The Treatment of the Nonresponse Problem," *Journal of Advertising Research*, vol. 1, no. 5, pp. 1–7, September, 1961.
18. Rex V. Brown, "Research Appraisal in Confusion: Where Can the User Turn?" paper delivered at the American Marketing Association Summer Conference in Philadelphia, June 18, 1968.
19. Tore Dalenius, *op. cit.*

SIXTEEN
Checking In Returns

THE FIRST RETURNS of most surveys consist of unopened mailings returned by the postoffice as undeliverable. The percentage of these "undeliverables" will depend on the quality of the mailing list and on the accuracy of the addressing of the outgoing envelopes. In a carefully conducted survey all undeliverables are checked against the mailing list and, if possible, against the original sources of the list, such as directories and subscription galleys. If an error in name or address is discovered, the mailing piece should be corrected and remailed at once.

In most surveys the percentage of response is calculated on the basis of net mailing, that is, total mailing less the undeliverables. However, the latter should always be shown: to some user of the survey the number of undeliverables may be important in evaluating the quality of the list or as indicating the mobility of members of the particular universe. Of course the "Moved without forwarding address" returns show only part of the mobility pattern because questionnaires *are* forwarded to known new (changed) addresses.

In a busy office it is advisable to have a keyed and easily identifiable reply envelope for each survey. A survey (or each survey, if several are coming in at once) can be identified even before opening the envelope by varying the name of the person to whom the reply envelope is addressed, the name of the department, room numbers, the position of each line of the address, or the color of the printing.

This identification will enable the researcher to get a quick daily count of replies. This is always advisable. For one thing, the table of daily counts will give an immediate and easy way to check the total returns on any given day, and this in turn may decide the timing of such subsequent operations as test tabulating, editing, and coding. Also, he can readily perceive when the returns are petering out. By indicating the total number of returns which he can expect from the mailing, this will enable him to decide whether or not he needs a follow-up mailing and, if so, when it should go out and what, if any, incentives it should contain. Finally, the daily counts may come in very handy at some future date if he should have to repeat the same survey or conduct a similar one, for he will know what percentage of response he can expect during given periods of time. For an example of a daily return sheet, see Figure 25.

OPENING THE ENVELOPES

The next step is the opening of the envelopes. If this is done by electric letter openers, it is advisable to shake down the contents of the envelopes, as otherwise you may find many of the questionnaires cut apart at the fold.

If the questionnaire has a question on the city and state where the respondent lives, it is good practice to make sure when taking it out of the envelope that this question has been answered. If not, the answer can be copied from the postmark. Where this question has not been asked, the easiest way to obtain such information is by copying the city and state from the postmark onto each questionnaire. The results will be approximately correct. Not entirely, however, because some postmarks will be illegible and in some cases respondents may mail the questionnaire from a place other than their home town or even their home state.

As the envelopes are opened, their contents can be sorted into two groups: (1) usable questionnaires and (2) all others. This latter group may include blank questionnaires and refusals. For all practical purposes these mean the same thing. Refusals should be carefully analyzed. Who the refusers are and their reasons for nonresponse can be very important to the final evaluation of the results. Partially filled-out questionnaires and letters from which such questionnaires can be constructed may represent borderline cases of usability, and the researcher will have to decide in each case whether to discard it or find some use for it. He will also have to decide whether or not to send a follow-up mailing to this nonrespondent and refuser group.

	JOB #
DAILY RETURN RECORD	
Client_____	Job Name_____
Project Director_____	Ass't Project Dir._____
Envelope size_____	Envelope size_____
Mailing_____	Mailing_____
Date mailed_____	Date mailed_____
Number mailed_____	Number mailed_____

Date	Returns for day	Cumulative return	Date	Returns for day	Cumulative return

Undeliverable_____   Undeliverable_____

Blanks, Refusals_____   Blanks, Refusals_____

Closing date_____   Closing date_____

FIGURE 25

PULLING MAILING CARDS

If there is to be a follow-up mailing or some type of validation procedure or if the mailing cards contain information which will be part of the analysis, the next step is the "pulling." In all such cases the questionnaire will contain either the name of the respondent or a key by which he can be identified. In the former case, the mailing cards should be in alphabetic order by the names of the addressees; in the latter, in numerical order by the key number. Whenever possible, the pulling should be a daily operation so as to keep a tight control on the flow of work and to have an up-to-date record. The mailing card corresponding to each return should be pulled and arranged in order within three groups: (1) undeliverables (which contain no addressing error and cannot be remailed), (2) refusals, blanks, and other unusable replies which may or may not rate a follow-up effort, and (3) usable questionnaires. The mailing cards may contain information which we want to transfer to the questionnaire and/or to the card which will be punched from the completed questionnaires. This may consist of the correct city and state information and already available data, such as sex, occupation, SIC number, sales volume. There are two ways of handling this transfer. In the case of a relatively low percentage of response, these data can be simply copied onto the questionnaire, to be coded and punched as though they were replies to additional questions. In cases of a high percentage of response, such as 70 percent or better, it is usually less expensive and certainly more accurate to code the mailout cards, punch a separate deck of cards containing the key number and the information which we want to use, and then reproduce this information mechanically from the punched cards created from the mailing cards into the deck punched from the questionnaires. The two decks of cards will be matched by the key numbers; therefore these numbers must appear on both sets.

If there is any danger that the pulled cards (undeliverables, refusals, and respondents) and the unpulled cards (nonrespondents) may get mixed up, it is advisable to mark all pulled cards. A simple way to do this is to snip off a corner of each card or to circle the key number.

If the returns are pulled every day, the researcher can decide at any time that he is ready to mail out the second wave, and his mailing list will be readily available; all he has to do is to serialize the unpulled cards, if he wants to key the next mailing, or just use them as they are, if no keying is needed. In the case of a keyed mailing the unpulled cards should be serialized, that is, keyed with a consecutive number.

156 Professional Mail Surveys

The consecutive number is needed to keep a ready check on quantities and to reduce the margin of error in matching cards, outgoing envelopes, and questionnaires. It is advisable to use a completely different series of numbers, a different color, and a different position on the cards for this second numbering in order to avoid confusion between the two sets of numbers. List cards can look quite complicated by the time they have served three waves of mailings and the coding and transfer of information which they originally contained (Figure 26.)

ORDERLY PROCEDURE

The pulled mailing cards should always be kept in numerical order in clearly labeled boxes. One can never be sure when they may be needed for another validation, for checking such information as city, state, or sex of respondent, or for later mailing of an ancillary survey to some or all of the respondents. If groups of the list cards have to be separated from the rest for any length of time, it is good practice to make a duplicate set of such subgroups and to keep the total respondent card file intact.

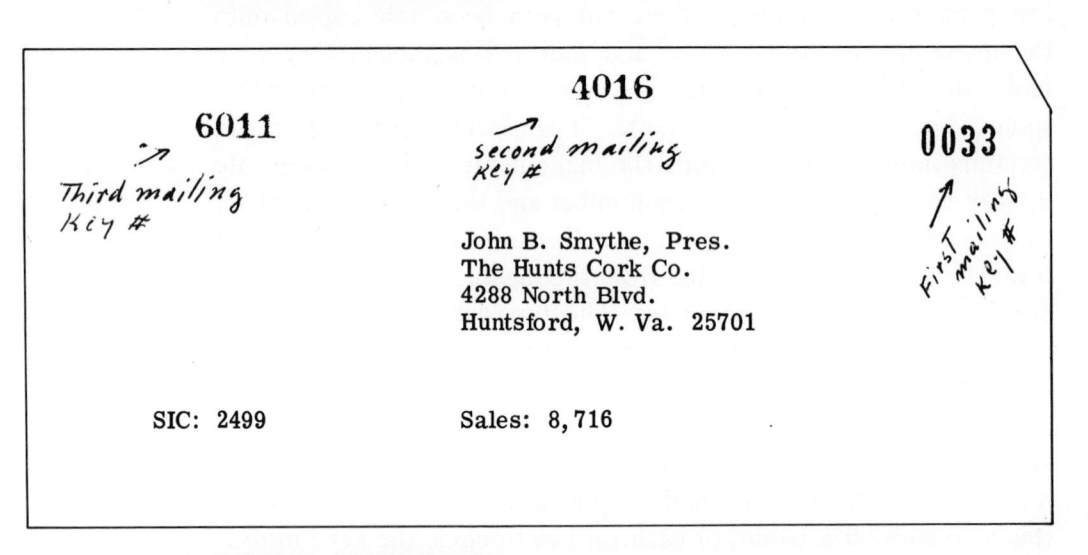

```
              4016
   6011    second mailing                0033
Third mailing   Key #
Key #
              John B. Smythe, Pres.          First mailing
              The Hunts Cork Co.             Key #
              4288 North Blvd.
              Huntsford, W. Va. 25701


SIC: 2499        Sales: 8,716
```

FIGURE 26   Mailing-list card.

Upon completion of a survey there will be much material to be filed away, in the form of completed questionnaires, source materials, punched cards, tabulations, etc. It is wise to box and label all such material adequately and clearly so as to prevent confusion and error and to allow quick identification and reference. Figure 27 shows a job label.

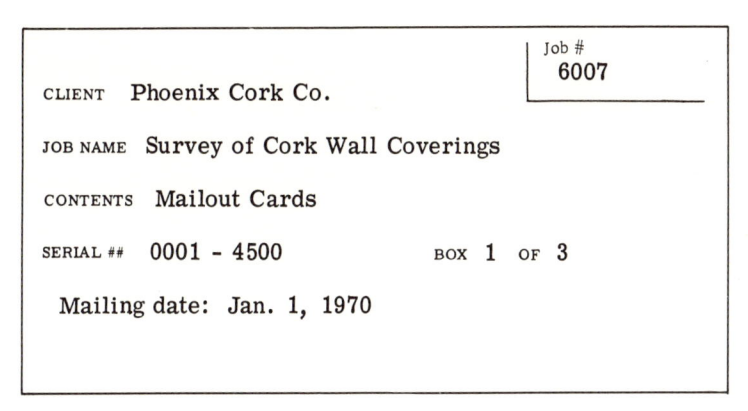

```
CLIENT    Phoenix Cork Co.              Job #
                                         6007
JOB NAME  Survey of Cork Wall Coverings

CONTENTS  Mailout Cards

SERIAL ##  0001 - 4500           BOX  1  OF  3

Mailing date: Jan. 1, 1970
```

FIGURE 27 Job label.

After the questionnaires have been taken out of the envelopes, city and state transferred, and (in the case of keyed mailings) the cards pulled, the returns should be made ready for the various data-processing operations.

When the questionnaire contains open-end questions, test tabulations will be needed (Chap. 19). A random sample must be selected and put in a separate batch for this purpose. The number of questionnaires needed for this operation depends on the nature of the job, as will be discussed later.

All other questionnaires should be counted and put into even batches for further processing. For convenience in handling, the number of questionnaires in a batch may vary from 100 to 300, depending on the number of the pages per questionnaire and the thickness of the stock on which it is printed. Every batch should have a "top sheet" (an example is shown in Fig. 28), which records who performed each operation and how long it took. This will indicate to the supervisor at a glance how much of the needed work has been completed and which coder's job is being checked; he can compute the time spent on these operations and gauge whether the performance is above or below average in speed and accuracy.

In the case of hand tabulations, the top sheets will contain a column headed "Hand tabs," with space for filling in the tabulator's initials and time spent on tabulating each question. Of course in this form all questions must be listed, as all questions have to be hand tabulated, while only some have to be coded for machine tabulation. (See Chap. 17 for hand tabulating and Chap. 19 for coding.)

| Job # | 643 | Job name: | SURVEY ON SCOTCH WHISKY |

Batch # 1 of 12   Quantity 100

Page #	Question Identi-fication	Coding & Editing			Checking		
		Coder's initial's	Hours	Mins.	Checker's initial's	Hours	Mins.
3	4						
	5						
	7 (Switch from–to)						
	7 (Reasons)						
	8 (Brand)						
	Q. 1 (Brands 1–3)						

Date finished _____

FIGURE 28. Top sheet for questionnaire batch (for questionnaire page shown in Fig. 7).

SEVENTEEN
Data-Processing

THE COMPLETED AND RETURNED QUESTIONNAIRES contain the answers which the researcher wants to analyze. Each questionnaire represents one respondent. The survey design often calls for thousands of questionnaires, and the individual data which each contains must be somehow counted and arranged into a meaningful form for the final analysis. Instead of individual answers, the analyst needs tabulations of large numbers of figures, tables of percentages, averages, medians, charts, and various groupings and breakdowns of all these for presenting the results of the survey. "Data-processing" is the collective name for all operations which combine and translate the individual replies into meaningful reports.

Human beings presumably started counting on their fingers, and there is a more or less straight line of evolution from these honorable ancestors to the digits of our numbers and all the way to our digital computers. The essential part of data-processing is tabulating, that is, counting the replies and presenting them in tabular form. Tabulations can be done by hand or by machine.

Suppose we have a batch of 2,000 questionnaires which include the following question: "What is the make of your family's principal car?" The respondents are all car owners, and we have to tabulate this question. There can be only one answer per questionnaire, and so we can give the questionnaires to a clerk to sort by make of car. We can tell him that we are only interested in ten leading makes and ask him to sort the questionnaires into twelve groups: the ten makes (Ford, Cadillac, etc.), an "all other makes" group, and a "no answer" group. Experience shows that the average clerical worker can sort, count, and check this kind of job at the rate of 600 questionnaires an hour. Once the answers to this question are punched on a card, a fast counter-sorter machine can sort out and count each of the groups, as well as total, at the rate of 1,000 per minute. A computer can work at great speed and can perform a number of operations simultaneously, including tabulating, percentaging, and projecting.

Hand tabulation still has its uses, although by now they are only marginal. Today nearly all tabulating work is done by machines, and most of this machine work is handled by electronic data-processing (EDP) equipment. However, it is still true that the researcher has to decide on the type of data-processing techniques he wants to use for each particular case. He will have to consider the number of questionnaires to be tabulated, the length and complexity of the questionnaire, the number and types of the cross tabulations needed, the available manpower and machines for various steps of the operation, the availability of existing computer programs which can handle his work, or the time and cost required for writing a new one to handle it, and so on.

No matter which one of several available data-processing techniques the researcher may choose, he will have to plan for several interrelated steps in data-processing:

1. Editing
2. Coding
3. Punching or electronic transfer (if machine tabulations)
4. Consistency checks, cleaning
5. Tabulating (runs, if machine)
6. Calculating (weighting, averages, percentages, medians, etc.)
7. Recapping (if other than computer printouts)

A survey, like a chain, is only as strong as each of its links. A good survey plan calls for consideration of the final tabulations and recaps needed, even before questionnaire construction starts. Starting with questionnaire construction and sampling, through all the steps of data-gathering and data-processing, each operation has to be carefully planned, executed, and checked. This of course is true also of the seven steps of data-processing just enumerated.

HAND TABULATING

Hand tabulating is usually used in the following circumstances:

1. When for some reason no machinery or machine time is available

2. For tabulating a very small number of questionnaires, such as the results of pilot studies

3. For test tabulating, the preliminary step needed to establish codes (this will be discussed in Chap. 19)

The counting of answers by hand can be accomplished by either of two methods: sorting or tabulating proper, that is, ticking off counts on a sheet of paper.

Sorting is the easier and more accurate method when a question can have only one answer. For example, the questions "Have you ever flown on a commerical airline?" and "If so, did you take such a flight during the past 12 months?" can each be answered only by "Yes" or "No." These answers can be easily sorted into five groups: Yes-Yes, Yes-No, Yes-No Answer, No to the first question, and No Answer to the first question. Once the questionnaires have been sorted into these groups each group can be checked to make sure that the sorting was done correctly. Next, each group can be counted, and the total should add to the total number of questionnaires. Counting answers by the sorting method gets more complicated when more than one answer is possible to the same question; for example, "What make(s) of car does your family now own?" In such cases one can sometimes devise a complicated sorting procedure or sort single-answer questionnaires only and tabulate (tab) double or multiple answers, but usually it is easier to tab, rather than sort, the questionnaires.

Once, many years ago, the author visited the market research department of a large publication. The first thing he noticed were three very long tables, with long, lined sheets of tabulating paper laid out on top of each. Several young ladies were walking the length of these tables, with questionnaires in hand, making tab marks on the long sheets. It turned out that they were hand tabulating the questionnaires by tallying each and *every question* of one questionnaire at a time. When they were finished with all questions of the questionnaire in hand, they started tabulating the first question of the next questionnaire.

This is the classic example of how *not* to tabulate. Both for accuracy and speed one should hand tabulate *one question* (or one continuous set of questions) at a time and finish the operation on the whole batch of questionnaires before going on to the next question. Each questionnaire will be handled many times, but both speed and accuracy will be gained, because the tabulator will be working with one tab sheet and will be able to concentrate on one question (or set of questions) at a time.

HOW TO TABULATE BY HAND

Figure 29 shows a system of hand tabulating called "making gates": Each answer of the same kind is marked with a short vertical line, up to four tabs. The fifth is a diagonal line across the first four, and the five together resemble a gate. Where hand tabulations (usually called "hand tabs") are frequently needed, it may be worth printing a specially designed tabulating paper, which can be padded. It is usually printed on eye-ease (light green) or light yellow stock and contains boxes divided across into units of five by wider, vertical lines. The advantages are that the neatness of this layout boosts the accuracy of the tabulator and that counting at the end will be easier because one can count in units of twenty-five (five gates, each containing five tabs).

It is not easy to check hand tabulations without actually doing a job twice. The tabs for single-answer questions should add to the total number of questionnaires. In the case of multiple mentions the tabulator can make a separate tab of double, triple, etc., answers as he goes along and check out the totals. The trouble is that the totals may check despite compensating errors; for example, a few mentions of "France" may have been tabulated under "Germany" (Fig. 29).

When check questions are tabulated by hand, the replies must be listed on the tab sheet in the same order as they appear on the questionnaire: any other arrangement would confuse the tabulator and increase the margin of error. "No Answer" should be tabulated on all questions.

Open-end questions can be quite simple (e.g., "How many adults over 18 years of age live in your household?" or "What make of car do you own?") or rather complicated ("What is the make and series name of your car?" or "Why did you buy this particular make of refrigerator?").

```
JOB #: 599        NAME OF JOB: Travel Survey

Q.7 (If "Yes" to Q.6) Which countries did you visit in the last 12 months?

    Canada                           ||||| ||||| ||||| ||||| ||||| ||||| ||||| ||||| ||||| ||||| |||||
                                     ||||| ||||| ||||| ||||| ||||| |||  (108)
    Mexico                           ||||| ||||| ||||| ||||| ||||| ||||| ||||| ||||| ||||| ||||| |||||
                                     ||  (77)
    Other Cent. Am. & Caribbean      ||||| ||||| ||||| ||||| ||||| ||||| ||||| ||||| ||||| ||||| ||||| ||||| |||  (68)
      (Bermuda, Bahamas, etc)
    Britain                          ||||| ||||| ||||| ||||| ||||| ||||| ||||| ||||| ||  (42)
    France                           ||||| ||||| ||||  (14)
    Germany                          ||||| ||||| ||||| ||||| |  (21)
    Italy                            ||||| ||||| ||||| ||||| ||||| |||  (28)
    Scandinavian countries           ||||| ||||| ||||| ||||| ||  (22)
    Other Europe                     ||||| ||||| ||||| ||||| ||||| ||||| ||  (32)
    Africa                           ||||| ||||| ||||| |  (16)
    Japan                            ||||| |||  (8)
    Other Asia                       ||||| |  (6)
    Australia & South Pacific        |||||  (5)
    All others                       ||||  (4)
    No answer                        ||||| ||  (7)

    Total mentions                   458

    Double mentions                  ||||| ||||| ||||| ||||| ||||| ||||| ||||| ||||| ||||| ||||| |||  (53)
    Triple mentions                  ||||| ||||| ||||| ||  (17)
    Quadruple mentions               ||||| ||  (7)

    Base                             350
```

FIGURE 29 Hand tabulation.

In the case of a question calling for a numerical reply, it is simple enough to tabulate the answers, keeping the groups of replies in numerical order.

TABULATING BRANDS AND REASONS

In hand tabulation of brand names, one can list the few leading makes which the researcher knows will show up most often and tab the others in approximate alphabetic order, leaving enough room between the letters of the alphabet for as-yet-unlisted brands. Occasionally respondents confuse make and manufacturer, and the tabulator may have to get counts for "Mustang," for other specified Ford makes, and for "Ford makes not further identified." In a situation like this, the researcher may decide that there is no way of telling how many Mustangs are included with the answers of respondents who just listed "Ford" and that all Ford makes should therefore be combined.

The same problem will be multiplied many times with the tabulation of make and series name of cars. Respondents may confuse the name of the manufacturer, the make, or the series name. Series names may not only disappear in the manufacturer's new line, but (at least in the case of some car makes) may represent different price ranges in successive years. This of course has little to do with tabulating techniques, but it shows that the job of a good tabulator or tabulating supervisor can be far from routine. He may need a sheaf of manufacturers' brand and model lists in order to set up a seemingly simple tabulation of makes and models of cars.

Finally, the hardest answers to tabulate are the replies to opinion questions and reason questions, which often start with "Why...." The difficulty here is in deciding what to tabulate verbatim and what to combine with what else. The language is rich enough to express the same thought in many different ways. If all these expressions were to be listed separately, the end result would be nearer to a listing of all answers than to a tabulation, and it could fill page after page with useless semantics. On the other hand, careless combining of answers may end in too few categories, too general to be meaningful. In one particular job, the basic meaning of the word or expression may be what is important. "I bought this refrigerator because of its capacity," "... because of its large size," "... because it takes a lot of food to fill it up," "... because of its giant size" might all be included in one category, as far as that job is concerned. In the case of a different project, where the question was asked in order to test advertising effectiveness, it would be essential to tabulate separately all mentions of "giant size," which happened to be the slogan used in an advertising campaign.

SUPERVISION AND CHECKING

In ordinary jobs the coding supervisor will have to tabulate the first batch of questionnaires; in important jobs the project director should do this first step. Only complete knowledge both of the aims of the research project and of the kind of answers which are actually listed by the respondents will enable the person in charge of tabulating to instruct the tabulators and to check their work.

The tabulating (or coding) supervisor has three concerns: (1) Do all tabulators understand their instructions and all the problems the job at hand can raise? (2) Having understood it, do they use the same interpretation and make the same decisions in the case of identical problems? (3) Is their work reasonably accurate?

The only way to make sure that all three requirements are met and maintained is to establish firm rules, illustrate them with examples whenever possible, put them in writing, and check the first batch of questionnaires tabulated by each tabulator by retabulating his work. In the rare case of a large job being tabulated by hand, spot checking of tabulated batches (that is, retabulating) would be appropriate.

Test tabulating and coding, which are normally parts of the machine tabulating process, will be described in Chapter 19. However, the hand tabulating of many types of answers, such as brands or reasons, can be made more accurate and easier to check by establishing codes and then coding all questionnaires (including the batch from which the codes were established). From the checker's point of view this will break down checking into two operations: making sure that the interpretation and uses of codes are correct and uniform among all coders and that the tabulating of the codes is correct. While for the second of these two operations he will still have to redo small batches of the tabulator's work, the coding job itself can be checked by inspecting individual questionnaires selected at random. Furthermore, if at the end of the job, or even months later, the researcher wants to check how individual answers were interpreted and tabulated, he can always go back to the questionnaires and inspect the codes.

When the tabulating is finished, all gates and tab marks must be counted and the counts checked for each item tabbed. Next a "recap sheet" will be made up of these checked counts. The order of the tabulated items on the recap sheet will depend on the nature of the question. In a tabulation of the months of the year, the recap sheet will show the twelve months, in order, from January to December. In the tabulation of brands, we may put all brands into descending order by the number of mentions or into descending order of mentions by manufacturer. Reasons may be arranged by order of mentions or into logical groups by meaning. (For an example of a recap sheet see Fig. 37.)

It is important that recap sheets be carefully proofread against the original tab sheets.

EIGHTEEN
The Punch Card and Its Use

IN ORDER TO USE any type of data-processing machinery, we have to create something that can be fed into a machine. This can be done, or at least started, even before the data-gathering process.

Mark-sense cards represent a special process, where the questions are printed on cards the size of punch cards, with spaces left for check answers. The answers have to be marked with a special pencil containing soft, highly conductive graphite which can be electrically "sensed", that is, picked up by the processing machinery. For various reasons this method is very seldom used in tabulating mail surveys.

Another system is used by the Census Bureau. Here the questionnaires are handled by an automated photographic process for ultimate electronic transfer of the information from microfilm to magnetic computer tape. In this process the design of the questionnaires is subject to a number of constraints in color, size, internal spacing, and folding. At present this process is not generally used in mail surveys.

In most mail surveys the questionnaires are printed on regular paper. These forms (questionnaires) will go through the data-gathering, editing, and coding operations and then be punched into cards, which in turn may end up as tapes before being fed into the tabulating machinery. Some questionnaires are punched directly on paper or magnetic tape.

The keypunch machine has a keyboard, which may contain three kinds of symbols: numeric, alphabetic, and special symbols for computer specifications (Fig. 30). The last type is for technical use,

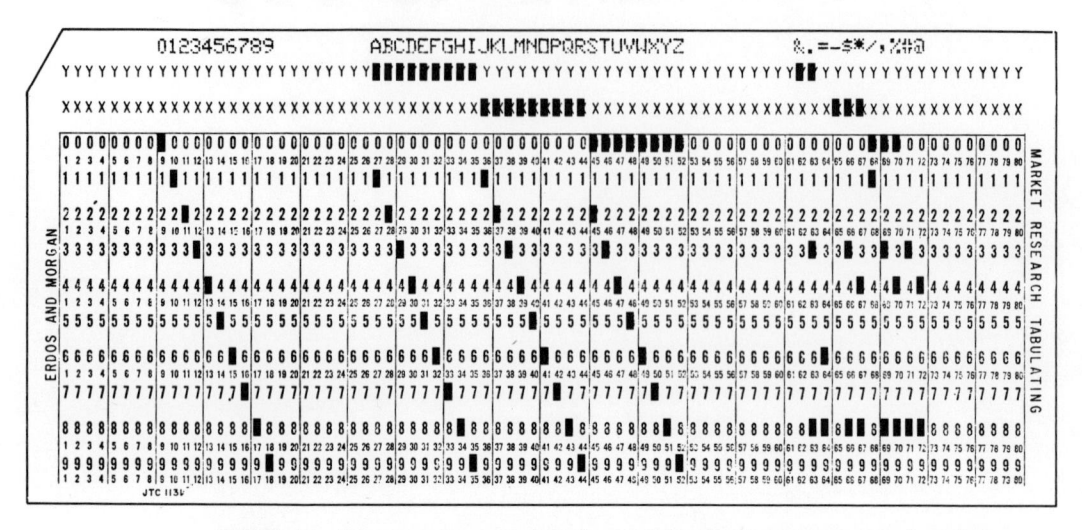

FIGURE 30 Interpreted punched card containing numbers, letters, and symbols.

which does not concern us now. Alphabetic punching is seldom used in mail surveys, except for the presentation of reports and tabulations.

DESCRIPTION OF THE PUNCH CARD

Nearly all tabulating is done with the help of numbers. Questionnaires must be translated into a system of numbers before we can tabulate them. The system generally used is based on the 80-column (IBM) card reproduced in Figure 31. It has 12 positions in each column: from 1 to 9 and O, X and Y. There are various other systems, using different numbers of columns and positions.

A "field" of columns (several columns used as a unit) can be assigned to a serial number or to answers to a question. In our example (Fig. 31) the first 4 columns contain serial numbers which identify the questionnaire, columns 5 and 6 show the age of the respondent, column 7 indicates whether or not he has traveled outside of the United States in the past 12 months, and the next 3 columns indicate which countries he visited if he did travel abroad. If we had our code sheets handy, to "decode" or translate the punched codes back into the answers which appeared on the questionnaire, we would see that respondent number 5694 is 24 years of age, has been abroad in the past 12 months, and has visited France, Italy, and Mexico. (Column 7, with a punch in position 1, means "yes"; columns 8, position 3, means France, punch 4 in the same column indicates Italy; column 9 was reserved for countries which this respondent did not visit in the past 12 months, therefore the column has no hole; and punch 2 in column 10 stands for Mexico. The X punch in the last column indicates here the end of the card.)

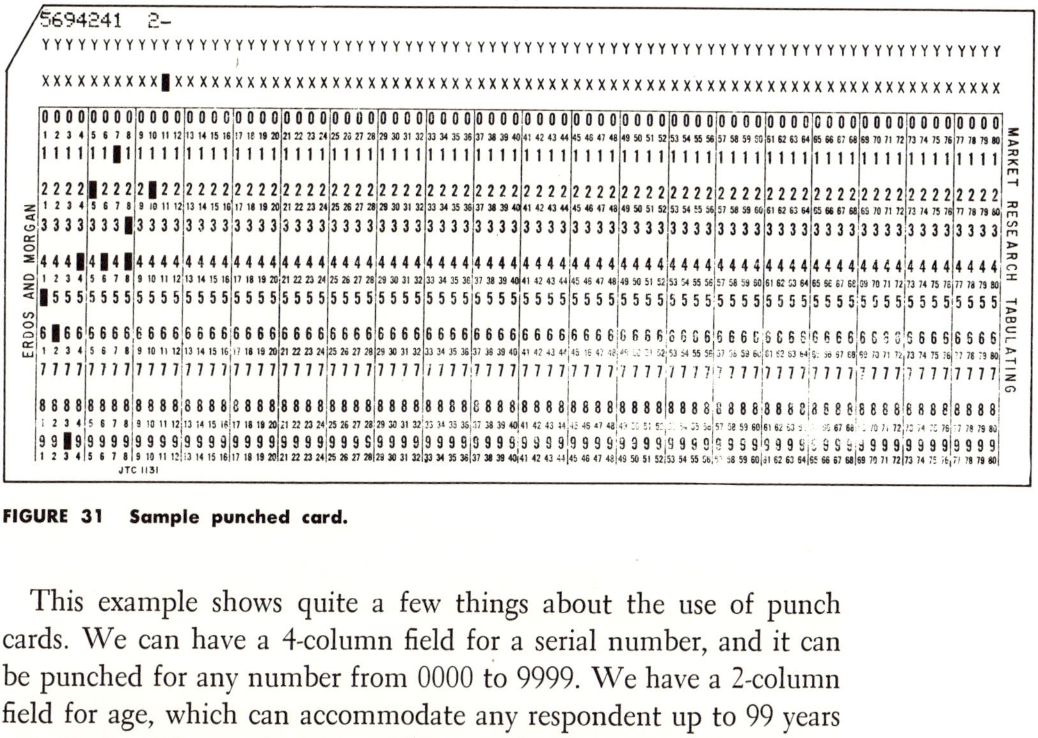

FIGURE 31 Sample punched card.

This example shows quite a few things about the use of punch cards. We can have a 4-column field for a serial number, and it can be punched for any number from 0000 to 9999. We have a 2-column field for age, which can accommodate any respondent up to 99 years old. Each of these columns could be punched in any of 10 positions, from 0 to 9. The next single column can be punched in only 2 positions, for "yes" and "no." Any other punch (unless the researcher decided to indicate "no answer" with a special punch, such as Y) in column 7 would be in error. In all columns so far, from 1 to 7, we could only have "single punches," that is only 1 hole in 1 column. The last field of 3 columns is set up for "multiple punching": each of these columns can have from 1 to 12 punches, which means that the field can accomodate a total of 36 answers. (In our example it would be 35 specific countries and then "all others.")

FLEXIBILITY IN THE USE OF COLUMNS

Actually, the researcher has an unlimited number of positions at his disposal. A single card represents 80 times 12 positions, or 960 codes, if he wants to equate code and position. He may choose to use 2 columns as a field, and this makes room for 99 codes even if we ignore the X and Y punches. On a brand question, which calls for single answers, these 2 columns can be used to code 99 brands, the first being code 01, and the last, 99. If more than 1 brand can be mentioned by the same respondent, he may leave a field of 2 columns for each mention. He may decide that all he wants to count are the leading 36 brands. In this case he can use 3 columns and multiple punch each of them. If he is using columns 11 to 13 for this purpose, the first brand will be code 1 in column 11, and the last, code Y in column 13. If he runs out of columns, he can always use a second, third, or any number of additional cards for a questionnaire, making sure that the same serial number is punched into each.

Tabulators sometimes try to save columns by coding more than one question in a column. This generally results in no saving at all because although card punching is a relatively fast operation, multiple punches slow it down, and the additional double punching of columns will waste more time than has been gained by saving a fraction of a card. Furthermore, the cleaning and card counting operations (described later) may become less efficient when unrelated answers are punched in one column. However, to speed up computer tabulations one can always "pack" a column by automatically transferring into it punches from one or more other columns.

Multiple punching in general is a very useful device, but two limitations must be considered: It may increase the margin of error and decrease the speed of a keypunch operator who is not accustomed to it, and some computer programs are not set up for double punches.

TRAILER CARDS

"Trailer cards," supplementary to the basic punch card, can greatly increase its flexibility. They usually cover one question, or the answers to part of one question, and they are often used in situations where a relatively small percentage of respondents are expected to give a particular type of answer. Question 1 of the automotive section of a questionnaire shown in Figure 9 is a good example of the use of trailer cards. If we know from experience that 80 percent of the respondents will list only one or two cars, we may decide to allocate the necessary number of columns for only two cars. If we plan a two-column field, or ninety-nine possibilities for coding make and series name, one column for model year (taking only the last digit), one column for "new and used," one column for the month of purchase and one for the "year bought," we will need twelve columns on our card to cover the first two cars, that is, the first two lines of the questionnaire. For the small percentage of respondents who will list a third car, or the even smaller number who will squeeze in four or five cars, it might be wasteful to add several times six more columns. The solution is either a hand tabulation of the small number of questionnaires listing these additional cars, or the use of trailers which will contain information on them. The trailer card will contain the serial number of the basic card, the information filled in on the third line of the auto question, plus a code in a specific column to indicate that this is the first trailer for this respondent. If the questionnaire has the description of a fourth car, another trailer card will be punched with a code identification specifying it as the second trailer. Occasionally there are several questions on a questionnaire where trailers are used, and in such cases the question number is added in a column reserved for it.

With this system we avoid a large blank space on 80 percent of our cards, we can count the number of answers and number of respondents and can always match the trailer card with the so-called basic card when required for cross tabulation or any other purpose.

PREPARING QUESTIONNAIRES FOR PUNCHING

Trained keypunch operators can do a very fast and accurate job if the questionnaire has been properly laid out and coded. Questionnaires can be prepared for punching in various ways:

1. Precoding
2. Hand coding
3. No coding, but careful layout (of check questions)

1. In precoding, the researcher decides in advance how many and which columns should be allocated to each question. The column numbers, and, in the case of check questions even the actual code numbers, are printed on the questionnaire next to the space left for answering. If precoding is used, it should be designed by an expert; badly planned precoding can hopelessly confuse keypunch operators.

172 Professional Mail Surveys

Precoding is very useful in the case of personal or telephone interviews, but for reasons stated earlier the author has not found it advisable to use precoding on mail survey questionnaires.

2. Hand coding is the method used on most surveys. It will be discussed in detail in the next chapter.

3. If the questionnaire consists entirely of check questions and proper care has been taken in laying out the answer boxes, keypunch operators trained in questionnaire work can punch the answers from it without the aid of any codes. Of course in most cases the questionnaire will include both check and open-end questions, and in this situation only the open-end questions will have to be coded.

CODED QUESTIONNAIRE AND MASTER

Figure 32 shows the filled-out last page of a questionnaire mailed to important people in the financial world. Figure 33, the "master questionnaire" prepared for the keypunch operator, shows the proper columns she has to punch for each answer and also the codes (that is, positions of the holes to be punched in the column) for each question which can be answered by checks. On this page there are only two open-end questions (Q. 9 and Q. 11a—"If Yes..."); both call for numerical answers. These are coded, as described later. With the help of the clear layout and the master questionnaire, a good keypunch operator can punch about 100 such pages per hour. The master page starts with a serial number, which identifies the respondent. Looking again at Figure 32, the operator simply punches 1 in the first column, 2 in the next one, 3 in the third column and 6 in the fourth. This questionnaire was too long for one card and the punching of its answers has to be spread over three cards. Column 5 on the master indicates which of the three cards we have in hand (in this case it is the third one), therefore column 5 will be punched 3. Question 9 will be punched the same way as the serial number, using columns 6 to 10 for punching the actual number listed. Question 10 is allotted three columns, and our respondent's reply will be punched 12–2. The "X columns"—14, 20, and 29—are automatically punched (keypunch machines can be set to punch given positions automatically) to help the keypunch operator make sure that she is on column: if she either skipped a column or missed a punch, the X column will fall in an unexpected space and rhythm and warn her of the error. The X columns are so spaced on a page that the operator can catch her error without wasting too much time in continuing to punch a card which

Page 4

9. About how many employees are there in your entire company or firm—that is, the total number of employees including all plants, divisions and branches? Total 350

10. Please check in which bracket you estimate your company's gross sales last year (including all plants, divisions and branches):

    Under $1,000,000 ☐ $ 25 to $ 49 million ☐ $250 to $499 million ☐
    $ 1 to $ 9 million ☐ $ 50 to $ 99 million ☒ $500 million and over ☐
    $10 to $24 million ☐ $100 to $249 million ☐

11. a. Does your company now own corporate aircraft? .... Yes ☒   No ☐
    If "Yes," how many such aircraft does it own? .... One (1)

    b. Does your company plan to buy any corporate aircraft? .... Yes ☐   No ☒

12. a. Do you yourself now own all or part of a franchise? .... Yes ☐   No ☒
    b. Are you presently considering such an investment? .... Yes ☐   No ☒

STATISTICAL DATA (to help us analyze our survey)

1. What is your age? .... Under 25 ☐   35 to 44 ☒   55 to 64 ☐
                                       25 to 34 ☐   45 to 54 ☐   65 or over ☐

2. What is the highest level of school you reached? (Please check one.)

   Grammar school .... ☐
   Attended high school ...... ☐
   Graduated from high school ☐

   Attended college .... ☐
   Graduated from college .... ☒
   Postgraduate college ...... ☐

3. Would you please check the bracket into which your total annual family income (before taxes) falls, including all members of your immediate household? (Please include all income from salaries, wages, interest, dividends, capital gains, rents, commissions, bonuses, pensions, etc.)

                                      $ 15,000 to $24,999 ☐
   Less than $5,000 ☐ $ 25,000 to $49,999 ☐
   $ 5,000 to $ 7,499 ☐ $ 50,000 to $74,999 ☐
   $ 7,500 to $ 9,999 ☐ $ 75,000 to $99,999 ☒
   $10,000 to $14,999 ☐ $100,000 or more ☐

4. Would you please indicate what is your immediate family's net worth? (Please include personal and household possessions, all real estate, bank accounts, securities, insurance, jewelry, automobiles and all other valuables.)

   Less than $5,000 ☐ $ 50,000 to $ 74,999 ☐ $ 250,000 to $ 499,999 ☐
   $ 5,000 to $14,999 ☐ $ 75,000 to $ 99,999 ☐ $ 500,000 to $ 999,999 ☐
   $15,000 to $24,999 ☐ $100,000 to $149,999 ☒ $1,000,000 to $1,999,999 ☐
   $25,000 to $49,999 ☐ $150,000 to $249,999 ☐ $2 million and over ..... ☐

THANK YOU VERY MUCH FOR YOUR COOPERATION

FIGURE 32 Filled-out questionnaire page.

Serial # 1-4
Card # 5

Page 4

9. About how many employees are there in your entire company or firm—that is, the total number of employees including all plants, divisions and branches? Total _____ 6-10

10. Please check in which bracket you estimate your company's gross sales last year (including all plants, divisions and branches):

    Under $1,000,000 ☐1 $ 25 to $ 49 million ☐1 $250 to $499 million ☐1   11-13
    $ 1 to $ 9 million ☐2 $ 50 to $ 99 million ☐2 $500 million and over ☐2
    $10 to $24 million ☐3 $100 to $249 million ☐3   (14-X)

11. a. Does your company now own corporate aircraft? .... Yes ☐1 No ☐2 15

    If "Yes," how many such aircraft does it own? .... _____ 16

   b. Does your company plan to buy any corporate aircraft? .... Yes ☐1 No ☐2 17

12. a. Do you yourself now own all or part of a franchise? .... Yes ☐1 No ☐2 18

   b. Are you presently considering such an investment? .... Yes ☐1 No ☐2 19

STATISTICAL DATA (to help us analyze our survey)   (20-X)

1. What is your age? .... Under 25 ☐1   35 to 44 ☐3   55 to 64 ☐5 21
    25 to 34 ☐2   45 to 54 ☐4   65 or over ☐6

2. What is the highest level of school you reached? (Please check one.)

    Grammar school .... ☐1 22
    Attended high school ...... ☐2
    Graduated from high school ☐3

    Attended college .... ☐1 23
    Graduated from college .... ☐2
    Postgraduate college ...... ☐3

3. Would you please check the bracket into which your total annual family income (before taxes) falls, including all members of your immediate household? (Please include all income from salaries, wages, interest, dividends, capital gains, rents, commissions, bonuses, pensions, etc.)

                      $ 15,000 to $24,999 ☐1 24-25
    Less than $5,000 ☐1 $ 25,000 to $49,999 ☐2
    $ 5,000 to $ 7,499 ☐2 $ 50,000 to $74,999 ☐3
    $ 7,500 to $ 9,999 ☐3 $ 75,000 to $99,999 ☐4
    $10,000 to $14,999 ☐4 $100,000 or more ☐5

4. Would you please indicate what is your immediate family's net worth? (Please include personal and household possessions, all real estate, bank accounts, securities, insurance, jewelry, automobiles and all other valuables.)

                          26-28
    Less than $5,000 ☐1 $ 50,000 to $ 74,999 ☐1 $ 250,000 to $ 499,999 ☐1
    $ 5,000 to $14,999 ☐2 $ 75,000 to $ 99,999 ☐2 $ 500,000 to $ 999,999 ☐2
    $15,000 to $24,999 ☐3 $100,000 to $149,999 ☐3 $1,000,000 to $1,999,999 ☐3
    $25,000 to $49,999 ☐4 $150,000 to $249,999 ☐4 $2 million and over ..... ☐4

THANK YOU VERY MUCH FOR YOUR COOPERATION   (29-X)

FIGURE 33 Page of a master questionnaire.

will have to be done over. Wherever the check questions seemed too difficult to punch, they were broken into several columns each, to match the number of columns of boxes. Keypunch operators well trained in questionnaire work have no trouble punching this page; the actual card punched from the sample questionnaire is shown in Figure 34.

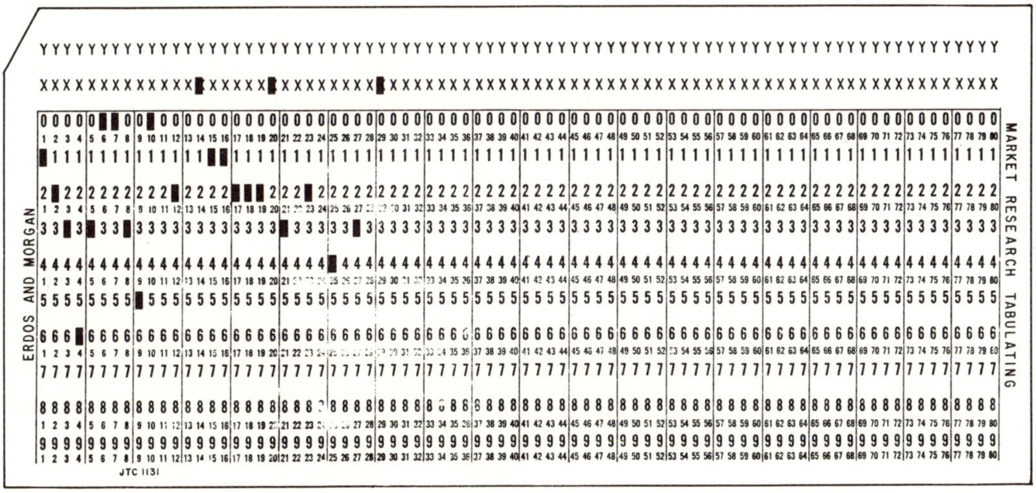

FIGURE 34 Card punched from questionnaire page in Figure 32.

NINETEEN
Editing and Coding

THE EDITING OPERATION brings the completed (filled-out) questionnaire to its maximum usefulness to the research project and facilitates all later processing. The work of the editor can be likened to that of the restorer of a work of art: He should bring to light all the hidden values and extract all possible information from a questionnaire, while adding nothing extraneous. His changes and additions must have a firm basis in some of the answers on the questionnaire and may not be the result of guesswork or far-fetched interpretation.

Editing has three main purposes:

1. To improve the accuracy and clarity of the answers to specific questions and eliminate inconsistent or obviously wrong or hopelessly ambiguous replies

2. To reduce "No Answers" or incomplete replies to some questions with the help of information found elsewhere on the questionnaire

3. To make the entries clear, consistently uniform, and comprehensible to coders and keypunch operators

Editing is essential in all survey work, but it is particularly important for mail surveys. Without the help of an interviewer, respondents may misread instructions, give sloppy answers, and send back incomplete returns. One of the aims of careful questionnaire construction, testing, and pilot surveys is to reduce these imperfections to a minimum, but the editing process will always be important to get the most out of the questionnaire.

EDITING FOR CONSISTENCY AND CLARITY

Let us consider some of the possible answers on the "Auto insurance" section of the questionnaire reproduced in Figure 5. One respondent may fill out the whole section and then explain in a note on the bottom of the page that the family car was sold three months ago, they do not carry any auto insurance right now, and that the answers refer to the last insurance they used to carry. The editor will change the "Yes" answer in Q. 1 to "No" and delete the answers to all other questions on the page. Another respondent may check "No" to Q. 1 and then answer all the following questions. In this case the editor may decide that the respondent made a mistake and change the "No" to "Yes." On the other hand, he may find out from some other question that the respondent does not own a car now and that the likelihood is that (like the note writer) his answers also refer to past insurance. In this case the "No" in Q. 1 was correct and the rest of the page has to be crossed out. Suppose the respondent checked three items in Q. 10 on the same page as types of insurance which he authorizes for his company and then indicated in the classification data on the next page that he is retired. The answers in Q. 10 must be eliminated.

On the last question of the questionnaire reproduced in Figure 3, a respondent might have listed H. & H. Pinch Bottle as a bourbon brand. It must be edited to Scotch. For coding and editing of this type it is a great advantage to have brand lists on hand to verify the types of products and brands which each manufacturer makes. In Figure 2 the last question concerns spheres of influence. The first three columns may be checked for the same item, because it is possible that an executive's sphere of influence includes recommending, specifying, and approving any one of the items listed. But if he checked one or more of the first three, he should not check the much less informative "Have some say;" and if he does, it should be deleted. Similarly if "Not my concern" is checked, no other box can be checked on the same line. Often the questionnaire requires numerical answers which have to add to a total. The editor must check that they do. Occasionally the editor will find a nonsensical questionnaire where the respondent (perhaps a child) had some fun giving silly answers to all or most questions. Such questionnaires must be discarded.

EDITING INCOMPLETE REPLIES

Looking at the questionnaire in Figure 2 we may find that a respondent wrote in "6" in Q. 3 but left the "Yes-No" part of the same question blank. The editor will check "Yes." In Q. 3 in Figure 3 someone may write "Bacardi" on the line next to rum, without checking the box. The editor will do so. In the first question on top of the same page a respondent may leave all the boxes blank and list "tennis" on the "What else" line. The editor will cross this out and check the box next to tennis. Suppose a respondent skipped the whole "Auto insurance" section on the questionnaire shown in Figure 5, but the editor can ascertain from his answers to questions on another page that he has a car and that he lives in a state where there is compulsory automobile insurance. He will certainly check the first "Yes."

CLARIFYING ENTRIES

The editor must make entries comprehensible to coders and keypunch operators. Some respondents will write words where the question calls for a check or for a number. To Q. 9 in Figure 32 most respondents will write an amount (e.g., 1,000) but some will write "One thousand" and a few may enter "1 M." The editor will have to make sure all these appear as 1,000. On the questionnaire shown in Figure 7 the answer to Q. 5 may read: "It has a smoother taste than brands I tried before." If there is no answer to the "Why did you switch?" part of Q. 7, or if the answer is less explicit, the editor will indicate for the coder (usually with an arrow) that the answer given for Q. 5 should also be coded for Q. 7.

The editor will have to decide (usually in a conference with the project director) which questions must be single mentions and which can have more than one answer. Obviously "How long has the brand you usually drink been your favorite?" can have only one answer, while the question "Why did you switch brands?" may result in three different but perfectly legitimate reasons. It is more difficult to make a decision when the question "Which would you say is the biggest selling brand of Scotch in the U.S.?" is answered by naming two brands. This may mean that in the respondent's opinion both sell equally well, or that he is undecided. The decision on something like this is a matter of policy and may have to be made by the project director. He can accept more than one answer, he can accept only the first mention and edit out subsequent entries, or he can edit out the whole entry and make it a "No Answer."

PROPER EDITING

These few examples will indicate that editing is a very responsible job and that it takes experienced and intelligent people to do it logically. Usually the project director or his assistant will scrutinize a batch of returns very carefully and make notes of problem areas from which the editing instructions can be developed.

Both editing and coding should be done in red pencil, for easy differentiation from the answers. Nothing written by a respondent should ever be erased or made illegible. One can never tell when some part of the editing work may be questioned and need to be checked.

It is not easy to do a proper editing job. Often a vexing problem is whether we are more interested in finding out the true facts or the strength of certain misconceptions people may have. In a survey among unskilled and semiskilled workers respondents were asked what the union term "closed shop" meant to them. The answers included such definitions as "A factory where they make clothes," "A place where you work and which is close to your home," "A lockout, a shop closed by the bosses." As one of the purposes of the survey was to establish whether or not the respondents were familiar with union terms, these answers were not eliminated but were carefully coded and tabulated.

It may be quite important for a manufacturer to find out that a sizeable percentage of potential customers thinks that his brand is made by another company. The manufacturer in this case will be much more interested in the mistake of the respondent than in the correct answer which an editor might think he should substitute for it.

The good editor must be not only intelligent, alert, and experienced, he should also be rather conservative as to how far he can go in changing an answer or completing one. If he is not absolutely sure of an interpretation, he should consult the project director, who in turn may wish to discuss the problem with the ultimate user or analyst of the survey. When there is more than one editor, there must be an editor-in-chief who discusses all problems with the editors and makes sure that any changes or additions to the editing instructions appear on each one's copy.

Editing and coding are separate operations when difficult questionnaires call for the undivided attention of an editor or when there is no coding required on a questionnaire (or on a page) which does need editing. Under other circumstances it is often possible to combine the editing and coding operations. This saves time and helps to correlate the two functions. Of course the checkers must watch out that neither operation suffers in the process. If the editing and coding are performed as two separate jobs, both operators must be thoroughly familiar with the work of the other, with the principles of the machine operations which will follow, and preferably, even with the purposes of the survey. The more that clerical operators know about the uses and purposes of a survey, the more likely they are to do a good job.

ESTABLISHING CODES

An open-end question is one which cannot be answered by checking a box or circling a number; the respondent has to fill in the space (which has been left for this purpose) with a number, a word, or one or more sentences. The purpose of coding is to translate these entries into numbers which are easily legible and intelligible to the keypunch operator, who should have to be concerned only with numerical codes, and not with the words written in by the respondent.

There are three common methods of establishing codes:

1. The researcher has limited and known objectives and can devise codes to fit them. For example, if the question "Which states have you visited in the past 12 months?" was asked simply to find out how many respondents visited each of the New England states, he may not be interested in any other information he could gather from answers to this question. He will therefore allocate a code to each of the six New England states and then add a seventh for "all others."

2. Previous surveys have established all the codes which the researcher needs for the study. As a matter of fact, he may consider it essential to keep the same codes in order to make the tabulation of subsequent surveys comparable. In that case he will use the existing codes, possibly supplemented by some new ones, such as for brands which did not exist at the time of the previous survey.

3. The most common method of establishing codes involves the use of test tabulations. The first step in this operation it to take a random sample of the questionnaires and hand tabulate all answers. Codes will then be assigned to the answers which come up most frequently. It is essential that the questionnaires selected for test tabulating represent a random sample of all returns. When time is

short, it is tempting to proceed by taking the returns of the first day or two as the test-tab sample. The result of course is heavily overbalanced with respondents who live nearby and are the kind of people who return questionnaires at once. The test tabulations will fail to record, for example, those regional brands which happen to be very important in more distant states.

HOW MANY TO TEST TAB

The number of questionnaires selected for test tabulations will be determined by several considerations:

1. *Whether or not all or most respondents answered the question.* A question such as "What make of toothpaste do you use?" will be answered by most people. However, if we list the ten leading makes on the questionnaire, with "Others (Please specify)" as the last line, we may find that most respondents checked the listed brands and that out of 500 questionnaires selected for test tabs only 40 have a write-in brand. In this situation we will need a larger number of questionnaires to find enough respondents to the particular question or section we want to test tabulate.

2. *The degree of stability desired for the results of the test.* If the researcher is interested in only a few top brands, he may not be bothered by the fact that the test tab will not show reliable figures for most other brands. He may feel that 100 or 200 questionnaires will give him the limited stability needed. On the other hand, suppose the question concerns the readership of newspapers and the researcher wants to list the leading newspapers in his report and then make the statement, "No other newspaper was listed by more than 2 percent of all respondents." In this case it is advisable that the test tabulation should include *all* returns, because even a large sample may not be reliable enough to catch every single paper which happened to receive more than 2 percent of the mentions.

3. *Whether the test tab will have any secondary uses.* If the researcher has reason to believe that an executive of the company will ask for "some quickie figures, just to indicate general trends...," he may consider it advisable to use a larger number of questionnaires for his test-tab sample.

TEST TABULATION

Test tabulations are hand tallies of answers to open-end questions in the test batch. It is advisable to mark each questionnaire in this batch with a red T so as to be able to find them if they should get mixed up with the other questionnaires.

If the subject of the tabulation is not something easily differentiated like brands or names of publications, it is hard to decide whether to tabulate all the answers verbatim or whether to exercise some judgment in combining answers which appear to mean the same thing. The latter can be done if the test tabulator is very experienced and has been well briefed on the purpose of the survey in general and of the question in particular. With less experienced tabulators it is safer to have all answers listed verbatim. This will result in considerably more listings and a more complicated recap, but it will assure the researcher that no important category has been lost through improper combining.

The easiest way to explain how a set of codes is constructed is to show the various stages of this operation. Figure 35 illustrates a test-tab page completed by an experienced tabulator. The questionnaire was mailed to people who had bought a refrigerator during the previous three months and returned the warranty card to the manufacturer. After setting up the sheet with clear headings and a rough division of the vertical space by letters of the alphabet, the tabulator listed each answer as it occurred in approximately alphabetic order. When the same answer was listed in the same words by another respondent, the tabulator merely added a tab mark to the first listing. If the same answer came up again but in slightly different phrasing ("could afford new one"—"had money for new one"), it is still only another tab in the same category. One respondent listed "had money for larger one," and this time the tabulator was not absolutely sure what the project director would want. He entered the phrase in a separate line after the "could afford new one" listing and put the word "larger" in parentheses. This is a reminder for later discussion, that in his opinion the two entries belong to the same code, while the second line should be double coded, once for "had money" and once for "wanted larger one." For answers which were closely related in meaning but where separate codes might be wanted by the project director, the tabulator listed the answers in groups, as in the case of the entries after "New home." The circles around the counts for each listing indicate that the additions have been checked, and the checks after each listing show that each has been entered on the recap sheet. The difference between the total mentions and the base (that is the number of questionnaires in the test-tab batch) indicates that a number of respondents gave multiple answers.

JOB #432   NAME OF JOB: Refrigerator Survey   TEST TAB 2

Q.3 Why did you, or your spouse, decide to buy a refrigerator at this time?

A	Could _afford_/had money for new one	ℍ̶Ⅱ	⑦	✓
	Had money for (larger) one	Ⅰ	①	✓
B	Was offered a _bargain_, sale	ℍ̶	⑤	✓
	Wanted _better_ one	ℍ̶ ℍ̶ ℍ̶ ℍ̶ Ⅲ	㉓	✓
F	_Family_ got larger, parents moved in	ℍ̶ ℍ̶ Ⅳ	⑭	✓
	More children, new baby	ℍ̶ ℍ̶	⑩	✓
	Needed _freezer_ section, larger freezer compartment	ℍ̶ ℍ̶ ℍ̶ Ⅰ	⑯	✓
H	New _home_, new apartment	ℍ̶ ℍ̶ Ⅲ	⑬	✓
	Just moved, husband got job here	ℍ̶ Ⅲ	⑧	✓
	Bought new house	ℍ̶ Ⅰ	⑥	✓
	Bought summer house, second home	ℍ̶ Ⅲ	⑧	✓
L	Needed _larger_, bigger one	ℍ̶ ℍ̶ ℍ̶ ℍ̶ Ⅲ	㉓	✓
M	Just got _married_	ℍ̶ Ⅲ	⑧	✓
	It was a wedding gift	Ⅰ	①	✓
	Wanted new _model_, they make them more practical now	{ ℍ̶ ℍ̶ Ⅰ	⑪	✓
O	One _not enough_ - needed two	Ⅲ	③	✓
R	_Replacement_	ℍ̶ ℍ̶ ℍ̶	⑮	✓
	Old one gave out	Ⅲ	③	✓
	Remodeled kitchen	ℍ̶	⑤	✓
	Installed new kitchen	Ⅱ	②	✓
S	_Saw_ new model in store, couldn't resist	Ⅰ	①	
	Good _salesman_ convinced me I could use one	Ⅰ	①	

Don't know, not sure   Ⅱ   ②
No answer   Ⅳ   ④

Total mentions   ⑱⑥

Base: 150

FIGURE 35 Test-tab page.

RECAPPING TEST TABS

Figure 36 shows the next step, the recap page made from the test tabs in Figure 35. The supervisor agreed with the tabulator's groupings; as a matter of fact he thought that two more categories could be combined on the recap. He also felt that for the purposes of this survey only broad categories were needed. The suggested code setup is a full one-column code. Some researchers prefer that "Don't Know" and "No Answer" should each have a code and be punched in the card. Others feel that when the two mean essentially the same thing, there is not much point in differentiating between them. "No Answers" can be counted as "Rejects" (no punches) by tabulating machines even if they have not been coded.

As shown in Figure 36, the test tabulator and his supervisor suggested to the project director that he use a single column and multiple punching which would furnish separate counts for eleven specific categories of answers. These categories included all answers given by at least 3 of the randomly selected 150 respondents. This code setup will furnish three further counts: a "Miscellaneous" which will include all answers that do not fit the eleven classifications, a "No Answer" category, represented by the "Reject" (that is, no hole punched in the column) count, and the "Base," which is simply a count of all cards run, which in turn means all respondents eligible to answer.

THE CODE BOOKLET

When the project director agreed with these suggestions, the code sheet was typed up and handed to every coder working on this question. This code sheet (Fig. 37) is one page of a uniformly organized "code booklet." It contains information essential to everyone who has anything to do with data-processing. After the usual job-classification data on top, it is divided into five columns. The first one indicates whether the coder should record a single answer or multiple answers to the question. The next column defines the base, that is, those who are eligible to answer the question. In this case it is "All," meaning all respondents. In the case of a section or question following a filter question (such as "Do you own a refrigerator? If 'Yes,' please answer the following questions"), the base would be restricted to those answering "Yes" to the first question. This is important for editing, coding, punching, runs, percentaging, etc. The third column specifies that the codes for this question will be punched in column 11. The

JOB #: 432   NAME OF JOB: Refrigerator Survey   TEST TAB RECAP 2

Q.3 Why did you, or your spouse, decide to buy a refrigerator at this time?

	No. of mentions	Suggested code
New home, new apartment	13	
Just moved, husband got job here	8	1
Bought summer house, second home	8	
Bought new house	6	
Family got larger, parents moved in	14	2
More children, new baby	10	
Needed larger, bigger refrigerator	23	3
Wanted a better refrigerator	23	4
Could afford it, had money for it	23	5
Replacement, old one gave out	18	6
Wanted freezer section, needed larger freezer compartment	16	7
Wanted new model, they make them more practical now	11	8
Just got married	8	9
It was a wedding gift	1	
Remodeled kitchen, installed new kitchen	7	0
One not enough, needed two	3	X
Miscellaneous single mentions (Saw new model in store, salesman convinced me.)	2	Y
No answer, Don't know	6	R
Total mentions	186	
Total in test	150	

FIGURE 36   Recap of test tab in Figure 35.

Job # 432	CODE BOOKLET	Card # 1
Client Adamant Advertising Agency		Card Ident. 5-1
Job REFRIGERATOR SURVEY		

S or M	Base (Eligible)	Col.	Code	Contents
M	All	11		Q. 3. WHY DID YOU OR YOUR SPOUSE DECIDE TO BUY A NEW REFRIGERATOR AT THIS TIME?
			1	For new home, new apartment, just moved, husband got job here, bought summer house, second home, new house.
			2	Family got larger, more children, new baby, parents moved in.
			3	Needed larger, bigger refrigerator.
			4	Wanted a better refrigerator.
			5	Could afford it, had money for it.
			6	Replacement, old one gave out.
			7	Wanted freezer section, needed larger freezer compartment.
			8	Wanted new model, they make them more practical now.
			9	Just got married, wedding gift.
			0	Remodeled kitchen, new kitchen.
			X	Needed two, one not enough.
			Y	Miscellaneous other mentions.
			–	Don't know, No answer

FIGURE 37 Page of a code booklet (1).

fourth column shows the codes which the coders are to use to code each of the categories listed in the last column.

The code book (and the master questionnaire shown in Fig. 33) are usually made up after all open-end questions have been test tabulated, because in some cases the test tabs will determine how many columns have to be allocated to a question.

NUMERICAL ANSWERS

Numerical answers seldom have to be test tabbed. In most cases enough columns can be allocated to these questions to punch the actual answers. When a numerical answer is allocated five columns and the respondent writes in a three-digit number, such as 350, the coder must fill in the missing digits with zeros, as in the example in Figure 33. The editor-coder will have to take care of such answers as "200 to 300" (generally coded as 250). Numerical answers are usually not coded by groups (1 to 500, 501 to 1000, etc.) because it is faster to punch the whole number than to code the breaks and save a column or two. Furthermore, averages and medians can be calculated more accurately if the actual answers are recorded.

Often the lowest digits (tens, singles, pennies) are not needed, and no columns are provided for them. In that case the coder can either cross out the superfluous numbers or circle (in red) the numbers which the keypunch operator should punch. The coding instructions may require some editing in such situations; for example, if the answers refer to the cost of shoes, we may take only dollars, but not cents. In this case we may edit to the nearest dollar and code $26.99 as $27.

Test tabulations must sometimes be used in order to establish how many columns are needed for a numerical field. This is a simple matter of tabulating or counting the number of one-, two-, three-, four-, five-, and six-digit answers which occur in the test batch. If we find that large numbers of five or more digits seldom or never occur, we can allocate four columns to the question, with an XXXX code for 10,000 and over. Should we want to have an accurate count of these few large numbers later, to calculate an average for example, we can always sort out the XXXX cards, find the questionnaires, and hand tabulate them.

Figure 38 shows another page of a code booklet. It contains codes and instructions for editing and coding two questions requiring numerical answers. There was no need to register in detail answers of less than 1 hour, and no answers were expected to reach 100 hours. In

Job # 6381		CODE BOOKLET		Card # 2

Client _____ Card Ident. 5-2

Job   Leisure Time Activities Study

S or M	Use: (Eligible)	Col.	Code	Contents
				Q. 8. About how much time did you spend watching TV:
S	All	23-24		a) Yesterday
			0X	Less than one hour (but watched)
			01	One hour
			02	Two hours
			03	Three hours
				and so on
			99	Ninety nine hours
			00	None
			0Y	Don't remember
			YY	No answer
S	All	25-26		b) Last week (including yesterday)
				Codes same as Cols. 23-24
				Note: If "None" checked or otherwise indicated, code 00 in the number area
				If no answer, code yy in the number area
				If the number is less than 10, prefix a "0" to make 2 columns and circle
				If the number is 10-99, circle the number
				Number in Cols. 25-26 cannot be lower than number in Cols. 23-24

FIGURE 38   Page of a code booklet (2).

this case the survey design called for separate codes for "Don't Remember" and "No Answer."

At all stages of code building, the project director and his supervisors must beware of any bias which may be introduced by the special views or preferences of someone working on the job. Even a simple decision, such as what constitutes a favorable, unfavorable, or neutral comment, may be influenced by the test tabulator's own opinion.

Interesting experimental work has been done at the National Opinion Research Center on the use of computers in coding answers to open-end questions. This work is based on a system developed at Harvard University and may lead to the reduction or, conceivably, the elimination of hand coding. Instead of code building and coding, as described in this chapter, "A large list of words—a dictionary of them—defined by an arbitrary number of concepts... is stored in the computer, which compares each word or phrase in the data with this dictionary." (The "data" are the verbatim answers, which must appear on the punched cards or tape.) The computer then proceeds to code the answers by "concept codes" assigned to each word of the "dictionary."[1] Although at this writing computer coding is still in the experimental stage, its further development may revolutionize coding in the future.

CODING

Ideal coders have a fairly unusual combination of abilities: They are willing to perform an essentially routine operation for a prolonged period of time. They have the alertness to detect the one case in twenty when an answer requires a nonroutine decision, as well as the good judgment to handle such cases. They have the intellectual curiosity to find out all they possibly can about the survey in hand and the ability to code rapidly with very few errors. Of course, gems of this sort do not remain coders very long.

On the other hand the good supervisor must assume that at least some of his coders will have none of the above attributes and that chances are none of the coders will have all of them. His responsibility therefore is to systematize the job as much as possible, to give the coders detailed instructions in writing, make sure that they work under the best possible physical conditions, get them interested in the job, encourage questions and answer them, listen to suggestions, and continually check the work.

Coding instructions should always be listed near the codes, on neatly typed sheets laid out for easy reading. It is advisable to make little "lecterns" (or pin-up boards) out of cardboard and have the code pages propped up on these in a slanting position on the coder's desk. This will add to the visual comfort of the coder.

The first batch of coding of each question completed by a coder should be checked 100 percent. This will show whether or not he understood all instructions and does a careful job. If the results of this initial checking are satisfactory, most coding operations will thereafter require only spot checking.

UNIFORM CODING PROCEDURE

Mistakes are often not as troublesome as lack of uniform procedure. It is quite important that the supervisor should keep a close check on the uniformity of interpretation and coding. When a coder asks a question which is of general importance, the answer should be made known to all coders working on the same question, preferably as an additional, written instruction.

A coder sometimes reports that an item for which no code has been established is coming up frequently. The supervisor, knowing that this will inflate the final "Miscellaneous" count, may decide to add a new code for this item (which somehow failed to show up with enough mentions in the test tab.) The new code will have to be added to every existing copy of the code instruction sheet. Also all previously coded questionnaires will have to be rechecked and every mention of the item found and recoded.

Because of the importance of uniform procedure and the time it takes for coders to become familiar with the codes and problems of a new operation, it is advisable to have as few coders (and/or editors) as possible work on the coding of a given question or set of questions. In this respect, time pressure always works against efficiency because more coders are needed.

Depending on complexity, one question or a group of questions may be coded in a single operation. If the coding is very simple, the coders can efficiently process several questions on the same page. If there are a number of questions of the same type, it is usually advisable to have the same operator code them, whether in one or several operations. In these situations it is an advantage to have the same code list for each of these questions, even if the number of codes has to be increased because some items may occur frequently as an answer to one of the questions, while others may come up more often in answer to a second, related, question. For example, in Figure 7 there are seven different places where brands of Scotch whisky are called for. The same set of brand codes was used for all of them, and they were coded in a single operation.

ACCURATE, EFFICIENT CODING

One would think that the coding operation becomes more efficient after the coder has learned all the codes by heart. This is not necessarily so. The most accurate coding is done if the coders are encouraged to glance at the codes, even though they may know them by heart. On a job involving hundreds or thousands of questionnaires, it not infrequently happens that a coder who has been doing a near-perfect job suddenly starts putting down the wrong code for an item and keeps on using the wrong code until caught by the checker. Frequent reminders to coders not to rely on memory helps to avoid this type of error.

Coding, wherever possible, should be done in the right-hand margin of the questionnaire in red pencil. In order to distinguish them, data for punching on trailer cards are usually coded in the *left*-hand margin, in a different color, or on a separate sheet of paper.

If questions still come up after the initial briefing, the efficient supervisor will ask the coders to place "problem questionnaires" on top of each batch. Toward the end of the day there will then be a question-and-answer session with all coders when the difficult questionnaires and questions are discussed and decisions made.

When the editing and coding operations are completed, the questionnaires should be marked with serial numbers (usually in the top right-hand corner, as in most code setups the serial is the first field punched). It is not advisable to serialize them before this stage of the work has been reached because questionnaires do get out of order during editing and coding. Serialization is needed to establish a continuous series of numbers by which the questionnaires can be matched with the cards which will be punched from them. This is essential for card cleaning operations (Chap. 20). It is desirable to check the final count against the cumulative count of the daily returns to make sure that no batch of questionnaires has been misplaced and that all usable questionnaires have been coded.

REFERENCE

1. Bruce Frisbie and Seymour Sudman, "The Use of Computers in Coding Free Responses," *Public Opinion Quarterly*, vol. 32, no. 2, pp. 216–232, summer, 1968.

TWENTY
Card Punching and Machine Tabulation

THE KEYPUNCH MACHINE OPERATORS transfer the codes from the questionnaire to the punch card. The code will now become a hole in a specified location in a standard-sized card.

All the operator needs for her work is a supply of blank cards, a master questionnaire, and the edited and coded questionnaires. Her speed will vary according to the format of the questionnaire (unusually large pages or a number of pages which have to be turned mean slower work), the layout, the type of coding, the clarity of the coding, the number of columns to be punched, the proportion of multiple punches, and her own skill and experience. Difficult punching of full (eighty-column) cards may take two or three minutes per card; but if a card consists of a few simple, single-punch columns, a good operator may produce several hundred punched cards in an hour.

Intelligent assistance by the planners of data-processing can greatly simplify the work of the keypunch operator. For example, if we know that a high proportion of respondents will not answer certain sections of the questionnaire, the master questionnaire can indicate this as a "skip field," which will enable the operator to skip a number of columns by hitting a single key in the appropriate cases. In answering Q. 7 in Figure 7, many respondents indicated that they had not switched brands in the previous two years and were therefore not supposed to answer further questions on the subject. This is the kind of situation where a "skip field" can save unnecessary work for the keypunch operator.

Another shortcut concerns repetitive information which has to be punched into a large number of consecutive cards, such as the card number, 3, in column 5 shown in Figure 32. The card punch machine can be set to punch this (or any other code or set of numbers) into every card automatically, just as it punches the X columns (Fig. 33). These operations are controlled by a master (program) card prepared by the operator and inserted into the keypunch machine.

Experienced operators specially trained for questionnaire work make very few mistakes on the average job, usually not enough to influence the percentages calculated from the final tabulations. However, there are tabulations where the greatest accuracy is needed. The extent of verification required is always a critical decision in planning data-processing.

CARD VERIFICATION

The verifier is a machine similar in appearance to the keypunch, but instead of punching holes, it passes a thin metal plunger through the holes previously punched in the card. The verifier operator repeats the keypunch operator's work; if the two do not agree, the verifying machine will indicate an error. For all practical purposes verification means doubling the time and cost of the keypunching operation.

The first batch completed by each keypunch operator on a new job should be verified 100 percent. Thereafter on usual market research survey work, when punched by qualified, experienced operators, it has been found that only spot checking or sample verification is needed.

The Bureau of the Census made a detailed study of errors in card punching, based on 25,000 wrongly punched cards. They established the error rate of qualified keypunch operators as below one wrong card per hundred (full) cards punched. They used 5 percent sample verification of the work of qualified punchers, while the other 95 percent went through the tabulation uncorrected. They came to the conclusion that "When sample verification is used, the net effect of wrong punches, as they occur in practice, is often negligible." They found two main reasons for this: There was a large proportion of compensating errors, and in the case of numerical fields the right-hand columns were punched wrong oftener than the left-hand ones. One effect of the second (in their opinion, psychological) phenomenon was that in a four-digit field the singles and teens were more affected by wrong punches than the hundreds and thousands, thereby resulting in a relatively small total error.[1]

When the punching of a job is finished, the first task is to make sure that every questionnaire has been punched and that none has been punched twice. The total card count must check out with the last serial number. To make sure that there is no compensating error, the cards will be put in serial order and checked for duplication of serials and for missing numbers.

Punches which are supposed to appear on all cards or on batches of cards can be sight-checked by lifting a batch of cards and looking through the common punch toward the light.

CONSISTENCY CHECKS

Cleaning operations, including consistency checks, are an essential part of all machine data-processing. When done thoroughly they can be quite time-consuming and expensive. If done poorly or not at all, the reliability of the survey can be greatly impaired.

Essentially, the cleaning operation is an extension of the editing, except that instead of just looking for the inconsistencies of the respondent, it also seeks to eliminate and correct errors made by editors, coders, and keypunch operators. The first step is called a "consistency" check because it is just that: a check to make sure that the cards do not contain punches which are manifestly wrong, illogical, or inconsistent.

Let us suppose column 55 has been allocated to the sex of the respondent, with code 1 for male and 2 for female; any other position punched in that column must be wrong. All columns must be checked for punches not justified by the code sheets; this operation is called "code-range" check.

If the answer to a question requires a check in one of three boxes (e.g., "Often," "Seldom," and "Never") the master questionnaire will assign a single-punch column to it. A double punch in such a column would indicate that the respondent has given an illogical answer which the editor failed to notice or that a punching error was made. All single-punch columns must be checked for multiple punches.

"Eligibility" checks must be made to make sure that only the proper cards are run on a column or set of columns. For example, only respondents who switched brands of cigarettes should answer questions which refer to previous brands. If the punches in one column indicated that the respondent never switched brands of cigarettes and in the next few columns he seems to report the name of the brand *from* which he switched and the brand *to* which he switched, obviously there is an inconsistency which has to be "cleaned." All "filtered" sections of the card must be checked for this type of inconsistency.

The important considerations in the cleaning operation are (1) how to find the inconsistencies and (2) how to eliminate them.

"Cleaning instructions" are usually made up by the project director or his assistant. It is a task which takes experience in all phases of data-processing and a working knowledge of the aims of the survey. Once again, anyone can make a quick job of it by listing some of the obvious inconsistencies to look for, but it takes a lot of thinking and checking to ferret out all possible problems and to give clear instructions on how to go about finding them and how to treat each.

Cleaning operations are usually programmed for computers, but they can be performed, if necessary, on other types of tabulating machinery, including counter-sorters. The cleaning specifications must be written in the "language" required by the machinery used and, to a certain extent, of the operator working it. However, the principles are always the same: What is required is logical consistency.

AN EXAMPLE OF CONSISTENCY CHECKS

Figure 39 shows the automobile question which we illustrated in Figure 9, but this time the column numbers are indicated as on a master questionnaire. The following is a list (in nontechnical terms) of the cleaning instructions needed for this question.

1. There may not be any multiple punches in columns 23 to 38.
2. Columns 31 and 38 are X columns and should be sight-checked.
3. Column 23 cannot have other than 1 or 2 (yes-no) punches (code-range check).
4. 23–2 punches ("do not own car") have to be rejects (not punched) in columns 24 to 37, except for 31–X.
5. All 23–1 punches ("do own car") must have a punch in column 24 ("*no answer*" was coded as "indefinite number").
6. All cards punched 24–1 ("own one car") must be rejects on columns 32 to 37 and cannot have trailer cards, which would indicate that the respondent owns more than one car. Also, cards punched 24–2 cannot have trailers (third or fourth cars).

7. The total number of cars indicated in columns 32 to 37, plus trailers, should check to the number of cards punched in column 24.

8. Code-range checks should be made on columns 25 to 30 and 32 to 37 to make sure that no impossible punches exist. For example, columns 28 and 35 can have only position-1 (new) or position-2 (used) punches. Any other punch is an error.

1. Do you (or any members of your household) own a car now?........... Yes [1] No [2] _23_
   If "Yes," how many?.. _____ _24_
   Please indicate the make, series name and model year of each car now owned and check how and when it was bought.

		Series name (New Yorker,	Model	How bought		When bought		
Make		F-85, Falcon, etc.)	Year	New	Used	Month	Year	
		_25-26_	_27_	[1] 28 [2]		_29_	_30_	_31-X_
		_32-33_	_34_	[1] 35 [2]		_36_	_37_	_38-X_
TRAILER 1 →		_32-33_	_34_	[1] 35 [2]		_36_	_37_	_38-X_
TRAILER 2 →		_32-33_	_34_	(1) 35 (2)		_36_	_37_	_38-X_

FIGURE 39 Car section of a master questionnaire.

9. The "Model year" and "Year bought" columns in each line of the questionnaire must be cross tabulated (column 27 by column 30, and column 34 by column 37) for consistency. No car can be bought years before it is first manufactured. With the help of columns 28 and 35 we can also check whether any make was bought "new" years after it came off the assembly line.

10. Since make and series name were both incorporated in a single code setup, there is no need for a consistency check between them. On the other hand, a cross examination of the make plus series-name codes against the model year (columns 25 and 26 by column 27, and columns 32 and 33 by column 34) will furnish another consistency check. With the help of the year-by-series-name lists of manufacturers we can spot inconsistent replies in the above cross tabulations.

CORRECTING ERRORS

Suppose we have just made ten consistency checks on one question of a four-page questionnaire. We are dealing with 3,000 respondents. Each of the ten checks may turn up a few score erroneous or inconsistent cards. The operator will have a list of the serial numbers of "wrong" cards and an indication of the inconsistency in each. What is the next step?

While nearly every data-processing supervisor feels that consistency checks are very important, there are two schools of thought about how to reconcile the inconsistencies.

Those people who are not too meticulous feel that extremely careful procedures are not worth their cost in time and money and that you can simply adjust the errors and inconsistencies "logically" without going back to the questionnaires. Inconsistent replies may be divided proportionately among other responses, or they may be changed to "Don't Know" or "No Answer." The users of the tables, including the analyst, might never know about these adjustments and how many of them were made, and there is a possibility that they have not seriously affected the usefulness of the tables.

Yes, but there is also a chance that at least in some cases they *have* affected the findings and that the "logical" adjustment would seem much less logical to anyone but the adjuster. In careful data-processing there can be only one sequel to the consistency check, and that is to go back to the questionnaires. Each of the listed questionnaires should be examined, and the origin of the inconsistency or error ascertained and corrected. In the case of a major survey these painstaking corrections may take a considerable amount of time and money, but in the author's experience they are almost always necessary.

MACHINE TABULATING

The punched card serves two major purposes: It contains the data gathered in a form which enables the tabulating machines to tally them, and it enables the researcher to store the data he needs in compact form for a very long time.

Punch-card tabulation operates on a simple principle. Each column of the card will run in the machines between a roller and a wire brush. Where there is a hole in the card an electrical impulse is created. These resulting impulses are then converted into output form, which may be holes punched into the same card or another, a printed line, a machine function, or some combination of these.[2]

There are a number of machines which are used to prepare cards for tabulation. The *interpreter* converts the holes punched into the cards into printed numbers or, in the case of alphabetic punching, into letters or words (Fig. 30). For example, it can print on the cards names and addresses which have been punched into them, thereby enabling the cards to be used as a mailing list. If for any reason visual checking of data (such as brands) is required, they can easily be interpreted (printed) on the cards.

The *collator* can match two decks of punched cards into pairs by serial number, or it can merge two decks of cards into one file. Two matched decks can be fed into a *reproducer*, which can transfer punches from one deck to matching cards in another. This is often done when a long questionnaire requires several cards and certain information (such as classification data) must be transferred into all cards for purposes of cross tabulations. (When using computers this transfer is not necessary, since the machine can cross tabulate information from two cards.)

EAM AND EDP

The machines which perform the final mechanical or electronic steps of data-processing—that is, tabulating and calculating operations—can be divided into two broad groups: EAM (electric accounting machines) and the rapidly expanding EDP (electronic data-processing) machines. This brings us to the world of the computer, to "families of machines," which are happily improving in successive "generations" and whose planners, programmers, and operators speak and write special languages created to answer the special requirements of machine and program designs.

EDP, specifically the computer, has created new possibilities in the analysis of survey results and greatly expanded the field of surveys. At the same time, because of the feasibility of having a very large number of simultaneous tabulations in subgroups at reasonable cost, they have created a need for larger bases, that is more questionnaires for a given job. Because of this, computers have given added impetus to mail surveys, which can provide large numbers of questionnaires at reasonable cost.

Whether the researcher will use EDP or EAM equipment to tabulate his survey depends largely on the complexity of the job and on the availability of a computer and a program which can handle it. Unless the survey is quite extensive, it is comparatively expensive to write a special program for it. The program is a set of instructions which will direct the computer to perform the tabulating and calculating operations and print out the tables required. Many extensive research programs exist which may very well fit the needs of a given survey tabulation. These programs can be stored in many ways—on tapes, disks, drums, punch cards, or in the computer storage unit itself. All these are used effectively and are available at the user's request.

Computers and their programs require specialized knowledge and experience. They also change and improve very rapidly. The research man considering computer work should discuss his problems with an expert in this field, unless he happens to be one himself.

When computers are not available, and for ancillary work such as providing card sorts and check totals, EAM equipment such as the *counter-sorter* is often used. It can sort the cards into as many as thirteen groups and give counts for each group and the total number of cards used. It does not calculate percentages, averages, and so forth, and it does not print out the results, but it can do an efficient tabulating job.

Regardless of what equipment is to be used for the final tabulations, the researcher must know exactly what he wants and how he wants it presented. Marginal, or straight tabulations (that is, a total count of every code punched on the cards of a survey, plus a card count for each column) is the first set of tables he normally wants to see.

These marginals are usually the final steps of the consistency checks: They are proof that the cards have been cleaned in every column and that no cards have been misplaced in the process. They are also very useful as check totals for all further tabulations, and they may change or influence the researcher's plans as to what breaks (cross analyses) to use.

TABULATING SPECIFICATIONS

In setting up his final specifications for tabulations and recaps (recapitulations), the researcher needs the following tools:

1. His original plans for the survey analysis with its dummy tabulations.
2. A master questionnaire. Usually this is also translated into a master card, a blown-up copy of the punch card with indications in each column or field of columns about what information has been punched into it.
3. A complete set of the code booklet, with editing and coding instructions.
4. The marginal tabulations just discussed.

The data-processing specialist will translate the analyst's requirements into specifications for tabulating machines, but he cannot do this unless he is informed in detail about each final recap sheet or tabulating sheet which the researcher will need.

The final specifications will depend on the requirements of the survey design and on the kind of equipment that will be used. There are a few general rules that always should be remembered:

The tabulator will have to be told which cards (what base) to use for each question. For instance, when tabulating the answers to a question about cars, it must be specified whether the base is all cards, that is, every respondent, or only those who stated that they owned a car, or owners of foreign cars only, or of Volkswagens, or of Volkswagens bought in the last two years. The base must be made clear on every run.

Do we need a "Total" line? In a table where there are multiple answers, do we want to show a total (all mentions) and a base (all respondents)? Do we want to include "No Answers" in the total or show it separately?

How about groupings (class intervals) on questions which asked for numerical answers and where the actual numbers given have been punched? For example, the actual dollar cost of an item may be punched in a three-column field. The marginal runs show 139 different prices listed. How should they be grouped in the tabulations? There are two important considerations in this matter: The intervals should be meaningful, and the distribution within them should be reasonable. In other words, if the product in question has a normal price range of from $75 to $250 and we decide on six price groups, there is no point in making the first break $1 to $25. It also does not make any sense to have one of the six breaks $75 to $149 and the next one $150 to $249; we know that all, or nearly all, answers would be distributed between these two intervals with practically nothing in the others. The breaks should be reasonable from a logical point of view and have a fairly well-balanced distribution of the answers. Occasionally there are so many different numerical answers listed that we will decide to group them even for the marginal tabs. In this case the intervals should be made narrow, and the groups numerous, to give us flexibility when combining them into broader groups later. The final combining may occur only at the recapping operation.

THE NEED FOR DETAILED, WRITTEN INSTRUCTIONS

Operators, being human, will often make mistakes, and even machines are not infallible. Wherever it is possible to build checks into the specifications, this should be done, even if it slows down the procedure. Furthermore, all specifications, whether for handtabbing or for the simplest kind of tabulating machinery or for the most recent generation of computers, should always be in writing. Of course EDP specs *have* to be in writing, but in the chain of command between the analyst and the specwriter, there can always be someone who shouts from one room to the next, "Incidentally, Joe, also get me some breaks on question 5 by classification data."

If you want Joe to get it done properly, don't shout; write. Also don't say "question 5" without further identification by page number and by writing down the actual question, because there might be several sections in the questionnaire each having a question 5. Furthermore, specify each item in the classification-data section which you want to use for your breaks, give the actual groups you want to use, specify how to handle "No Answer" and "Don't Know" figures. Also indicate the base(s) you wish to use for the runs, for percentaging, for averages, and for other calculations, and finally, specify the layout you want. (Should age and income be distributed across the top, with the answers to Q. 5 going down the side, or the other way round?) In other words, you must be clear and specific, even though the specifications writer is a specialist who knows his job.

Breaks or cross tabulations (that is, the analyzing of one question by another question, or by groups of the original sample, or by any other known information) should add to the check total whenever possible. For example, if we have a marginal run on a question and then want to crosstab it by the education of the respondent, we may not be interested in the answers of those respondents who failed to indicate their educational level. Nevertheless, these answers should be counted, otherwise the breaks would not add to the marginal figures, and we would lose the advantage of having a check total.

The same principle holds when tabulating a subsample, such as running special tabs on a number of questions on only those respondents who have yearly family incomes of $25,000 or more. "All other respondents" should be run as a group at the same time on the same questions in order to be able to check out each line of the run. (These procedures are important in EAM operations. In computer work all checks are built into the program or the specifications.)

If there is any chance that the results of the tabulation will represent final or semifinal sheets which will be looked over by other than data-processing personnel, care must be taken to have clear and meaningful titles for each table and for column headings, stubs, or line headings (describing each line across). As a matter of fact, most of the recapping functions would have to be considered in advance when computer printouts are to take the place of recap sheets.

The author has seen very expensive tabulations, including computer runs, which were useless because the initial requests, the specs, and their checking were ambiguous or erroneous. It is advisable to check all specs by three different criteria:

1. Do they include all the runs needed with the bases and layout specified as required?
2. Do they have all possible checks and check totals?
3. Do they contain any erroneous instructions?

All tabulating sheets should be numbered so as to make certain that no page can be misplaced and to facilitate any checking and recapping operations which may be required later. They must also include the card number on multicard jobs. The job number should appear on the tabulating sheets (and on all other material connected with the job), because in busy offices sheets have an odd habit of hiding in the wrong job folders.

REFERENCES

1. W. Edwards Deming, Benjamin J. Tepping, and Leon Geoffrey, "Errors in Card Punching," *Journal of the American Statistical Association*, vol. 37, nos. 217–220, pp. 525–536, December, 1942.
2. "An Introduction to IBM Punched Card Data Processing" (student text), IBM Technical Publications Department, White Plains, N.Y., p. 9 (undated).

TWENTY-ONE
Recaps and Calculations

RECAP SHEETS REPRESENT, in effect, the final form in which the data will appear; this is so even if they are to be subsequently typed or printed. In the case of hand tabulations or counter-sorter runs, the recapitulations will be made from the tab sheets and will be checked before calculations (percentages, averages, medians, etc.) are made from the figures on the sheet. In computer work, the printout is often (but not always) the final sheet for which no further recap is required. However, in this case the principles of the recap sheet are usually incorporated in the computer specifications.

The purpose of the recap is to present the tabulations in the clearest and most useful form to the analyst and other users of the survey results.

Recaps will involve one or more of the following operations:

1. Eliminating from the running sheets any numbers or notes which serve the purposes of tabulation but have no relevance to the report, such as code and column numbers and running instructions.

2. Decoding, that is, translating codes back to their original mean-

ings. The resulting code descriptions are usually not quite the same as those on the code page because the recap descriptions can be shorter and may include fewer examples. However, there should be no omissions that would limit the full meaning of a code.

3. Combining columns (vertically) and/or lines (horizontally). For example, as shown on Figures 40 and 41, four age groups (vertical columns) can be combined into two, if the more detailed breakdown does not seem to be meaningful. A comparison of the same pages also illustrates how horizontal lines (Q. 9, "Five or more") can be combined, when the numbers appearing in one or more of them seem too small to serve any useful purpose.

4. Inverting tables by changing the position of lines and columns. One setup may be easier for the tabulator, while the other may be clearer to the reader of the report. For instance, in Figure 41 the age breaks are distributed on top, each becoming a vertical column. For the purposes of the analyst it may be more desirable to have the answers to Q. 8 (company ownership of aircraft) listed across the top of a page and the age groups down the side.

5. Changing the order of lines or columns to make them easier to read or more meaningful. The most commonly used arrangement is the numerical order (descending order of mentions). Other ways of listing, such as alphabetic order, logical sequence (for example, listing months from January through December), and logical groupings (as of brands listed by their manufacturers) are usually included in the code setup and will so appear on the machine tabulating sheets. However, some of the possibilities for grouping may have been overlooked, and therefore the final order of lines and columns may still have to be established in the recapping operation.

6. Adding subtotals, which may bring out important factors for the analyst. For example, a detailed "title and position" setup may include scores of codes, from "chairman of the board" to "unskilled worker." Subtotals for such groups (policy-making executives, administrators and managers, professional and technical people, etc.) would help in quickly summarizing this table. Often such subtotals are shown as separate summary tables. In these cases, however, the original table should be shown as well; not everyone may agree about just who is a "policy-making executive."

7. Adding page titles, captions, column headings, descriptions of totals and bases, explanatory notes.

8. Recapping two or more runs on one page. This may be a matter not only of saving space but also of meaningful juxtaposition (for

example, makes of car now owned, owned in the past, and "plan to buy").

"NO ANSWER" COUNTS

In the author's opinion the best procedure is to show "No Answer" figures and base percentages on all those who were supposed to answer the question. If then a user of the report wishes to distribute the "No Answers" proportionately among the responses, he can easily do it himself.

The distribution of "No Answers" can often be done without affecting the reliability of the findings. For example, all respondents are either male or female, and if 4 percent failed to check the sex question, it is quite reasonable to distribute these proportionately. Again, suppose we have found from a filter question that of 1,000 respondents, 450 own boats, and the next question asks the type of boat owned now. We know that all boat owners own some type of boat, and so the chance of distortion is not great if we distribute a small number of "No Answers" to this second question among the answers given by the other boat owners. The simplest way of effecting such distribution is to get a subtotal of all those who gave an answer and base the percentaging on this group (by considering them 100 percent). In such case the "No Answer" count is shown as a separate entry without a percentage figure.

There are cases where "No Answer" definitely should not be distributed because there is reason to believe that they would *not* break down the same way as the answers. For example, if to the question "Do you own a swimming pool?" 200 respondents check "Yes," 400 check "No," and 400 fail to answer, it is very likely that the proportion of owners will be much smaller among nonrespondents than among respondents. As a matter of fact, it is reasonable to believe that respondents who answer the other questions on the same page but fail to answer this one simply skipped it because they do not own a swimming pool. It would then be more correct to combine "No" and "No Answer" than to distribute the latter.

Unfortunately, many questions are not as clear-cut on this problem as sex or swimming pools. What about a question like age? Is it possible that the "No Answer" group includes a large proportion of older women? It is because of such borderline cases that the decision should be left to the user of the report and that it is preferable to include the "No Answers" in the base.

JOB NO. **668**
JOB NAME **Survey on Aviation**

QQ 8-10 × Q.12   Run p. 12

Q.8 Does your company now own one or more aircraft?	COL. CODE	TOTAL	Q.12 Age of Respondent				
			Under 30	30-44	45-54	55 or over	No Answer
			72-1	72-2	72-3	72-4	72-R
Use all cards	36-1	87	3	32	38	12	2
	-2	693	51	363	145	133	1
	-R	63	8	22	18	3	12
	Total	843	62	417	201	148	15
Q.9 If "Yes," how many?							
Use cards punched 36-1 for cols. 37 & 38	37-1	25	1	9	12	2	1
	-2	20	–	10	6	4	–
	-3	13	–	5	7	1	–
	-4	16	–	6	7	3	–
	-5	–	–	–	–	–	–
	-6	1	–	–	1	–	–
	-7	–	–	–	–	–	–
	-8	–	–	–	–	–	–
	-9	–	–	–	–	–	–
	-0	2	–	1	1	–	–
	-X	6	1	–	4	–	1
	-R	4	1	1	–	2	–
	Total	87	3	32	38	12	2
Q.10 What is your connection with your company's aircraft?	38-1	7	1	5	1	–	–
	-2	7	1	4	2	–	–
	-3	13	–	4	3	5	1
	-4	10	–	4	4	2	–
	-5	7	–	2	5	–	–
	-6	6	1	2	2	–	1
	-Y	24	1	10	10	3	–
	-R	20	–	5	13	2	–
	Base	87	3	32	38	12	2

FIGURE 40 Run sheet.

Job #668	SURVEY ON AVIATION				Recap P. 32	

Q. 8. Does your company now own one or more aircraft?

Q. 12. Age of Respondents

	Under 45		45 or over		Total*	
	#	%	#	%	#	%
Yes	35	7	50	14	87	10
No	414	87	278	80	693	82
No answer	30	6	21	6	63	8
Total sample	479	100	349	100	843	100

Q. 9. If "Yes," how many?

	#	%	#	%	#	%
1	10	29	14	28	25	29
2	10	29	10	20	20	23
3	5	14	8	16	13	15
4	6	17	10	20	16	18
5 or more	1	3	2	4	3	3
Don't know, no answer	3	8	6	12	10	12
Total respondents whose companies own aircraft	35	100	50	100	87	100

Q. 10. What is your connection with your company's aircraft?

	#	%	#	%	#	%
Use as passenger	4	11	8	16	13	15
Authorize flights	4	11	6	12	10	11
Pilot or co-pilot	6	17	1	2	7	8
Maintenance or service	5	14	2	4	7	8
Decide type and make when buying	2	6	5	10	7	8
Other (authorize budget, etc.)	3	8	2	4	6	7
No connection, none	11	31	13	26	24	28
No answer	5	14	15	30	20	23
Total respondents whose companies own aircraft**	35	100	50	100	87	100

*Some lines do not add across because 15 respondents who failed to answer Q. 12 are not included in this tabulation.

**Columns may add to more than 100% because of multiple answers.

FIGURE 41   Recap of run sheet in Figure 40.

Figure 40 shows the results of a counter-sorter run in the form of a tab or run sheet. Figure 41 is a percentaged and typed recap sheet of the same tabs. The differences between the two illustrates the recapping operations listed in items 1, 2, 3, 5, 7, and 8 of this chapter. Figure 42 is a computer printout from another survey; it already incorporates needed recap features.

```
                                                              E & M JOB NO. 1058
                                                              TABLE   12
Q. PLEASE WRITE IN THE TOTAL NUMBER OF ACCOUNTS OF EACH OF THE FOLLOWING TYPES HELD BY
   YOU AND OTHER MEMBERS OF YOUR HOUSEHOLD.  (IF NONE, WRITE IN '0'.)

                                                                          SAVINGS
                                           SAVINGS       SAVINGS         ACCOUNTS AT
                              PERSONAL     ACCOUNTS      ACCOUNTS AT      SAVINGS
                              CHECKING     AT SAVINGS    COMMERCIAL      AND LOAN
                              ACCOUNTS     BANKS         BANKS           ASSOCIATIONS
                              ----------   ----------    ----------      ------------

                              NO.  PCT.    NO.  PCT.     NO.  PCT.       NO.   PCT.

1                             598  49.3    279  23.0     186  15.3       264   21.8
2                             291  24.0    167  13.8     101   8.3       137   11.3
3                              81   6.7     77   6.4      37   3.1        46    3.8
4 OR MORE                      62   5.1     84   6.9      33   2.7        58    4.8

HELD--NUMBER NOT SPECIFIED     82   6.8     58   4.8      32   2.7        38    3.1

TOTAL WITH ACCOUNTS          1114  91.9    665  54.9     389  32.1       543   44.8

'NONE,' NOT STATED             98   8.1    547  45.1     823  67.9       669   55.2

TOTAL--ALL HOUSEHOLDS        1212 100.0   1212 100.0    1212 100.0      1212  100.0


AVERAGE (AMONG ALL
        HOUSEHOLDS)             1.5          1.2           0.6            0.9
```

FIGURE 42 Computer printout.

Good recaps will save the analyst time and work and may even give him some new ideas. However, he should make it his business to keep all the detailed run sheets on file. His ideas about what to combine and what bases to use may differ from those of the data processor's.

PERCENTAGING

Most research is more meaningful when its results are expressed in numbers and percentages, rather than in numbers alone. There are other types of calculation which are also often used in showing survey results, and these will be discussed later.

The most useful tool for the analyst is a table which contains both numbers and percentages. Percentages are what he is usually looking for, but any reader of a table or report should be able to tell at a glance how many respondents a percentage represents. The conclusions to be drawn from a 10 percent entry representing 3 respondents and another 10 percent representing 3,000 respondents will be quite different. If both numbers and percentages cannot be shown, the next best procedure is to list percentages only, but also to indicate on every table the number of cases on which they are based. This is less desirable than the first procedure because it takes a small mental calculation for the reader to arrive at the numerical value of each percentage. The next tolerable method is to list percentages only, but with a very clear column heading indicating the exact base for percentaging, such as "Percentage of all respondents" or "Percentage of all owners of hi-fi equipment." This time we really make the poor reader work. If he wants to see what the percentage stands for, he has to turn to the page showing total returns. Or, for the second example, he will have to figure out from a percentage the number of hi-fi owners and use this as his base for the table he is scrutinizing. What is *not* tolerable (but is still occasionally done) is to present or print a report containing only percentages, without any indication whatever of the numerical bases. Such a presentation is meaningless.

Percentages can be shown without decimals or with one or more digits after the decimal. Usually there is no statistical reason to show any decimal place. The listing of two or more decimal places can be misleading by implying a greater degree of accuracy than the report actually has.

The last digit of the percentage figure is usually the result of rounding—increasing the last retained digit of a percentage by one, if the digits following amount to half a unit or more, or by ignoring the digits following it if they amount to less than half.

Answers to questions requiring single mentions only should add to 100 percent. In many reports percentages in such cases are "forced" to make them add to exactly 100 percent (by increasing or decreasing the last digit of one or more percentages in a column.) This is a perfectly acceptable procedure.

AVERAGES AND MEDIANS

Averages or arithmetic means are often very useful in expressing the results of numerical questions. They are especially valuable in comparing tables, such as the family incomes of respondents in various groups, numbers of children, and dollar amounts spent. However, there are pitfalls to look out for. As the average is simply the total of all numerical answers divided by the number of respondents who gave those answers, a small number of very high figures can seriously distort the results. If the income of 499 respondents ranges from $5,000 to $15,000 but one respondent made $5,000,000 during the period surveyed, the answer of that one respondent would just about double the mean income of the group. This can conceivably be a freak incident, which would not be repeated in any other 500 sample drawn from the same universe. If such a situation is detected, it is advisable to call attention to it in a footnote or not to use the average at all.

Another important matter is clear labeling. Are we talking about the average number of cars owned by all respondents or the average number owned by automobile-owning respondents? The word "average" followed by a number is often meaningless unless clearly labeled or unless the reader wants to make his own calculations, if he can, to figure out what the average means. It should also be made clear how the problem of indefinite answers (many, few, etc.) was handled, as well as that of "Don't Know" and "No Answer." In some cases they may be left out of the calculations, while some researchers give them the weight of the average figured on the specific responses.

Medians are often used instead of, or in addition to, averages. As they represent a midpoint, with half the answers higher and the other half lower, they are not as susceptible as averages to fluctuations due to a few very high numbers.

Whenever possible, averages and medians should be calculated from actual answers, and not from frequency-distribution groups. The danger of calculating from groupings is that such calculations must necessarily make assumptions about the distribution of responses within groups. These assumptions frequently are quite different from the actual distribution. In calculating averages from groupings we would also have to set arbitrary values for the highest and lowest groups. In some cases, when the use of breaks is unavoidable (for example in the case of income questions, which people are more willing to answer when asked in check-question form), we can still do better than use midpoint figuring. We can often find United States census figures with detailed income breaks which may be applicable to our problem and help us decide, for example, that a $10,000-to-$14,999 interval should be given the value of $12,000 or $12,200, rather than $12,500.

The recap sheet shown in Figure 41 is a good example of a situation where averages or medians cannot be used. The survey in question was mailed to individuals at their home addresses. The replies to the three questions on company-owned aircraft represent the answers of individuals, and not those of companies. It is possible that a number of the respondents work for the same company, and thus one company's planes can be included several times in the replies. Under these circumstances it would be wrong and misleading to project or average the number of aircraft owned by the respondents' companies.

WEIGHTING AND PROJECTION

Weighting (counting an answer as more or less than 1) is often needed to compensate for disproportionate sampling and occasionally to adjust disproportionate returns from various subsamples. Weighting can be done either arithmetically or by duplicating cards, as, for example, to punch two cards for each respondent whose answer is to receive a weight of 2. The method will depend on the number of cards involved and the type of tabulating equipment used. Weighted returns are sometimes called effective or expanded returns.

Projection is often used to emphasize the significance of the findings. Within limits, it is a useful tool. But once again, it is important that the actual number of answers be available to the reader. It can be dangerous to project small figures, especially single mentions. The author once conducted a survey for a leading publication in which a questionnaire was received from approximately every 500th subscriber. There was some disagreement about whether every single response should be projected to the total number of subscribers. The argument ended when a return was received from a former president of the United States, who so identified himself in answer to the occupation question. The publication's report could hardly have claimed 500 ex-presidents of the United States among its subscribers.

TWENTY-TWO

Final Checking and Presentation

THERE ARE A NUMBER of useful checks which can be made before delivery of the final tabulations.

1. Is the set of tables complete? Does it include all tabulations which were requested?

2. If anything was copied, typed, or typeset, has it been proofread? Every page should be initialed by the proofreaders.

3. Where columns should add down or lines should add across to a 100 percent total, has this addition been checked? If any column or line may add to *more* than 100 percent because of possible multiple mentions, has it been checked to make sure that it does not add to *less*?

4. Does the correct base appear at the beginning or end of every table, and is it clearly and fully described?

5. Have there been thorough checks of page titles, column headings, stubs (line descriptions), and any other descriptive matter used to identify numbers and any other entries on the page? (It is possible that wrong code sheets were used for decoding, column headings

were mixed up, titles or pages were interchanged, lines are missing or misplaced, etc.)

6. Have footnotes been added whenever they can contribute to the clarity of the table? (For example, "Adds to more than 100% because of multiple mentions," "Percent not shown because response totals less than 0.5%," "Continued on next page.")

7. Have averages and/or medians been added wherever they are meaningful? Were they calculated on the correct base, and are they clearly and fully described?

8. Have all proper names, such as brands, names of companies, individuals, or publications, been checked for completeness and correct spelling?

9. Have all bases, totals, and other figures which may have a relationship with other answers been cross checked against their counterparts on other pages to make sure that the relationship is correct? If number, percentage, and projection are shown, has this relationship been checked for all three? (For instance, number of cars owned can be the same or more, but not less, than the number of respondents who own them. If the total number of cars is the base for subsequent questions on year model, how bought, yearly mileage per car, etc., each of those tables must add to the same total number of cars.)

10. Was there a previous survey of similar nature against which all or some of the results can be checked? If there are significant differences, can they be explained? Are there any other existing data against which results can be checked, such as census data, industry figures, United Nations data? Such checks are often most useful, in a negative way, in checking suspiciously high or low figures.

After all these checks (plus all other systematic probings that the researcher can think of) have been completed, there is one last check, that of common sense. The researcher should read carefully through the whole set of tables, keeping his eye and his mind open for anything that "just looks wrong."

PRESENTATION OF THE FINDINGS

Many years ago the first president of the American Marketing Association, Frank Coutant, said of survey reports: "Because there are many types of minds to be reached by a presentation, the ideal report uses three avenues to the mind: figures for the reader who likes to follow up the details; simple words for the man who remembers his arithmetic only as a series of painful lessons; and pictures for the fellow whose mind tends to wander."[1]

Actually the findings of most surveys are presented to one or more of three types of audience:

1. Analysts, market research men, statisticians, businessmen, and others who know about surveys and have the background and experience to understand and use the figures without any special effort by the researcher to simplify or "sell" his findings.

2. People who ordered the survey; in the case of marketing research these would be businessmen or government officials and their colleagues or superiors to whom they'll want to show the results. These people will be interested in the findings of the survey, but they will leave the evaluation of the techniques and details to others.

3. In the case of published reports (especially those of promotional nature such as media studies), a general or specific audience. The sponsor of the survey hopes these people will read the report and retain the particular findings which he considers important. Members of this audience may or may not have any experience with surveys or be particularly interested in the specific survey presented to them.

Members of the first audience may not require a formal report or analysis; they may prefer to draw their own conclusions and write their own report. They will often ask for the recap sheets and the run sheets and may make their own requests for cross tabulations and calculations. However, they will certainly want a detailed description of the methodology, including the sampling plan and its execution, the source of the mailing list, mailing and closing dates, number of mailings, incentives used, number and percentage of returns, samples of all materials used in the mailing and in all other data-gathering and data-processing techniques. In general, the report to this group of people can be short on interpretation and fancy presentation, but it must be long on detailed, technical information and complete, basic findings.

Coming now to the second group, the executive who ordered the survey is primarily interested in the results and only secondarily in how the research specialists arrived at them. If he did not have confidence in the researcher, he would not have entrusted him with the survey in the first place. He should have the technical data, just in case he wants to check some phase of it, but he is a busy man, and what he will want to see in a hurry are the most essential findings, the analyst's conclusions about them, and possibly recommendations about actions the sponsoring company or department should take as a result of the findings. He will want a presentation which is short, to the point, has visual aids such as charts to increase the speed or scope of understanding (not just for decoration), and represents a concise briefing in the language of *his* field (rather than that of marketing research).

Reports intended to be published and distributed among specific groups of people who are important to the sponsoring organization usually need to contain only very basic data on methodology, a short summary of findings, and the percentaged tabulations—all of them in as interesting and simple a form as possible. Even if the survey is promotional, it is advisable to keep the report just a clear presentation of the research findings. The advertising or promotional "sell" can either be printed as a separate brochure referring to the survey report and interpreting its findings, or it can be attached to the report and clearly labeled as not part of the actual findings.

No matter who will read the presentation of a competitive or promotional survey, it is highly desirable that all marginal tabulations be reported, and not only those which the researcher or the sponsoring organization consider important or advantageous for their purposes.

CONTENTS OF THE REPORT

Various ingredients of mail survey reports can be drawn upon to fit the requirements of any of the three types of audience we have just discussed:

1. Description of the purpose of the survey: Who ordered it, what the general problem is, in what specific way the survey is supposed to be helpful.

2. Description of the method and scope of the research. This part of the report will include a definition of the universe, the source of the list, the sampling method used, and the size and distribution of the sample. It should state the name of the organization which appeared on the stationery and describe any incentives used.

This section must show the overall gross and net mailings and the number and percentage of returns. In addition to the number of mailings, including the kinds of follow-ups and validations used, it should indicate the number of questionnaires mailed and returned.

In some cases the methodology may show limitations on the use of figures; for example, if the sample consisted of "best customers and prospects" of a number of manufacturers, it may point out that the results should not be projected to the total market.

This part of the presentation of the research findings can be a relatively short and simple description or a very detailed one, including checks on stability, validation, sampling error, etc. In the latter case the section is usually placed at the end of the report as a "technical appendix."

3. A summary of findings. This is desirable in any kind of report. It is a concise presentation of the most important data and offers a quick way for the reader to absorb the highlights of the survey results.

4. Conclusions. These can consist of a few short paragraphs saying, in effect, "You have just read the highlights of this survey, and in our opinion, here is the general pattern which emerges from these findings...." On the other hand the conclusion may be a very detailed analysis of all findings.

5. Recommendations. These are not always requested, and the researcher must be familiar with the sponsor's business before he can make useful recommendations.

6. Tabulations and calculations. These can be shown as typed pages or as a computer printout. If the former, they would be typed copies of the recap pages. Often the tables are shown both in the numerical form and as charts.

7. Analysis. When the findings of a survey are studied in depth in order to arrive at detailed conclusions and recommendations, the analysis will take the place of items 4 and 5, and possibly 6. This is a job for a trained analyst who knows both survey work and the sponsor's problems. The analysis is more than a verbose rehashing of the findings; it must have insight, originality, and clear and interesting presentation.

8. Samples of the mailing pieces: The questionnaire, letters, cards, and any other material used in the mailings.

9. Letter of certification. If the survey was conducted by an outside organization, it is usual to submit its report with a letter of certification, which is often printed in published reports. It usually includes the basic facts on method and scope. Figure 43 shows an example of this type of letter.

FORMAT OF THE REPORT

The cover of the report should include the name of the survey. A good survey title should inform the reader of its subject matter. The cover may also include the date of the survey, the name of the sponsoring company or department, and if the survey was conducted by an outside organization, the name of the research house as well. If only a very simple cover is desired, some of the informative material can be shown on the title page of the report.

> **PROFESSIONAL MAIL SURVEYS COMPANY**
>
> 7432 East Court Avenue
>
> Elveron, California 90101
>
> 213 991-5550
>
> (Date)
>
> To whom it may concern:
>
> In January, 19xx Professional Mail Surveys Company was retained by The National Prestige Newspaper to determine the businesses, positions and functions of its subscribers and identified readers; to measure the business buying-influence of subscribers, their family income and net worth.
>
> In compliance with specifications set up by Professional Mail Surveys Company, a random selection was made from the complete subscriber galleys. An explanatory letter, the accompanying questionnaire and a stamped reply envelope were mailed on March 15, 19xx to each subscriber so selected—a total mailing of 20,000.
>
> Returns were received directly by Professional Mail Surveys Company. After two mailings a total of 13,803 questionnaires, or 69.0% of the mailout had been received and were tabulated. All questionnaires returned up to May 13 were used, and no questionnaire received after that date was included.
>
> The size of the sample provides large enough bases for the tabulation of the complete questionnaire by the four regional editions of the publication.
>
> All tabulations, percentages and projections published in the foregoing report were computed by Professional Mail Surveys Company, employing established research practices.
>
> PROFESSIONAL MAIL SURVEYS COMPANY
>
> *James B. Jones*
>
> James B. Jones, Director

FIGURE 43 Letter of certification.

The title page is usually followed by a table of contents. The main consideration in constructing this index must be the convenience of the user; the wording and layout should enable him to locate any subject in the report with the least time and effort.

The physical shape of the presentation can vary from typed pages and computer printouts to hardcover books printed on letter press. If the researcher wants the recipient of the report to file it and keep it in his library after reading, it is advisable to choose a format which fits on a bookshelf. Outsize reports usually get banished to some stock room, while very small ones have a tendency to disappear without a trace.

Neat and economical reports can be prepared by using the carbon-ribbon typewriter, and then if more than a few copies are needed, they can easily be reproduced by photo-offset. The cover can be printed in the same way, with a spiral or plastic binding to complete the process.

REFERENCE

1. Frank R. Coutant, "Market Research Must Hold Executive Attention," *Journal of Marketing*, vol. 10, no. 3, pp. 288–289, January, 1946.

TWENTY-THREE

Recognition Studies and Corporate-Image Surveys

WE'VE COME A LONG WAY from the era of the "robber barons" and "the public be damned" to the increasing economic interdependence of the modern era. Business and industry are very much concerned these days with the attitudes of a great many groups which may influence not only their business but their very existence. Stockholders, labor, competitors, customers, government, financial leaders, and the public at large are some of the groups that business and industry have to reckon with. The larger the company, the more intricate becomes this web of interdependence.

The first problem of a new company is to become known. Once it is known, the next worry will be "Known as what?" The company at this stage has an "image," which it "projects" toward the groups of people who are in any kind of contact with it. The image can be good, bad, or indifferent; it may improve or deteriorate; it may or may not be a reflection of the truth. It is partly based on tangible evidence, such as size, quality of products, profits, growth, diversification; or it can be based on such intangibles as reputation, notoriety, or "leadership." It can be influenced by an advertising campaign, a rumor, or world politics. It can also be measured by survey techniques.

How well is our company known; who knows it; what kind of image does it project to various groups; how does a sales campaign, an advertising campaign, or the meteoric rise of a new competitor influence or change the image? If a change has taken place, what is its nature and extent? Can we measure the effectiveness of our past efforts and obtain guidance for future actions to improve our company image?

A large and increasing number of companies are now conducting recognition studies and corporate-image surveys. Some are simple, one-shot surveys; others are "before and after" studies to measure the effects of a merger, a new product line, or an advertising campaign; while still others are continuous studies. It is easy to conduct some such survey—it is harder, and sometimes quite costly, to do a good and reliable job.

A NOTE OF CAUTION

The following "red flag" primarily concerns "before and after" surveys but must be kept in mind for all research of this nature. A change is accurately measurable only if there is a single variable, while all other elements of the measured object or situation remain constant. We must recognize that one cannot measure the changes in a company's image caused by any single event or chain of events such as an advertising campaign. There are always a large number of variables in any such situation which cannot be held constant, and therefore it is usually impossible to define precisely what caused a given change.

Suppose a corporation spends a million dollars in a period of six months on advertising a specific line of products, emphasizing the reputation it enjoys for making quality merchandise. A survey before and after this campaign seems like a good way of judging the results of this effort. Let us assume that it was a well-conducted survey and that from the researcher's point of view it was a technical success. What happens if, during the campaign, the company has a real debacle in another product line, which gets a lot of publicity? How will the results be influenced by the fact that a competitor has just introduced some new products in the same line which are better and cheaper than the line advertised? Suppose press accounts of a strike at the company's main plant during this period put the company in a bad light? Suppose another company spends not one, but ten, million dollars in the same period, advertising a competing line?

This warning does not mean that "before and after" surveys are useless. It means that it takes an astute analyst to evaluate the results and to ferret out all the factors which may have caused the apparent change or lack of change.

AREAS OF CONSIDERATION

In discussing this type of survey, we can talk about four general areas in some depth:

1. WHAT are the objectives; what do we want to find out?
2. WHOM do we want to survey; what is the universe?
3. WHEN and how often should the survey be done?
4. HOW should it be accomplished? (Questionnaire construction.)

Let us look at the structure of each of these areas. The following are only some of the common degrees and variations of recognition and attitude:

Setting the objectives. Progressing from the general to the specific, the following can be listed as frequent research objectives:

1. Measuring recognition of the company's name (Fig. 45).

2. Measuring awareness of what the company produces. How many respondents are aware of any products made by the XYZ company? How many know that the AZ corporation makes not only plastics, for which they are famous, but also fertilizers? (See Fig. 45.)

3. Measuring recognition of the company's brands (Fig. 49).

4. Establishing attitudes toward the company. How do respondents think of the ABC company in terms of product quality, growth potential, diversification, efficiency of management, labor relations, customer service, and so on? Do they see the company as modern, profitable, helpful, dull, immoral, as a follower, or as a leader? The sum total of all such attitudes represents the company image. (See Figs. 51 and 52.)

5. Measuring the extent of advertising penetration. Have respondents seen or heard the company's ads, and if so, how much do they recall? (See Fig. 48.)

6. Checking specific problems which are important at a given time or place, such as the effect of a new sales approach on people in test-market areas, the penetration of a specific message of an advertising campaign, the recognition of a new slogan, a threat from a competing product.

THE UNIVERSE

Whom do we want to survey? There are always several possible universes for any recognition or corporate-image study, and many surveys use more than one. The following are examples:

1. Present customers of the company. They are sometimes separated into major and minor customers.
2. Prospective customers, representing the potential, as against the present market.
3. Financial leaders, such as security analysts, bankers, brokers, who can influence the standing of the company's stock and its ability to obtain expansion capital.
4. Opinion makers, such as top executives and officials in business and government.
5. The audience of a specific medium which an advertising campaign will use, such as the subscribers to one or more publications.
6. Particular interest groups, such as businessmen in cities or counties where a special sales effort will be made. In these cases it is always advisable to conduct the same research among a control group.
7. The public at large.

TIMING AND FREQUENCY

When and how often should the universe be surveyed? Once again the depth and complexity of useful research is usually limited only by the budget.

A one-shot survey is the easiest way to gauge current recognition of the company and the image it projects. Lacking any other data to compare it with, however, we find it very difficult to evaluate the results.

A much better type of research would consist of a "before and after" survey, to measure the effects, if any, of an advertising campaign or of major changes in production, sales policy, or company structure. Proper timing is, of course, very important: The "before" phase should be conducted before the actual changes take place or before the campaign starts, and the "after" phase of the survey should take place when the planned changes have been made or the campaign is over.

A more thorough way of surveying the penetration of an advertising campaign, especially if it is one of long duration, is to have a "before," "during," and "after" survey to check the effects of the campaign in its various stages.

There is a fourth degree of depth: a retention survey conducted six months or a year after the "after" survey. This is meaningful if the "after" survey showed significant changes and if we want to explore how long these changes will last. Suppose an effective advertising campaign has succeeded in persuading a group of business leaders of the growth potential of the ABC company: Will they still feel the same way a year later?

If the budget permits, the best measure of recognition and of corporate image is the continuous or "tracking" survey, conducted at fixed time intervals and furnishing management a handy mirror in which to see the current image of the company.

STRUCTURING THE QUESTIONNAIRE

How should the questionnaire be constructed? A combination of the objectives of the survey and the desired depth of analysis will determine the simplicity or complexity of the questionnaire structure.

The simplest and shortest questionnaire will ask the questions determined by the objectives of the survey about the sponsoring company only. Such oversimplified research may be biased and does not offer any possibility of analysis in depth. (See Fig. 44.)

It is advisable to ask questions about several companies in addition to the sponsor, not only to avoid bias, but also to permit analysis in depth. For example, in a "before and after" study (conducted before and after an advertising campaign) all the objectives surveyed can be analyzed first by comparing the company's present position with its own "before" status, next by measuring the company's present and past standing against that of the other firms listed, and finally by analyzing the "before" and "after" comparative positions of the other firms listed.

These comparisons can be made by using mail questionnaires with check questions, some of which may represent simple scales (Fig. 47). For more sophisticated comparisons, a real scaling system may be used. In our experience an eleven-point, illustrated scale gives a sensitive measuring device to the analyst, which is still not too complicated for the respondent (Fig. 51).

These scales can be applied to attributes measured for each company listed, to characteristics of materials or products supplied by various companies, and so on.

Using averages and percentages derived from the responses to the scaling questions, we can make analyses of various facets of the company image as measured against competitors or, in the case of "before and after" surveys, as measured against itself and its competitors after a specified time lapse.

With the help of the scaling method, and if we are dealing with sufficiently large numbers of questionnaires, we can also analyze whether respondents seem to have set opinions about a company and all its works (as all good, or all bad), or whether they are selective. Do they tend to give the same ratings to all companies listed, or do they give different ratings to different companies?

Word-association questions can be very helpful in comparing the images of several companies (Fig. 52).

Various other questions can be helpful for analysis in depth. For example, how involved is the respondent with the company? Does he know its name only, or also its products and facilities? Is he a customer or a supplier of this company? Is he a stockholder, or does he work for it? (See Fig. 51.)

Other questions may establish the exposure of the respondents to various media, their titles and functions, their lines of business, the size of their company, etc.

The attributes of the surveyed companies can also be analyzed with the help of one or more *ranking* questions. The characteristics attributed by respondents to the top-ranked companies may be helpful in establishing which of the attributes they consider really important.[1] (For ranking versus rating, see Chap. 7.)

GENERAL CONSIDERATIONS

As in all mail surveys, the most important considerations are the following:

1. Definition and planning, based primarily on the points just discussed and shown schematically in Figure 53.
2. The selection of random samples of individuals from the universe we want to survey.
3. Sufficiently large numbers in each sample unit to ensure stability and comparability.
4. The construction of precise and unbiased questions.
5. Adequate data-gathering procedures, including a letter and questionnaire. These minimize possible bias, such as nonresponse by people who are not familiar with the companies listed on the questionnaire, by encouraging them to return it in any case.
6. The highest possible percentage of returns.

CASE HISTORIES

The following questionnaires represent illustrations of the points discussed and actual case histories.

The questionnaire shown in Figure 44 was mailed to 1,400 subscribers to a magazine. A single mailing with a 25¢ incentive yielded a 62.3 percent response. This short questionnaire represents the minimum approach. Respondents know the identity of the sponsoring company. We do not know what bias this may introduce, and there can be no comparison with other companies.

The survey was repeated twelve months later.

Have you heard of the ▬▬▬▬ Corporation? .... Yes ☐ No ☐

If "No," please check the proper box and return the questionnaire in the stamped reply envelope. Your answer is very important to us. Thank you.

If "Yes," please continue.

Listed below are several statements which might apply to ▬▬▬▬. For each statement, simply check whether you Agree Strongly, Agree, are Not Sure, Disagree or Disagree Strongly.

	Agree Strongly	Agree	Not Sure	Disagree	Disagree Strongly
▬▬▬ is a growth company	☐	☐	☐	☐	☐
▬▬▬ is a poorly managed company	☐	☐	☐	☐	☐
▬▬▬ produces high quality products	☐	☐	☐	☐	☐
▬▬▬ is not interested in research	☐	☐	☐	☐	☐
▬▬▬ is a sophisticated engineering company	☐	☐	☐	☐	☐

Would you please make an estimate of the annual sales of the ▬▬▬▬ Corporation? (check one)

Under $100 million ☐ $100 million - $499 million ☐

$500 million - $900 million ☐   Over $900 million ☐

Thank you for your help.

FIGURE 44 Corporate-image questionnaire (one company).

The next questionnaire (Figs. 45, 46) was used in a survey conducted for a large chemical company on a worldwide basis. Two thousand questionnaires were mailed to a random sample of subscribers to *Time International*. A choice of three inexpensive incentives was offered to respondents.

WORLD WIDE SURVEY

1. In your opinion, which of these industries is contributing the most to improving the standard of living of the world's people?

    Drugs ☐   Electronics ☐   Chemicals ☐   Automotive ☐

2. How well do you know each of the following companies? Please check one box for each company.

    I know this company:

	Well	Moderately well	Somewhat	Hardly at all	Never heard of
Esso Chemical	☐	☐	☐	☐	☐
Farbwerke Hoechst AG	☐	☐	☐	☐	☐
ICI (Imperial Chemical Industries)	☐	☐	☐	☐	☐
Shell Chemical	☐	☐	☐	☐	☐
Union Carbide	☐	☐	☐	☐	☐

    IF YOU HAVE NOT HEARD OF ANY OF THESE COMPANIES, PLEASE SKIP TO QUESTION 6 ON PAGE 2.

Please answer the following questions about each company you have heard of.

3. Have you seen or heard any advertising for chemicals recently by any of the following companies?

	Esso Chemical	Hoechst	ICI	Shell Chemical	Union Carbide
Yes	☐	☐	☐	☐	☐
No	☐	☐	☐	☐	☐

4. For each of these companies, please check the products listed you believe they make. Check as many products for each company as apply.

	Esso Chemical	Hoechst	ICI	Shell Chemical	Union Carbide
Fertilizers	☐	☐	☐	☐	☐
Man-made fibers	☐	☐	☐	☐	☐
Petrochemicals	☐	☐	☐	☐	☐
Plastics	☐	☐	☐	☐	☐
Solvents	☐	☐	☐	☐	☐
Synthetic rubber	☐	☐	☐	☐	☐

    (Please turn)

FIGURE 45 Corporate-image questionnaire (several companies).

Page 2

5. Please check the one company you regard as best for each of the factors listed. (Please check one for each line across.)

	Esso Chemical	Hoechst	ICI	Shell Chemical	Union Carbide
Leadership in developing new and better products	☐	☐	☐	☐	☐
Growth potential	☐	☐	☐	☐	☐
Product quality	☐	☐	☐	☐	☐
Serves many different industries	☐	☐	☐	☐	☐
World-wide facilities	☐	☐	☐	☐	☐
Overall reputation	☐	☐	☐	☐	☐

6a. In what type of business or profession are you mainly engaged? (For example, manufacturing, retail, law, government, armed forces, student, etc.)

_____

b. What is your job title, rank or position in your main occupation? (For example, managing director, partner, sales manager, etc.)

_____

c. If you are engaged in manufacturing, what product(s) does your company make?

_____

7. Please check whether you read each of the following magazines regularly, occasionally, or not at all.

	Read regularly	Read occasionally	Do not read
Chemical Week	☐	☐	☐
Fortune	☐	☐	☐
Industrial World	☐	☐	☐
International Management	☐	☐	☐
Life	☐	☐	☐
Newsweek	☐	☐	☐
Time	☐	☐	☐

Thank you for your help.

FIGURE 46 Page 2 of questionnaire in Figure 45, with readership question.

The first mailing closed with a 63 percent response, and a single follow-up mailing to nonrespondents brought the total response up to 76.5 percent. The questionnaire contains questions on familiarity with the company and four of its competitors, including simple questions on advertising and products. Attributes are not rated, but merely listed (Q. 5) for respondent's company preference.

The questionnaire headed "Company Recognition Study" (Figs. 47, 48) was sent to a random sample of 1,000 subscribers to a general magazine. It received a 51 percent return after a single mailing, using a 25¢ incentive. It illustrates the simplest type of rating of three attributes and some advertising penetration questions. This was a "before and after" survey, conducted before the start of an advertising campaign and after its conclusion. (The percentage of response was similar in both waves.)

The questionnaire used in the "Survey of Oil Field Chemical Suppliers" (Figs. 49, 50) was mailed to a relatively small number of the most important potential customers of one of the chemical companies listed.

The first mailing (with a 25¢ incentive) brought a 47 percent return. After a follow-up mailing, returns totaled 65.6 percent. This questionnaire shows brand and product recognition questions, a somewhat more sophisticated rating scale for attributes, and a personal involvement question.

The questionnaire shown in Figures 51 and 52 is a composite of several questionnaires actually mailed. This illustrates the most complete kind of rating scale, which can furnish a very sensitive grading for comparisons. This type of questionnaire has been mailed to customers of large companies, to subscribers to general and business publications, and to business executives listed in *Poor's Directory*.

The percentage of response of businessmen to this type of questionnaire (using a 25¢ coin incentive) has been between 38 and 45 percent on one mailing, and from 50 to 62 percent after one follow-up mailing, in the author's experience.

Of course a sufficiently large mailing of this type of questionnaire permits the researcher all sorts of analyses, including most of those described in this chapter.

COMPANY RECOGNITION STUDY

1. Are you familiar with these company names?

	Yes	No
Avco	☐	☐
Bendix	☐	☐
Honeywell	☐	☐
Hughes	☐	☐
Raytheon	☐	☐
Sperry	☐	☐

2. Please check the area(s) that you feel each company does business in:

	Automation	Aviation	Communication	Electronics	Missiles and Space	Automotive
Avco	☐	☐	☐	☐	☐	☐
Bendix	☐	☐	☐	☐	☐	☐
Honeywell	☐	☐	☐	☐	☐	☐
Hughes	☐	☐	☐	☐	☐	☐
Raytheon	☐	☐	☐	☐	☐	☐
Sperry	☐	☐	☐	☐	☐	☐

3. How would you rate these companies in:

	Progressiveness				Research Abilities			
	EXCELLENT	GOOD	FAIR	POOR	EXCELLENT	GOOD	FAIR	POOR
Avco	☐	☐	☐	☐	☐	☐	☐	☐
Bendix	☐	☐	☐	☐	☐	☐	☐	☐
Honeywell	☐	☐	☐	☐	☐	☐	☐	☐
Hughes	☐	☐	☐	☐	☐	☐	☐	☐
Raytheon	☐	☐	☐	☐	☐	☐	☐	☐
Sperry	☐	☐	☐	☐	☐	☐	☐	☐

4. How would you rate each company as a potential investment?

	Excellent	Good	Fair	Poor
Avco	☐	☐	☐	☐
Bendix	☐	☐	☐	☐
Honeywell	☐	☐	☐	☐
Hughes	☐	☐	☐	☐
Raytheon	☐	☐	☐	☐
Sperry	☐	☐	☐	☐

(Please turn)

FIGURE 47 Corporate-image questionnaire with ratings.

5. Do you recall seeing or hearing any advertising for one or more of these companies? .... Yes ☐ No ☐

   IF YES:

Please check the company whose advertising you remember.	Where did you see this advertising? (If in a magazine, please name magazine. If on TV, please name program.)	What points did the advertising make?
Avco .... ☐	_____	_____
Bendix .... ☐	_____	_____
Honeywell .... ☐	_____	_____
Hughes .... ☐	_____	_____
Raytheon .... ☐	_____	_____
Sperry .... ☐	_____	_____

6. AND FOR CLASSIFICATION PURPOSES: What is your title or position? _____

   If in business, what does your company make or do at your present location? _____

   Thank you for your help.

FIGURE 48 Page 2 of questionnaire in Figure 47, with advertising-penetration questions.

```
┌─────────────────────────────────────────────────────────────────────────────┐
│                   SURVEY OF OIL FIELD CHEMICAL SUPPLIERS                    │
│                                                                             │
│ 1. How well do you know each of the following suppliers of oil field        │
│    chemicals? (Please check one box for each company.)                      │
│                              I know this company:                           │
│                         Moderately            Hardly          Never         │
│                 Well       well    Somewhat   at all       heard of it      │
│    Aquaness .......      □         □          □             □          □    │
│    Enjay Chemical ....   □         □          □             □          □    │
│    Sinclair ........     □         □          □             □          □    │
│    Tretolite .......     □         □          □             □          □    │
│    Visco ..........      □         □          □             □          □    │
│                                                                             │
│    (Please answer questions 2 through 6 only for those companies you've     │
│    heard of. If you haven't heard of any, please skip to question 7.)       │
│                                                                             │
│ 2. Have you seen or heard any advertising on oil field chemicals recently   │
│    by any of these companies?                                               │
│                          Enjay                                              │
│             Aquaness   Chemical    Sinclair    Tretolite      Visco         │
│    Yes        □           □           □           □            □            │
│    No         □           □           □           □            □            │
│                                                                             │
│ 3. Please check which of these companies you believe are mainly captive     │
│    suppliers selling principally to parent crude oil companies, and those   │
│    which sell to the entire crude oil producing industry. (Please check     │
│    one box for each company you've heard of.)                               │
│                          Captive supplier      Sells to                     │
│                          selling mainly to   entire crude oil               │
│                          parent company    producing industry   Don't know  │
│    Aquaness .........         □                    □                □       │
│    Enjay ............         □                    □                □       │
│    Sinclair .........         □                    □                □       │
│    Tretolite ........         □                    □                □       │
│    Visco ............         □                    □                □       │
│                                                                             │
│ 4. Check which of the companies listed to the left uses these brand names.  │
│    (Only one check mark in each column.)                                    │
│                                                                             │
│              Breaxit   Coat   Corexit   Cronox   Drop   Kontol   Surflo     │
│    Aquaness ..  □       □       □        □       □       □        □         │
│    Enjay .....  □       □       □        □       □       □        □         │
│    Sinclair ..  □       □       □        □       □       □        □         │
│    Tretolite .  □       □       □        □       □       □        □         │
│    Visco .....  □       □       □        □       □       □        □         │
│    Don't know   □       □       □        □       □       □        □         │
│                                                                             │
│                                                         (Please turn)       │
└─────────────────────────────────────────────────────────────────────────────┘
```

FIGURE 49 Corporate-image questionnaire with brand question.

Page 2

5. Please rate each of the following companies using the scale at the left. Take Aquaness, for example. If you think they rate "very good" on product performance, mark the company 5; if you think they're "very poor" mark them 0. Of course you may want to rate them any number in between. Please rate each of the other companies the same way on product performance.

5	Very good
4	
3	
2	
1	
0	Very poor

	Aquaness	Enjay	Sinclair	Tretolite	Visco
a) Product performance	____	____	____	____	____

Using the same rating scale above, please rate each of these companies with a number on each of the following factors:

	Aquaness	Enjay	Sinclair	Tretolite	Visco
b) Technical service	____	____	____	____	____
c) Lowest possible cost to do the job	____	____	____	____	____
d) Sales service	____	____	____	____	____
e) Completeness of product line	____	____	____	____	____
f) Reputation as a supplier	____	____	____	____	____

6. For each company, please check the products listed which you believe it offers. Check as many products as apply for each company:

	Aquaness	Enjay	Sinclair	Tretolite	Visco
Bactericides	☐	☐	☐	☐	☐
Demulsifiers	☐	☐	☐	☐	☐
Scale chemicals	☐	☐	☐	☐	☐
Anti-foulants	☐	☐	☐	☐	☐
Paraffin chemicals	☐	☐	☐	☐	☐
Corrosion inhibitors	☐	☐	☐	☐	☐
Surfactants	☐	☐	☐	☐	☐

And now, for tabulating purposes only,

7. What is your job function? (Please be specific, e.g., purchasing department manager, district engineer, etc.) _____

8. Please check the statement below which most closely defines the degree of your involvement in the selection of individual oil field chemical suppliers. (Please check one.)

Have final say .... ☐
Make decisions subject to approval .... ☐
Approve products from a technical point of view only .... ☐
Place order, but not otherwise involved.... ☐
Not involved .... ☐

Thank you for your help.

FIGURE 50   Page 2 of questionnaire in Figure 49, with 6-point scale.

U.S. SURVEY AMONG EXECUTIVES

1. Please check what relationship or connection, if any, you (or your firm) have with each of the following corporations:

	Alcoa	DuPont	U.S. Plywood
We sell to this company	☐	☐	☐
We buy from this company	☐	☐	☐
Other relationships or connections (own stock, self or relative works for it, etc.)	☐	☐	☐
No relationship or connection	☐	☐	☐

Please continue, your answers are equally important to this research whether or not you have any connection with the companies listed.

Excellent, highest rating	10
	9
	8
	7
	6
Average	5
	4
	3
	2
	1
Very poor	0

2. Please use the rating scale on the left side to indicate how you feel about the soundness of management of <u>each</u> of the following companies. Take Alcoa for example. If you think Alcoa has excellent management, mark it 10; if you think its management is very poor, mark it 0. Of course you may want to rate it any other number in between these two extremes. Please rate each of the other two companies the same way on soundness of their management. Ratings may be based on your experience with these companies, or on anything you may have seen or heard about them.

	Alcoa	DuPont	U.S. Plywood
Sound management	___	___	___

3. Using the same rating method based on the scale at the left, please rate each of these three companies with a number on each of the following items:

	Alcoa	DuPont	U.S. Plywood
Diversification of product line	___	___	___
Product quality	___	___	___
Research and development program	___	___	___
Expanding markets by developing new product applications	___	___	___
Growth possibility	___	___	___
Intelligent use of natural resources	___	___	___
Meeting delivery deadlines	___	___	___
Labor relations	___	___	___
Efficient, modern production facilities	___	___	___
Service to their customers	___	___	___
Technical help to customers	___	___	___
Informative advertising	___	___	___
Pricing	___	___	___

(Please turn)

FIGURE 51 Corporate-image questionnaire with 11-point scale.

Page 2

4. Please check each of the following descriptive words for each of the listed companies to which, in your opinion, it applies. (You may check more than one company for a word. If you think the word does not apply to any of them, please check "None of these".)

	Alcoa	DuPont	U.S. Plywood	None of these		Alcoa	DuPont	U.S. Plywood	None of these
Competitive ...	☐	☐	☐	☐	Inconsiderate	☐	☐	☐	☐
Conservative ..	☐	☐	☐	☐	Modern	☐	☐	☐	☐
Dependable ...	☐	☐	☐	☐	Old-fashioned	☐	☐	☐	☐
Enterprising ..	☐	☐	☐	☐	Overbearing ..	☐	☐	☐	☐
Friendly	☐	☐	☐	☐	Profitable	☐	☐	☐	☐
Inflexible	☐	☐	☐	☐	Timid	☐	☐	☐	☐

5. Please check each of the following materials which your company uses:

Aluminum ☐   Plywood ..... ☐
Plastic .. ☐   Stainless steel ☐

Excellent highest rating | 10
| 9
| 8
| 7
| 6
Average | 5
| 4
| 3
| 2
| 1
Very poor | 0

6. Please consider each material listed below in terms of its use as a component of your principal finished product. Following the scale on the left, rate each of the materials for lightness. E.g., if you think aluminum is excellent in this characteristic, mark it 10; if very poor mark it 0, or you may use any other number in between. Please rate each of the other materials the same way for lightness. Then do the same in each of the next three lines.

	Aluminum	Plastic	Plywood	Stainless steel
Lightness	___	___	___	___
Strength	___	___	___	___
Comparative cost ...	___	___	___	___
Availability	___	___	___	___

7. Which of the following publications do you read or look through regularly (at least 3 out of 4 issues)? Please check all that apply.

Business Week .... ☐   Purchasing .... ☐
Chemical Engineering .... ☐   Purchasing Week .... ☐
Contractors and Engineers ☐   Time .... ☐
Fortune .... ☐   The Wall Street Journal .... ☐
Metalworking News ...... ☐   Wood & Wood Products .... ☐

8. For purposes of analysis please tell us:

Your title _____ and your job function _____

Thank you for your help.

FIGURE 52 Page 2 of questionnaire in Figure 51, with word-association question.

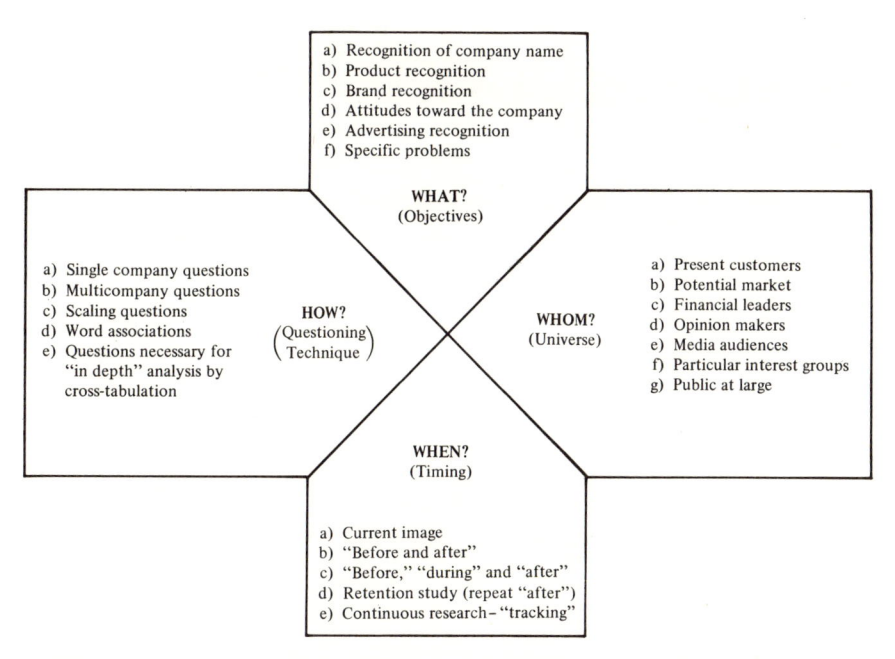

```
                    a) Recognition of company name
                    b) Product recognition
                    c) Brand recognition
                    d) Attitudes toward the company
                    e) Advertising recognition
                    f) Specific problems
                              WHAT?
                           (Objectives)

a) Single company questions                         a) Present customers
b) Multicompany questions                           b) Potential market
c) Scaling questions         HOW?        WHOM?      c) Financial leaders
d) Word associations      (Questioning) (Universe)  d) Opinion makers
e) Questions necessary for  Technique               e) Media audiences
   "in depth" analysis by                           f) Particular interest groups
   cross-tabulation                                 g) Public at large

                              WHEN?
                             (Timing)
                    a) Current image
                    b) "Before and after"
                    c) "Before," "during" and "after"
                    d) Retention study (repeat "after")
                    e) Continuous research-"tracking"
```

FIGURE 53 Schematic design for definition and planning of corporate-image surveys.

REFERENCE

1. Louis Cohen, "The Differentiation Ratio in Corporate Image Research," *Journal of Advertising Research*, vol. 7, no. 3, pp. 32–35, September, 1967.

Note: This chapter is based largely on a talk given by the author at the 13th Annual Conference of the Advertising Research Foundation.

TWENTY-FOUR
International Mail Surveys

IN MANY RESPECTS the principles and techniques of domestic surveys hold as well or better for international mail surveys.

This is true of both the advantages and the limitations of mail surveys. It has not proved difficult to have mail questionnaires completed by such diverse groups of people as leading industrialists of Common Market countries, doctors in Egypt, best Asian customers of a large American manufacturer, and foreign subscribers to the *National Geographic* magazine. International postal service is generally very efficient, and there is no insoluble problem in covering a large number of countries in a survey. One does not have to worry about the uniformity of procedures, the adequacy of supervision of the work in all countries which have to be included in a sample, or the synchronizing of the interviewing in each. On the other hand, it is sometimes difficult to find suitable lists, and problems of language and literacy must be considered in international mail surveys. While these surveys are more expensive than their domestic counterparts (largely due to postage and to language problems), they are usually still well below the cost of the same research conducted by other data-gathering methods. Most international mail surveys take more time than similar domestic studies because respondents in some countries are likely to take more time in answering than in the United States and because postal service to and from small places located in distant parts of the world may take somewhat longer.

Today, international mail surveys are used by the United Nations, by industrial and business firms with interests and markets abroad, by publications with a substantial number of foreign subscribers, and by institutions and organizations interested in the opinions of people in various countries.

INTERNATIONAL MAILING LISTS

The greatest limitation on the use of international mail surveys is the relative difficulty in obtaining reliable mailing lists for the whole universe in which the researcher is interested, or at least for a significant segment of it. While international lists can often be bought or compiled, it may not be simple or inexpensive to procure them.

Of course the number of available lists increases each year as more and more directories are published all over the world. Some types of lists used for international marketing research include:

1. Subscriber lists of international publications, as in the survey described on page 225. If the subscribers to a "prestige" publication happen to represent a desirable universe for a survey, the researcher knows that he has an excellent mailing list. It is up to date, and it includes people with international interests, whose socioeconomic level is usually high. All this adds up to the likelihood of a good response rate.

2. Directories of industrial and business firms of various countries, which include the names of top executives. These are equivalent to United States directories such as Poor's, Dun & Bradstreet's, and Thomas' *Register*. Information about such publications usually can be obtained from the consulates of the various countries.

3. "Who's Who" types of books published in various countries.

4. "Best foreign customers" or potential customer lists maintained by many industrial firms—usually, of course, for their own exclusive use. Drug manufacturers carefully maintain lists of physicians in various countries, appliance manufacturers usually have lists of jobbers or dealers, manufacturers of oil-drilling equipment are likely to keep up-to-date lists of foreign companies and subsidiaries who are exploring for oil in various parts of the globe.

5. Lists of specific groups of industrial firms and their executives, published in special issues of foreign trade publications.

6. Lists of members of various professions which have been compiled in many countries.

7. Lists of government officials of foreign countries (similar to our Washington "Blue Book").

8. Lists and informative material available from international organizations such as the United Nations, the Common Market, the Organization of American States (OAS).

9. U.S. Department of Commerce lists of foreign companies doing business with United States firms.

10. Attendance lists at international conferences and conventions.

11. Membership lists of organizations or clubs which are sometimes procurable.

PROBLEMS OF LANGUAGE AND CUSTOM

The sampling operations in international surveys follow the same principles as in domestic research, but it is an advantage if the samplers know the language of the country concerned. (For example, if you do not speak Finnish or Turkish, you may have difficulty in distinguishing between the name of a firm and that of an individual.)

Someone quite familiar with the language should mark the list cards for correct addressing and personalizing. In some languages the last name is written first; in Spanish the "last" name is usually in the middle. Sr. José López García should be addressed in the salutation "Estimado Sr. López" and not "Sr. García."

It is also important to recognize "Miss" and "Mrs." in various languages, as well as titles requiring special salutations, such as "Your Excellency." For another example, Indian names may be preceded by "Shri" or "Mr.," but not both.

In all international surveys some familiarity is required with the customs and language of the countries involved. One must know that Spanish is not the language of the Philippines and, when mailing a survey to Latin America, that Brazilians resent being addressed in Spanish. In mailing to Switzerland the careful researcher will sort his list cards by cantons; a self-respecting Swiss may not mind receiving a questionnaire from the United States in English, but would certainly resent getting a German or Italian form if he happens to be from Geneva or any of the other French-speaking cantons.

Careful observation of local customs should extend to the smallest detail, down to the addressing of the reply envelopes. For example, some Latin Americans resent our acting as though we were the only "United States" and ignoring the Estados Unidos Mexicanos and Estados Unidos do Brasil. The reply envelope from a Latin American country should say "EE. UU. de N.A." (United States of North America), although their post offices will normally recognize and forward mail to "U.S.A." Brazilians, whose airmail envelopes have green and yellow borders, do not react favorably to air-mail reply envelopes with red and blue borders.

POSTAGE

Most researchers use air mail both ways on all international surveys, which means that postage will constitute a large part of the total budget. If the mailing goes to one country only, it is often possible to order reply stamps from a local post office; for example, the Canadian post office at Niagara Falls will mail stamps to the United States. However, in most surveys where a large number of countries are involved and only a small number of stamps is required from most of them, it would be wasteful to try to buy or order these stamps from each country. In that case the stamps have to be ordered from stamp dealers in the United States, and adequate delivery time and money needed for this purpose must be allocated. For worldwide surveys, one must order the foreign stamps about six weeks before the mailing date, and the reply postage for the average mailing may cost about twice as much as the outgoing postage. The stamp dealer will usually know the postage rates of various countries. Except for mail to Canada and Mexico, which may be sent at domestic rates, the minimum United States air-mail charge for a foreign letter covers half an ounce (about 15 grams), while in many other countries the basic air-mail postage covers only 5 or 10 grams. This means that a questionnaire and reply envelope which weigh just under half an ounce will be over the minimum weight in some countries and additional postage must be affixed.

In addition to air-mail envelopes and letterheads, the researcher should also use special light-weight paper for the questionnaire. This paper has to be opaque, to prevent the printing from showing through, and sturdy enough to take writing and handling wear. A 14-pound opaque bond is usually adequate.

The question often arises, Why not mail from abroad to reduce mailing costs? The answer is that the percentage return is higher if the mailing is done from the United States. Consider the relative attention-getting value of a letter which you receive from your own city as against one which you may get from New Delhi, Santiago, or Oslo. On some international surveys the effect of pro-American or anti-American bias may be lessened by sending the mailing out with United Nations postage stamps. However, in that case the questionnaires must be mailed from the United Nations post office in New York.

There is no easy way of saving postage. Omission of the stamped reply envelope reduces returns. This is also true even if international reply coupons are enclosed in place of the stamps. The coupons have to be exchanged at the post office for stamps, and people do not like to be inconvenienced.

RESPONSE RATE AND LANGUAGE

The author has found that people in any free country are as likely to answer a mail questionnaire as those of similar socioeconomic groups in the United States. On international surveys the aim should be a better than 50 percent response. This may often require several mailings and an incentive either offered to respondents or sent with the questionnaire. As in domestic surveys, the prestige of the sender may take the place of incentives. For example, a four-page questionnaire mailed by the *National Geographic* magazine to a random sample of 3,000 of its foreign subscribers in 32 countries was completed and returned by 78 percent of the sample. No incentive was used and just one follow-up mailing was sent to nonrespondents.[1] However, this is unusual. Normally a premium (incentive) is needed to get a high return—just as in the case of mail surveys in the United States. Incentives can range from ball-point pens, lighters, prints, and maps to books, stamps, and money. Postal and customs regulations of each country should be checked to see that the premium intended to be used is admissible, and not subject to duty.

The language of the survey is always a question. In some areas, such as Holland and the Scandinavian countries, most people read English. In other areas only a very small segment of the population would understand a questionnaire in English. There is no problem when the mailing list consists of the subscribers to an English language publication, like *Time International*, but in other cases the language of the country to which we are mailing should be used. Some international mail surveys are sent out in half a dozen or more languages. In a survey mailed to banking experts who attended an international conference in Japan (where the official languages of the conference were Japanese, French, and English) the questionnaires were printed with English text on one side and French on the reverse side. Of course this questionnaire was not sent to the Japanese bankers. Unless there is a specific reason to use English in a mailing to another country, it is not advisable to do so. It may cut down the rate of response because those who do not read and write English will not answer, and the results will be biased because the characteristics of the (English-speaking) respondents may be quite different from those of the nonrespondents (most of whom may not speak English).

The ideal person to translate the questionnaire and the accompanying letter is a bilingual native of the country surveyed. For example, a letter may be adequately translated into Spanish by someone who has mastered the language. His translation may be grammatically correct, but he may not be familiar enough with Spanish customs to realize that Spanish business correspondence requires more polite (to our eyes, more flowery) forms and expressions than English and that a "correct" translation may sound rather brusque to the recipient. Going one step further, a translator born and educated in Spain or Argentina is unlikely to to know that in Puerto Rico a United States quarter is called "una peseta."

If the survey is addressed to an English-speaking audience (for example, subscribers to an English language publication), it is still important to scrutinize the letter and questionnaire for words and expressions which may be ambiguous or even offensive to a non-American. Words like "apartment" versus "flat", measurements such as "mile" versus "kilometer," and expressions such as "household head" have to be examined to make sure that the questions will be understood and that the answers will be specific. "Far East" is not a term to be used in surveys mailed to Japan or any other "Far Eastern" nation. They ask, "Far East from where?"

THE INCOME QUESTION

It is not easy to word a question on income which (1) will be answered at all and (2) will be answered with a minimum of bias or ambiguity. The question has to be rather explicit to achieve this result. The following question, which the author has often used in international surveys, gives good results, with an average of only about 8 percent "No Answers."

> What do you estimate is the total income of yourself and your immediate family living in your home (including salary, interest, dividends, rents, royalties, etc.)? You may give this on an annual, monthly or

weekly basis, whichever is most convenient. (Please show it in the currency in which you are paid and specify the monetary unit below, e.g., Rupees, Yen, Francs, etc. Do not use $ sign.)

___ annually   ___ monthly   ___ weekly

Of course the respondent cannot be asked to list his income in United States currency. The conversion must be done in the tabulating phase of the survey. Up-to-date conversion tables may readily be obtained for this purpose. It is important not to misinterpret $ signs; they do *not* always mean United States dollars (they can stand, for example, for Mexican pesos).

As a help in tabulating the income question, and possibly a number of other questions, we must know the country of residence of the respondent. If this has not been specifically asked and the questionnaire is not keyed, the country of origin should be taken from the reply envelope and marked on the questionnaire. It is usually helpful to sort the returns by country before editing and coding.

OPEN-END QUESTIONS

Of course if there are open-end questions, such as occupation, reasons, opinions, the editors and coders must be able to understand the language in which the replies are written. They must even know that a European 1 looks very much like our figure 7 and that their (handwritten) number 7 has a stroke across it: 7. They must know something about the educational vocabulary of the countries involved and have at least a nodding acquaintance with such terms as "licencié," "Privatdozent," and "don" as used in England if they have to tabulate the answers to questions on education or degrees. Job titles vary greatly; for example, in Europe the executive title "director" is very common and sometimes hard to reconcile with an American equivalent. In short, it helps if you know what you are doing.

Most people are cooperative all over the world, but they are more likely to be responsive if one takes the trouble of studying and understanding their point of view.

REFERENCE

1. "Outside USA. National Geographic Atlantic Edition and Pacific Edition Subscriber Characteristics" (research report), March, 1967.

Note: Parts of this chapter were contained in an article by the author published in the English and French language *Newsletter* of May, 1966, of the World Association for Public Opinion Research.

TWENTY-FIVE
Evaluating Mail Surveys

NUMEROUS LISTS OF CRITERIA EXIST for the evaluation of various types of surveys or of specific phases of survey work. Checklists and guidance booklets have been published by associations such as the Advertising Research Foundation,[1] the American Marketing Association,[2] the Associated Business Publications,[3] and the Marketing Communications Research Center.[4] Publications such as the *Journal of Marketing Research*[5] and *Media/Scope*[6] have also published checklists for evaluating surveys, or articles on the evaluation of some phases of survey work.

The checklist which follows, is an attempt to enumerate the essential considerations for evaluating a mail survey. For more detailed discussions of any of the points listed, the reader can consult the appropriate chapter of this book.

This checklist has two uses. The researcher may consult the list when planning and executing his survey to make sure that he has not overlooked any important consideration. The user of the findings of a survey or the reader of a research report may want to check the list to see that the survey in question is not deficient in some important area. Of course most reports would not contain answers to all the questions raised in the following list, but if the reader considers any such question important, the researcher should always be able to furnish the information needed even if it is not printed in the report.

SPONSOR, PURPOSE, AND SURVEY DESIGN

1. Who is the sponsor of the survey? Who ordered it and who is paying for it?

2. What is the purpose of the survey? If not stated, is it obvious? If stated, is it reasonable to expect such a purpose to be fulfilled by a survey, and more particularly, by a mail survey?

3. What is the universe surveyed? Is it really relevant for the purposes and goals stated? Does the universe include all people who are important for the stated purposes of this research and few or no others?

4. What is the sampling plan? Is it acceptable in method and scope?

5. Who did the sampling: the sponsor of the survey, an outside research organization, or the owner of the lists? Whose plan was it? Who prepared the sampling specifications?

6. What was the origin, composition, date, and previous use, if any, of the mailing lists?

7. How was the actual sampling operation done? By hand? By computer? Some other way? How was it supervised and checked? Were there any data available for the universe, such as geographic distribution, against which the sample could be checked? Was it checked?

8. Who conducted the survey? Does the company have the proper qualifications to do the job, such as experience with similar surveys, sufficient trained staff and equipment? Does it do its own tabulating? If it farms out tabulation, what supervision does it provide? Did a qualified project director handle the survey?

9. In whose name and on whose stationery was the survey mailed? Can this name introduce any kind of bias in a survey of this type by influencing answers or by making it likely that one specific segment of the sample is more apt to return the questionnaire than another?

10. What was the timing of the survey, and could it have biased the results in any way? Can the results unwittingly reflect a seasonal

pattern? Were there events shortly before or during the survey period which could have influenced replies?

11. Was there a pilot study? What was its method and scope? Who conducted it? Were the returns from the pilot study included among the questionnaires tabulated in the mail survey? Are the questionnaires used for the pilot study and those used for the main survey identical?

12. What was the actual data-gathering method? Did the various waves include advance notice, reminders, follow-up mailings with another questionnaire, further follow-ups with other data-gathering techniques? Is each of these steps described? Are they all sound?

THE QUESTIONNAIRE

13. Does the questionnaire include all questions which can be important for the purpose of the survey as well as those needed to provide classification and other data important for analysis? Are all questions relevant to the purpose of the survey or needed for some other reason?

14. Was the layout of the questionnaire such that it encouraged clear answers?

15. Was the questionnaire construction satisfactory? Were all questions of a nature that the respondent can be expected to answer without guessing? Would they strain his memory unreasonably? Would any question concern confidential information? Is there a judicious choice between open-end and check questions? Can the answers listed on check questions limit or bias information?

16. Is the questionnaire clear of bias? Can there be any bias resulting from the title of the questionnaire? Does any question give away the identity of the sponsor when this could be a biasing factor? Was any effort made to avoid subject bias? Can a lack of filter questions introduce bias? If there are long lists of check-question answers, were the listed items rotated (using a split sample) to avoid fatigue bias? Could any bias have crept in because of psychological reasons, such as respondents showing off or not wishing to be embarrassed? Could the order of questions introduce bias by making one question influence the answers to a subsequent one? Could any of the questions themselves, an expression or a word, have a biasing influence?

17. Does the questionnaire avoid any ambiguity? Are the questions, headings, and instructions in the body of the questionnaire helpful in getting precise answers and minimizing the need for editing?

18. Can it be reasonably expected that the questionnaire elicited complete and meaningful answers and that these were of a nature which could be tabulated and analyzed without omissions or distortions?

DATA-GATHERING

19. Was the text of all cards, accompanying letters of various waves of mailing and any other communications made in connection with the survey, truthful and free of biasing elements?

20. If any incentives were used, what were they, and were they enclosed or promised upon return? Could they have introduced any bias?

21. To whom was the reply envelope addressed? Can there be any biasing factor in the name of the person, of the organization, or of the address? (A survey among subscribers to a denominational publication was mailed from New York. Some of the recipients protested to the publication against receiving their questionnaire from such a sinful place. The follow-up mailing was sent out from the city where the main church is located.)

22. Are mailing versus return figures given for each wave? What was the number of undeliverables? Was an attempt made to readdress and remail them whenever possible? How many refusals, blank returns, and incomplete returns were there, and how many usable answers? Are the mailing and closing dates given for each wave?

23. What is the number of final completed returns? What percentage is this of the total net mailing? Were all these returns used in the tabulations?

24. Is the percentage of response high enough to be representative of the sample as a whole? Can the returns be checked against mailouts by geographic distribution, by subsamples, or by any other known characteristics?

25. If the response rate is not considered high enough to be representative of the total sample, was any attempt made (*a*) to establish the answers or, at least, the characteristics of nonrespondents by interviewing a random sample, using telephone or personal interviews or (*b*) to arrive at similar results by weighting nonresponse by some system developed from successive waves of returns? Was any such method clearly described, and does it meet statistical and research standards?

26. Who opened the envelopes, the sponsor or the research firm? If there were several waves of mailing, was proper care taken to avoid

tabulating duplicate questionnaires from the same respondent or the same respondent-household? Was the state of origin established by a question, a code, or information copied from the reply envelope?

DATA-PROCESSING

27. Was the editing of the questionnaires a carefully planned operation? Do written editing instructions exist? Was all editing of all questionnaires done under the supervision of one chief editor? How was it checked?

28. Who built the codes for open-end questions? How was this done? Did the sponsor approve the codes? Is there any chance that the code setups (or precoding) may have introduced a bias?

29. Was a single supervisor in charge of all coding? Did all coders have written codes and coding instructions? How was the coding checked?

30. Was the punching and verifying done on the same premises as the coding? If not, how were they controlled? How was verification handled, and what percentage of the work was verified? What was the result of the verification?

31. What check was employed to ensure that all answers to all questionnaires were punched and that none were punched twice?

32. Were consistency checks made on all columns? How were the corrections made for any inconsistencies found during this process?

33. What kind of equipment was used for tabulation? Were all possible checks built into the tabulating programs?

34. If any weighting was done, what was the principle and how was it done—mechanically or arithmetically? Was it checked?

35. How were all other calculations, such as percentages, averages, and medians arrived at? How were they checked? Were the actual answers used for calculating averages and medians, or were these figured from frequency distributions?

THE FINAL REPORT

36. Who prepared the final report—the sponsoring organization, the research house, or someone else? If it was published, who published it?

37. Does the report list its publication date, the date(s) of the survey, the name of the sponsoring organization, and the name of the company which conducted the survey?

38. Does the report show the actual questionnaire, the accompany-

ing letter for each wave, any advance or reminder cards or letters, and any other follow-up material?

39. Does it give a clear methodology describing all important steps of the survey? Does it describe the possible limitations of the study?

40. Does it give confidence levels, and if so, is the response rate high enough to make these meaningful?

41. Is there any comparison with existing census figures, industry information, or the results of other surveys? Is this comparison relevant?

42. Is there a summary of the findings of the survey? Are these findings new and meaningful in terms of the stated purpose of the survey?

43. If there are an analysis and recommendations, are these clear, concise, and supported by the data of the survey? Is the representativeness of the the survey high enough to justify drawing these conclusions and making the recommendations?

44. Are the tabulations of answers to all questions included in the report? If not, why not? Are all relevant cross tabulations shown? Is the report cluttered with irrelevant breakdowns?

45. Are both numbers and percentages shown? If only percentages are reported, are the numerical bases shown for all tabulations? If the tables show weighted figures, are the unweighted bases shown?

46. Are any of the "Miscellaneous," "Don't Know" or "No Answer" figures unusually large? If so why?

47. Are "No Answer" figures shown on all questions? If they were distributed, was this justified? Is it always made clear what was done with "No Answers"?

48. Are all totals and bases indicated, and are they fully and clearly described?

49. Do all the averages and medians shown justifiably reflect the distributions from which they were calculated, and are they fully and clearly defined?

50. Are all titles, captions, and other descriptive copy correct and complete?

51. Are all cross tabulations meaningful in terms of the size of each subgroup?

52. Are all tables numerically consistent among themselves?

53. If charts are shown, are they correct and relevant?

54. If projections are shown, are they justified and correct? Do they imply greater accuracy than they should?

55. If there is any promotional material included in the report, is

it clearly distinguishable from the results of the survey? If figures are used from other sources, are these sources clearly stated?

56. If the researcher is checking his own survey, has he compared the estimated with the actual cost breakdown for various operations?

Because of limitations of time, money, and other ingredients and wherewithals of good research, few if any surveys are perfect. Imperfections in a survey need not render it useless. The user of the survey, if he is capable of evaluating both its strengths and its shortcomings, can determine the extent to which he should be guided by its results.

REFERENCES

1. "Criteria for Marketing and Advertising Research," report of the Advertising Research Foundation, New York, pp. 1–7, (undated).
2. "Criteria to Assist Users of Marketing Research," the American Marketing Association, pp. 1–21, 1962.
3. "Full Disclosure Form for Business Paper Research (Approved by the Business Paper Committee of the Association of National Advertisers, the A.A.A.A. Committee on Business Publications and the A.B.P. Advertiser/Agency Relations Committee)," Association of National Advertisers, Inc., pp. 1–6, January, 1966.
4. "Yardsticks for Evaluating Industrial Advertising Research," Industrial Advertising Research Institute (now Marketing Communications Research Center), pp. 1–11, 1954.
5. Charles S. Mayer, "Evaluating the Quality of Marketing Research Contracts," *Journal of Marketing Research*, vol. 4, no. 2, pp. 134–141, May, 1967.
6. Arthur J. Morgan, "How to Judge Media Research Done by Mail Surveys," *Media/Scope*, vol. 3, no. 2, pp. 76–79, February, 1959; also, "Media/Scope's Media Research Check List" (foldout), *Media/Scope*, vol. 9, no. 8, August, 1955.

TWENTY-SIX
Ethical Standards in Mail Research

IT IS NOT THE PURPOSE of this chapter to preach a sermon. The unscrupulous are not impressed by lectures, and honest people do not need them. However, the author's many years of experience seem to indicate that in the research field there exist more "crimes" of omission than of commission. Some people who conduct surveys, and many more who use and promote survey findings, do not even realize that what they are doing may be improper. It may be useful to list some of the obligations which the researcher has (1) to the sponsor of the survey, (2) to the respondents, (3) to readers of the report other than the sponsor, and (4) to businesses, organizations, or persons who might be hurt through improper use of the findings.

The following are the ethical considerations the researcher ought to keep in mind concerning the sponsor of the survey:

THE SURVEY AND THE SPONSOR

Can the survey be conducted by mail, and if so, is this the most desirable method under the circumstances? Chapter 2 lists the limitations of mail surveys, and the researcher should not suggest or accept the job if any of these limitations might jeopardize the reliability of the survey.

The researcher should conduct the survey according to accepted research standards. Beyond acceptability, he should do his best to conduct the optimum survey within the budget and time span available for it. If in his opinion the money and time available are not sufficient for an adequate survey, he should refuse the job; but once he accepts the assignment, he should try to do as nearly perfect a survey as he can.

He should refuse any job which is biased in any way. This is always in the best interests of the sponsor in the long run, although the latter often fails to appreciate it. A few examples from the author's experience follow:

A survey conducted among the subscribers to a publication was closed after one follow-up mailing. The response rate was quite high. When the survey was repeated two years later, the publisher remarked that the follow-up mailing seemed to result in replies from subscribers who had a lower average income than the respondents to the first mailing. Consequently he questioned the value of the follow-up mailing, as it not only cost more money, but weakened the publication's story to its advertisers. The researcher explained that the weaker story happened to be the true one and that no self-respecting research man would consent to omit the follow-up mailing when such an omission would obviously result in distorted findings. When it was put to him in that way, the publisher had to agree.

The manufacturer of an industrial product needed a survey to establish the image of the company and of the product among actual and potential users. He wanted to mail a questionnaire to all people on their promotion list. He was told that his plan would give his company biased results because their list included only a small fraction of all potential users of the product and these people were likely to be influenced by the promotional material previously sent to them. The sponsor decided to have two subsamples: one from his own list and another of potential users not on his list.

The publisher of an industrial magazine decided to conduct a survey among engineers. The proposed questionnaire mainly concerned engineering and various aspects of the engineer's work. This was followed by a readership section which listed ten publications: five engineering and industrial magazines (including the sponsor's) and other general magazines such as *Business Week, Newsweek,* and *Time.* Several questions were proposed on the frequency of reading each publication and their usefulness to the respondent. The researcher turned down the assignment on the ground that the questionnaire created a general frame of reference which biased the answers to the readership questions in favor of the industrial and against the general publications.

These three examples illustrate three common types of bias: those of method, those of the sample, and those of the questionnaire. It is the researcher's duty to detect them and either eliminate them or reject the job.

OBLIGATIONS TO THE SPONSOR

Once the researcher is satisfied that the requirements of the sponsor are acceptable and that he can design a reliable survey, he should adhere to the instructions of the sponsor and not change any specifications without his agreement.

Confidential information should never be divulged without the permission of the sponsor. Such information may include the name of the sponsoring organization, information about its business obtained in connection with the research, lists of other data purchased or compiled for the survey, and the results of the project.

The researcher must be willing and able to stand behind his method of research and his findings and furnish any explanations about them required by the sponsor. Any material used for the survey, such as completed questionnaires, punched cards, and tabulations, should be made available to the sponsor upon request. No such material should be destroyed without his permission or without due notice.

Estimated costs should not be increased without the agreement of the sponsor. If he specifies a change in the research design or execution, he should be informed of any effect it may have on cost.

THE PUBLIC AND THE RESPONDENTS

The rescarcher cannot ignore obligations toward the public in general and respondents in particular.

A survey cannot be a disguise for any other activity, such as sales or establishing data on individual firms important to the sponsor. Even if the respondent's name is typed on the questionnaire before mailing, or even if he himself furnishes it upon request, none but statistical use should be made of any findings, unless such use was clearly and unequivocally spelled out in the questionnaire or the accompanying letter.

If a questionnaire is keyed in any way, the letter and the text of the form itself should not call it "Anonymous" and should not imply anonymity by using a phrase like "There is no need to sign your name."

If the letter or questionnaire states that the information is confidential, the answers of individual respondents should never be identified to the sponsor or any other person or firm unless the mailing was sent out in their name.

It is the researcher's obligation to fulfill any promise made to respondents for completing the questionnaire, such as the sending out of premiums or copies of the report.

The researcher also has certain obligations toward users of the findings or readers of the survey report other than the sponsor.

He should not endorse a report which in any way misrepresents the findings or contains inaccuracies.

He should require that any published report contain a full disclosure of methodology and sampling plan as well as answers to all questions asked.

He should not tolerate the publication of misleading partial findings.

PROPER USE OF THE FINDINGS

In connection with this last point there is one further group which is of concern to the ethical researcher, and these are the persons, firms, or organizations that may suffer damage due to unprincipled use of the findings. This often happens in competitive surveys sponsored by manufacturers and media. It is the researcher's duty to advise against, try to prevent, or protest against publicity, promotion, or advertising which uses findings in a misleading way or makes unfounded promotional claims supposedly based on the survey. This kind of problem usually arises not because someone wants to be dishonest, but because nonresearchers do not always realize the importance of precision when quoting survey findings. It may not be obvious to the publisher or promotion director of a magazine that it makes all the difference in the world whether a sample is identified as "top executives" or "top executives on our complimentary list." The advertising manager of a manufacturer may miss the point that not 20 percent of all housewives use his brand, but 20 percent of all housewives *who use this type of product* are users of his brand. The difference between the two statements can be several million housewives.

A number of associations connected with surveys and research have adopted codes of ethics, including the American Association for Public Opinion Research,[1] the Market Research Society of Great Britain,[2] and the World Association for Public Opinion Research.[3]

In the conduct of mail surveys one should always be conscious of these rules and avoid breaking any of them by acts of either commission or omission.

REFERENCES

1. "Code of Professional Ethics and Practices," Article IX of the Certificate of Incorporation and By-laws of the American Association for Public Opinion Research, pp. 14–16, filed Nov. 1, 1963.
2. "Code of Standards in Market Research" (as adopted by the Market Research Society of Great Britain), A. H. Davies and O. W. Palmer, *Market Research and Scientific Distribution*, London, Blanford Press, pp. 206–209, 1957.
3. "Code of Professional Ethics and Practices" of the World Association for Public Opinion Research, in the "directory" of WAPOR, pp. 7–9, October, 1968.

APPENDIX
Percentage and Speed of Response

It may interest the reader to look at the percentage-of-response statistics of questionnaires sent out on all domestic surveys conducted by the author's market research company during a period of about four years.

The following table is based on 415 separate studies and surveys and represents a total mailing of 771,004 questionnaires. The jobs range from small pilot studies of 200 or fewer questionnaires to major research projects with mailings to 10,000 or 20,000 people. They include surveys of subscribers to publications, industrial surveys, research among businessmen and professional groups, consumer surveys, and a variety of other types of research. A few of the surveys included some mailings to Canada.

Percentage of return (one mailing)	Number and % of jobs	
Less than 30%	20	5%
30 to 39%	30	7%
40 to 49%	73	18%
50 to 59%	128	31%
60 to 69%	99	24%
70 to 79%	56	13%
80% or more	9	2%
Total Jobs	415	100%
Total number of questionnaires mailed	771,004	
Median response to one mailing	57%	

The above figures do not include follow-up mailings of any kind. Some of the response rates are low. A number of these represent pilot surveys or experimental mailings of small samples. In some cases the results of the pilot study resulted in the discontinuance of the survey; in other instances they led to the use of follow-up mailings with proper incentives.

Incentives were included in many of these original mailings. The most frequently used incentive was a new 25¢ coin, which was included in 330 of the 415 surveys. Since incentives influence the response rate quite strongly, this large group of surveys with the unused quarter incentive has been selected for further analysis. Other incentives used on some of the other surveys included dimes, dollar bills, the offer of books or reports to respondents, etc.

SIZE AND NUMBER OF PAGES

The next table shows the response rate to the 330 surveys analyzed by size of page and number of pages in the questionnaire. "Small" size means smaller than 8½ by 11 in. (usually monarch size). "Large" size means 8½ by 11 in. with the exception of three surveys for which slightly larger questionnaires were used. In the "more than two pages" group four-page questionnaires were used in seventy surveys, five-page forms in three studies, and a three-page questionnaire in one case.

Of course each survey's response rate is influenced by many other factors, such as respondents' interest in the subject and the nature of the sample. Nevertheless, the above analysis by size and length of the questionnaire indicates that the number of pages can make a difference. Compare one-page (one-side) questionnaires with those of two or more pages. Size of the page seems to be a very important factor in the case of one-page questionnaires.

Actually the differences in the rate of response caused by the size and length of the questionnaire are considerably larger than this table would indicate. The research house always aims at high rates of response and would recommend the use of a long questionnaire *only*

	One-mailing response rate				Number of surveys (100%)	Median response rate
	Under 50%	50% to 59%	60% to 69%	70% or over		
All surveys with 25¢ incentives	26%	33%	24%	17%	330	57%
Questionnaire:						
One page (one side)						
Any size	11%	28%	28%	33%	116	63%
Small	9%	27%	27%	37%	101	65%
Large	20%	40%	33%	7%	15	58%
Two pages (one, leaf two sides)						
Any size	35%	33%	23%	9%	140	56%
Small	26%	38%	29%	7%	70	56%
Large	44%	27%	19%	10%	70	52%
More than two pages						
Any size	32%	39%	22%	7%	74	54%
Small	35%	28%	30%	7%	43	55%
Large	29%	55%	10%	6%	31	54%

How to read this table: Of 116 surveys with one-page questionnaires, 33% achieved a 70% or better response after one mailing.

when favorable circumstances, such as specific interest in the subject matter of the questionnaire or the prestige of the sponsoring organization, make a high return rate possible. This explains why the median response rate of the large-sized four-page questionnaires is higher than that of the large-sized two-pager. Everything else being equal, these particular results would be reversed.

The purpose of this table is to demonstrate that (1) using proper techniques respectable response rates can be achieved on the first mailings of questionnaires of various lengths and (2) that despite the best efforts of the research man, the longer questionnaires will in general not obtain as high a response rate as the short ones.

THE SECOND WAVE

The chart in Figure 54 shows the response pattern to the first and second waves of 103 surveys, which represent all mail surveys with two or more waves conducted by one research house in a given time period. Once more these include all kinds of mail surveys, incorporating many variables. Figure 54 indicates the effect of a second wave (some with incentives and some without) on these jobs. It shows, for example, that on the surveys where the response to the first mailing was 50 percent, the total response after two mailings would be approximately 60 to 65 percent on the same kind of survey.

Again, because incentives play such an important part in getting high rates of return, separate charts are shown according to some of the incentives used.

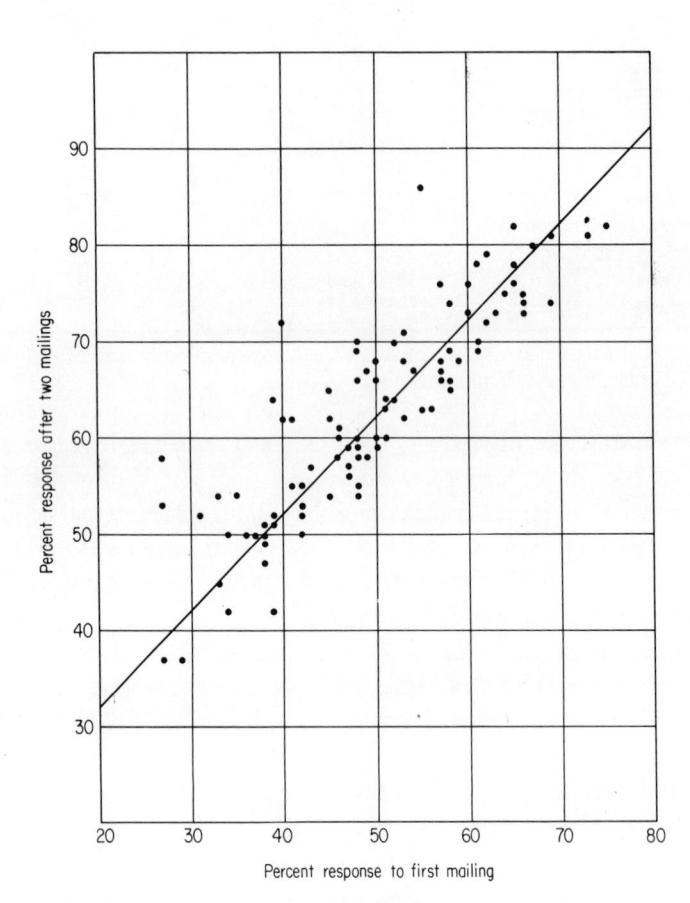

FIGURE 54 Response pattern to the first and second waves of 103 surveys. How to read this chart: On a survey where the response to the first mailing was 50%, the return after two mailings would be between 60 and 65%.

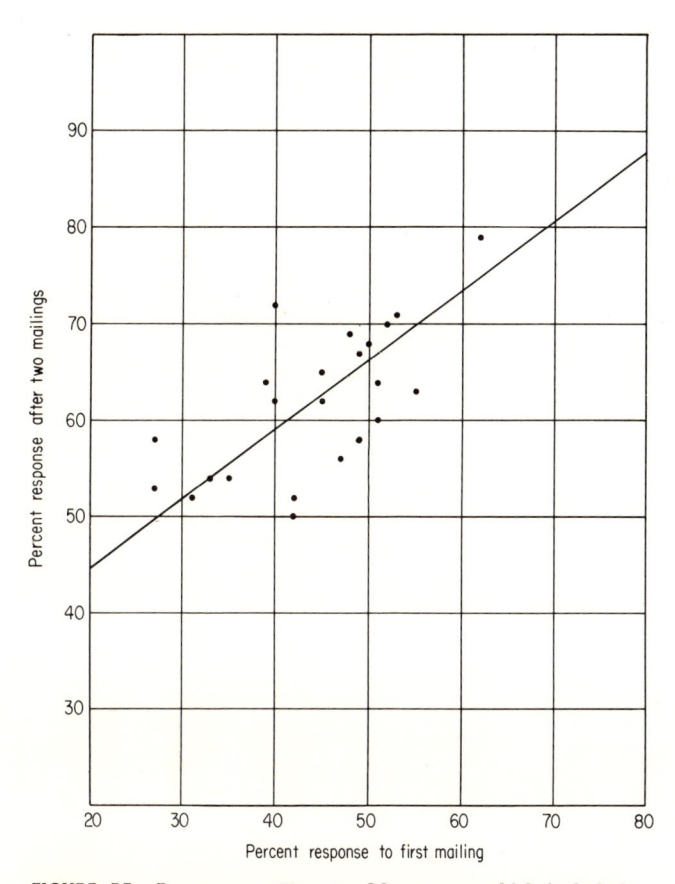

FIGURE 55 Response pattern to 23 surveys which included a 25¢ incentive in the first mailing and a dollar bill in the second wave.

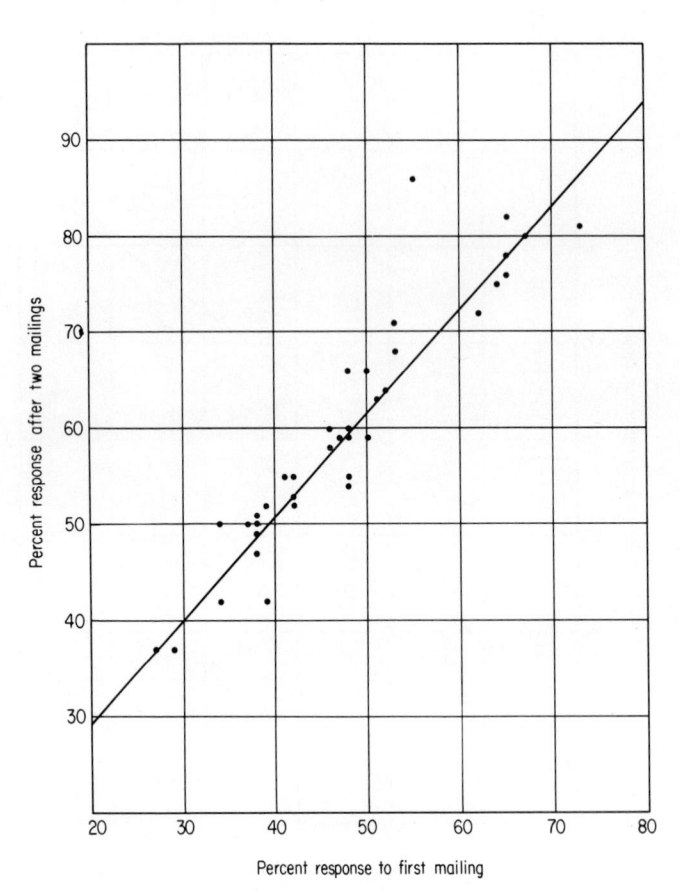

FIGURED 56 Response pattern to 39 surveys which included a 25¢ incentive in both the first and second mailings.

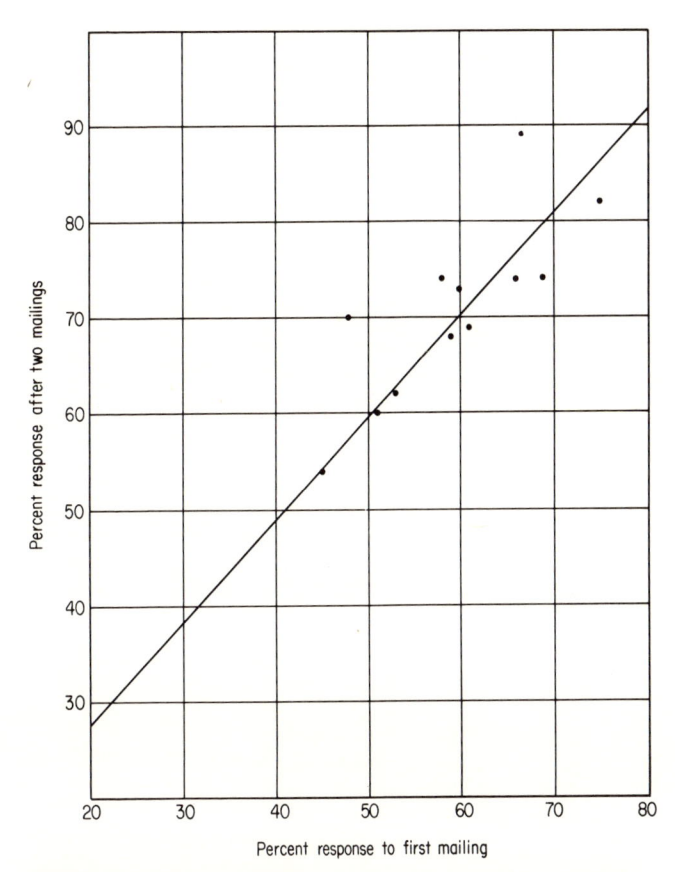

FIGURE 57 Response pattern to 11 surveys which included a 25¢ incentive in the first mailing and no premium in the second.

Figures 55, 56, and 57 are based on seventy-three surveys which were mailed out with a 25¢ coin incentive in the first mailing and were followed up by a second wave, which included a crisp new dollar bill, or another 25¢ coin, or no incentive.

The charts show the effect of the various incentives—and the importance of the first mailing results in determining the total return, including follow-ups.

THE SPEED OF RESPONSE

The research man must often estimate how soon a survey can be closed for processing or how soon a particular mailing can be closed and a follow-up wave sent out. Actual experience is valuable for this type of estimating.

The following table is based on the daily counts of reply envelopes received on fifty surveys. These fifty studies totaled 44,645 returns, and include various types of surveys conducted by the author's research company. They were nationwide, the mailings were made from New York, and returns were sent to the same city. In all cases of distant addresses questionnaires went by air both ways: this affected the speed of response. Many surveys can be closed after three weeks: on these fifty surveys the additional response after three weeks was less than 3 percent.

Number of days (after mailing date)	Average percentage (of the total returns received by the 21st day after mailing date)
7 (1 week)	72%
8	78%
9	83%
10	86%
11	88%
12	89%
13	92%
14 (2 weeks)	94%
15	95%
16	96%
17	98%
18	98%
19	99%
20	99%
21 (3 weeks)	100%
Base: (Number of surveys)	50
Total number of questionnaires returned on these surveys	44,645

How to read this table: On the 50 surveys, an average of 94% of the total 3-week response had already been received 14 days (2 weeks) after the mailing date.

The table shows the average percentage of replies to the fifty surveys received each day from the seventh to the twenty-first day after the mailing. Percentages for individual jobs were based on the total number of returns received by the twenty-first day, and the table shows the average of these percentages. Analysis by the day of the week on which mailings were made shows no important differences in the speed of return caused by the day of mailing.

Glossary

The definitions given in the glossary describe the meanings of words as used in this book.

ADDRESSEE A person to whom a mail questionnaire is sent in the hope that he will become a respondent. He is an addressee, however, whether or not he chooses to answer.

ADDRESSOGRAPH (Trademark) A machine using metal or plastic plates for addressing.

ADVANCE CARD OR LETTER A communication sent to advise people that they will shortly receive a questionnaire.

ALPHABETIC PUNCHING The keypunching of letters, as opposed to numbers, on the punch card.

ANALYSIS (1) An examination of component parts in their relationship to the whole. (2) A report which is more interpretive and in greater depth than a mere summary or tabulation of the findings.

ANCILLARY SURVEY Further research among a specific group of respondents to a previous survey.

AUDIT BUREAU OF CIRCULATION (ABC) An organization which receives and verifies statements regarding the circulation figures of print media.

AVERAGE (1) In statistics, a number which in some definite way represents all numbers of a group (such as a mean, median, or mode). (2) Commonly used as a synonym for the arithmetic mean. (see MEAN.)

BASE (1) A number used as a standard of reference; usually the total number of individuals or items whose characteristics are described in a table. (2) In a percentaged distribution, the number which is equal to 100 percent.

BASIC CARD In machine tabulation, the punched card containing the main data from a questionnaire (as opposed to TRAILER CARD).

"BEFORE AND AFTER" SURVEYS Surveys conducted before and after a special event, such as a sales effort or advertising campaign, in order to gauge its effect.

BIAS A systematic distortion in the collection, processing, analysis, or interpretation of research data (as opposed to a random or chance error).

BOLD TYPE Type face in which the strokes are broader than normal, making the copy stand out.

BREAK, BREAKDOWN See CROSS TABULATION.

BUREAU OF THE CENSUS A bureau of the U.S. Department of Commerce, responsible for decennial censuses of the population and other censuses and surveys for business, agriculture, etc.

BURSTING Separating the pages of continuous printout forms from each other.

CAPS Capital letters, uppercase type.

CASE HISTORY (1) The description of a special event or series of events used as an example, such as a particular survey. (2) The answer requested to some open-end questions concerning a specific experience of the respondent.

CENSUS A complete enumeration of a group (universe) at a point in time with respect to specific characteristics; as contrasted with the partial enumeration associated with a sample.

CENSUS DISTRICTS (U.S.) The nine geographic divisions of the United States used by the Bureau of the Census: New England, Middle Atlantic, East North Central, West North Central, South Atlantic, East South Central, West South Central, Mountain, and Pacific.

CHART An illustration representing a table in graphic form by means of bars, graphs, or other visual aids.

CHECK BOX A square for checking off an answer on a questionnaire.

CHECK QUESTION A question which is to be answered by placing a check or X in spaces or boxes provided for that purpose.

CIRCULATION FIGURES The total number of copies of a publication sold at newsstands plus those delivered to subscribers or other eligible recipients.

CLASS INTERVAL   In a table or distribution the difference between the lower limit of a group (class) and the lower limit of the next higher group; e.g., in the age groups 35 to 44 years and 45 to 54 years, the class interval is 10 years.

CLASSIFICATION QUESTIONS   Those designed to elicit classification data.

CLASSIFICATION DATA   Demographic or other information used to describe the composition of a sample.

CLEANING (CARDS)   The elimination of inconsistencies and erroneous punches found by means of consistency checks and normally corrected by reference to the questionnaires.

CLOSING DATE (OF A MAILING OR SURVEY)   The date after which no further questionnaires are counted as returns to that wave or survey.

CLUSTER SAMPLING   A random selection of a group of contiguous individuals or families instead of the separate random selection of each individual or family (e.g., a sample may consist of clusters in specific cities).

CODE   (n.) A number or symbol employed to express a word or a sentence. (v.) To convert written answers into codes. An operation performed by coders.

CODE BOOKLET   A set of code sheets or pages which contain all the codes used for a questionnaire and the instructions for using them.

CODE-RANGE CHECK   A part of the cleaning operations which ascertains that columns of a punched card have no punch in any position other than those specified in the coding instructions.

CODER   See CODE.

COLLATING (CARDS)   Comparing and merging two or more similarly ordered decks of cards into one ordered deck.

COLLATOR   A machine which merges sets of punched cards into a sequence and performs other card selecting and matching operations.

COLUMN   (1) A vertical single digit arrangement in a tabulating card. (2) A vertical series of figures in a table.

COLUMN HEAD, HEADING   Descriptive material at the top of a column defining the group to which the data apply.

COMPETITIVE SURVEY   A survey in which respondents are asked to compare media, products or companies.

COMPUTER   An electronic device capable of solving problems by accepting data, performing prescribed operations on them, and supplying the results of these operations.

CONCEPT TEST   A survey which seeks to determine attitudes toward a novel product or service which may not yet exist.

CONFIDENTIAL DATA, INFORMATION   (1) Information which respondents may not wish (or be permitted) to give. (2) Information whose dissemination or use is limited by the terms under which it has been given to a researcher or obtained from a questionnaire or survey.

CONSISTENCY CHECKS   The systematic comparison of data to eliminate logical inconsistencies.

CONTROL   An accepted standard, against which a survey or test is measured.

CONTROL GROUP   A group against which the results of a survey are matched. Usually they are so selected that all known characteristics are the same as (or similar to) those of the research or test sample except for the single item under study.

CORPORATE IMAGE   The pattern of beliefs and attitudes held by the public or a segment of it in relation to a company.

CORPORATE-IMAGE SURVEY   Research designed to reflect corporate image at a point in time.

COUNTER-SORTER   A data-processing machine which sorts cards according to the position punched in a given column and simultaneously counts the cards and all punches in that column.

CREW LEADER   Supervisor of a group of interviewers working on a specific job.

CROSS TABULATION   Tabulating subgroups for purposes of comparison.

DATA-GATHERING   The obtaining of information by one or more survey or research methods.

DATA-PROCESSING   The combining and translating of individual replies into meaningful tables or summaries.

DECENNIAL CENSUS   The census of the United States population taken by the Bureau of the Census in all years ending in zero.

DEMOGRAPHIC DATA   Basic data, such as age, income, family composition, describing a population.

DEPTH INTERVIEW   An extensive personal interview in which the respondent is encouraged to talk freely on a given subject.

DIGITAL COMPUTER   An electronic device which transforms or tabulates discrete data by applying arithmetic or logical processes to them (as opposed to analog computer).

DISK (COMPUTER)   A flat circular plate on which data can be stored by selective magnetization.

DOUBLE PUNCH   See MULTIPLE PUNCHES.

DISTRIBUTION   The way in which the units of a group are divided as shown in a frequency table.

DRUM (COMPUTER)   A cylinder with a magnetic surface on which data can be stored.

DUAL-SAMPLE SURVEY   A survey conducted among two samples, each representing a different universe, for purposes of comparison.

DUMMY TABLE   A tabular setup, showing stubs and headings but lacking the figures, prepared in advance of tabulation.

EAM (ELECTRIC ACCOUNTING MACHINE)   Data-processing equipment, such as sorters, collators, and tabulators, generally using electromechanical means for processing data.

EDITING (OF QUESTIONNAIRES) The elimination of errors and inconsistencies and the correcting or completing of the answers wherever justified.

EDP (ELECTRONIC DATA-PROCESSING) The handling and processing of data by electronic devices, such as digital computers.

EFFECTIVE RETURN The response rate after weighting.

ELECTRONIC TRANSFER Reproducing information electronically from microfilm into magnetic computer tape.

ENUMERATOR A term applied to an interviewer as for example in the United States Decennial Census.

ETHICAL BRAND (DRUGS) A brand promoted only to members of the medical, dental, and pharmaceutical professions for use in prescriptions.

EXPANDED (RETURN, FIGURE) Weighted returns or figures, counting each answer as more than one.

FACSIMILE SIGNATURE Reproduction of a signature on form letters.

FIELD (ON A PUNCHED CARD) A given number of columns on a punch card set aside for the recording of a particular type of classification or information (e.g., multidigit numerals or name and address).

FILL-IN (MATCHING) Part of an accompanying letter, usually the personalized salutation, typed to match the body of the letter.

FILTER QUESTION A question whose answer determines whether a succeeding question or section should be answered or skipped by the respondent.

FOLLOW-UP MAILING A second, third, etc., mailing to addressees of a mail survey. Usually sent to nonrespondents and frequently containing another copy of the questionnaire.

FORMAT The size, shape, type, and general appearance or makeup of a piece of printed or graphic material.

FRAME A list, map, or other specification which physically designates every element in a population; used for sampling.

FREE RESPONSE See OPEN-END QUESTION.

GENERATION (OF COMPUTERS) A somewhat arbitrary division of successive types of computers, marked by substantial improvements in technology; e.g., the replacement of vacuum tubes by transistors.

GROSS MAILING The total number of questionnaires sent out in a mailing (as opposed to NET MAILING).

IMAGE See CORPORATE IMAGE.

INCENTIVE A gift either enclosed with a questionnaire or promised to the respondent as an inducement to cooperate in a survey.

INDUSTRIAL SURVEY A survey conducted among officers and employees of manufacturers or other companies, usually about products and services they use (as opposed to "consumer survey").

INTERPRETER   An EAM machine (or keypunch device) which prints out the data punched in a tabulating card onto the card.

INTERVIEWER   The person who asks the questions and records the answers in a telephone or personal interview survey.

KEY, KEYED MAILING   A key is a number or code which identifies a questionnaire with the respondent or addressee. A keyed mailing is one which uses keys on the questionnaire or reply envelope.

KEYPUNCH   A keyboard-operated device which punches holes in a tabulating card to represent data.

KEYPUNCH OPERATOR   A person who operates a keypunch machine.

LAYOUT   The size, shape, and arrangement of print and other elements of a questionnaire, or other piece of graphic material.

LETTERPRESS PRINTING   Printing accomplished by pressing an inked raised surface to the paper.

LOGO   The characteristic name design of a publication or product printed from a "logotype" plate or block of type.

MAGNETIC TAPE   A tape with a magnetic surface on which data can be entered and stored by selective polarization of the surface.

MAIL SURVEY   A survey in which the questionnaires are returned by mail, after having been, in most instances, distributed by mail as well.

MAIN MAILING   The survey mailing in which the main bulk of the questionnaires are sent out, as contrasted with TEST or FOLLOW-UP mailings.

MARGINALS, MARGINAL TABULATIONS   The straight counts of a survey without reference to any breaks or cross analyses.

MARKETING RESEARCH (MARKET RESEARCH)   Systematic research activity conducted for purposes such as reducing costs, increasing sales and maximizing profits.

MARK-SENSE CARDS   Tabulating cards marked with a highly conductive graphite pencil. When these cards are fed into a special machine, the marks are converted into punched holes.

MASTHEAD UP   A questionnaire folded so that its title is showing.

MASTER QUESTIONNAIRE   A blank questionnaire marked to show the assignment of columns (and, where possible, coding positions) for answers to each question.

MEAN (ARITHMETIC)   A summation of a set of values, divided by the number of cases. Commonly referred to as the AVERAGE.

MEDIA STUDIES   Surveys designed to measure the extent and quality of the audience, the impact and other characteristics of publications, or other advertising media.

MEDIAN   The middle value of a group of values arrayed in ascending or descending order.

MEDIUM   A unit used to convey an advertising message, such as TV, radio, publications (pl. MEDIA).

MESSAGE (ADVERTISING) The story or impression which an advertiser wishes to convey to his audience.

MONARCH SIZE A common size of stationery, 7¼ by 10½ in. (with matching envelope 3⅞ by 7½ in.).

MULTIPLE ANSWERS More than one answer to a question by a respondent.

MULTIPLE-COLUMN CODE The use of more than one column to code the answers to a question.

MULTIPLE-PUNCHED COLUMN Two or more holes punched in a single column of a punch card, each representing a separate item of data.

NET MAILING The total number of questionnaires sent out, less the number which were undeliverable by reason of death, moving, etc.

NONRESPONDENT An addressee who fails to return a questionnaire.

NUMERICAL REPLY The answer to an open-end question which calls for a figure as a reply; e.g., number of years, dollars.

NEWSSTAND BUYER A purchaser of a publication at a newsstand, stationery store, supermarket, etc. (as opposed to a subscriber).

NEWSSTAND COPY A copy of a publication sold at a newsstand or similar outlet.

NO ANSWER The frequency of nonresponse to a question on a questionnaire.

MAKING GATES The method of hand-tabulating in which the first four tabs are vertical lines and the fifth a diagonal line across them.

OFFSET PRINTING A process in which the impression is transferred photographically to a plate, and then printed from the plate.

OPAQUE STOCK Printing paper on which printing doesn't show through on the opposite side.

OPEN-END QUESTION A question which calls for a free response (write-in) answer, rather than a check mark or the circling of a printed answer.

PACK To compress the answers to several questions into one column of a punch card.

PANEL A fixed sample whose members have agreed to be surveyed repeatedly or to report activities (such as purchasing) over a period of time.

PASSALONG READER A reader of a publication who has received his copy from a subscriber, a newsstand buyer, or another reader.

PENETRATION (ADVERTISING) The impact of an advertisement or campaign upon readers, viewers, or listeners.

PERSONAL INTERVIEW The completion of a questionnaire by an interviewer, who asks questions and records the answers of the respondent.

PERSONALIZED LETTER A printed or processed letter containing a (matching) fill-in of the addressee's name.

PILOT STUDY (PILOT MAILING) A small-scale test preceding a survey.

PLATE SIGNATURE See FACSIMILE SIGNATURE.

POINT (TYPE)   A unit measure for type bodies, equal to about $\frac{1}{72}$ in. This line is printed in 10-point type.

POLL   (1) A survey. (2) A survey of public opinion, often on political preferences. (See SURVEY.)

POPULATION   (1) In statistics, any finite or infinite collection of individuals. Also known as the universe. (2) In surveys, all individuals in the group to be studied.

POSITION   In card punching, the row location of a punched hole in a specific column of a punch card.

PRECODE   To print on a questionnaire the column numbers and, wherever possible, the position codes assigned to each question.

PREMIUM   See INCENTIVE.

PRETEST   See PILOT STUDY.

PRINTOUT   The output printed by a computer or other tabulating machine.

PROBABILITY SAMPLE   A sample selected according to the rules of the theory of probability. The likelihood of any unit being selected must be known.

PRODUCT TESTING   Surveying the acceptance of and preferences among products.

PROJECTION   The extension of data derived from a sample survey to a total population or universe.

PROGRAM (COMPUTER)   A plan or routine for solving a problem on a computer. "Software."

PROGRAMMER   A technician who writes or devises computer programs.

PULLING   The process of withdrawing address cards representing respondents from the pack of all mailing cards.

PUNCH CARD   A card of constant size and shape suitable for punching in a pattern. The most common arrangement contains eighty columns with twelve positions in each, but a number of other configurations exist.

RANDOM NUMBERS   An array of numbers chosen by chance where all digits occur with about equal frequency.

RANDOM SAMPLE   Sample chosen by a chance method in such a way that each individual or element in the universe has a known chance of being picked.

RANKING QUESTION   A question which requires the respondent to array items according to his preference or his belief as to their relative value. There should be only one "first," one "second," etc.

RATE OF RETURN (OR RESPONSE)   The percentage obtained by dividing the number of completed questionnaires returned by the number mailed.

RATING QUESTION   A question which calls for an evaluation of one or more items on a defined scale. The same rating may be given to more than one item.

RECAP A common abbreviation for "recapitulation." In research, the final or semifinal step in the preparation of report tables.

RECOGNITION STUDY A type of survey measuring how well companies and their products or services are known.

REJECT In machine tabulation, a card which has no punch in a particular column.

REMINDER POSTCARD A postcard follow-up to a questionnaire mailing.

REPRESENTATIVE RESPONSE A distribution of answers reflecting similar results to those which would have been achieved with a 100 percent response.

REPRESENTATIVE SAMPLE A sample which reflects the characteristics of the population from which it has been chosen.

REPRODUCER A machine which punches data from one card into another and performs other punching and comparing operations on groups of cards.

RESEARCHER One who undertakes systematic inquiries or surveys.

RESPONSE See RATE OF RETURN.

ROUNDING Limiting the digits of a percentage or figure to the smallest number relevant to the purposes of a table. The last retained digit is increased by one if the following digits amount to half a unit or more, but remains unchanged if the following digits amount to less than half a unit.

RUN (v.) To put source data (cards, tape, etc.) through a tabulating device. (n.) Tabulation, as in "marginal runs."

RUN SHEET A page on which machine tabulations are entered by hand.

SAMPLE A segment of the population (universe) selected for the purpose of drawing inferences concerning the total population.

SAMPLE BIAS A systematic distortion in sample selection, as contrasted with chance errors.

SAMPLING The process of selecting samples for use in research.

SAMPLING ERROR The difference between a value in a population and its estimate from a random sample, which exists because of the use of a sample instead of the total population.

SCALE A series of graded values which give a comparative rating or order to responses.

SCOPE The extent of a survey, including the description of the population surveyed, the size of the sample used, and the number of completed questionnaires.

SECTIONALIZING Breaking up a questionnaire into coherent parts (sections) with the use of subheadings.

SELF-ADMINISTERED QUESTIONNAIRE A questionnaire which the respondent fills out himself, as contrasted with a personal interview.

SELF-ENUMERATIVE PROCEDURE See SELF-ADMINISTERED QUESTIONNAIRE.

S.I.C. CODE Standard Industrial Classification code prepared by the U.S.

Bureau of the Budget and printed in a manual of codes representing the various industries, trades, and lines of business.

SIGHT CHECKING A procedure for sighting through the punched holes of a group of tabulating cards, all of which have (or should have) a punch in a particular column and position.

SINGLE-PUNCH COLUMN A punch-card column which may not contain more than one punch.

SKIP FIELD A section of a tabulating card omitted (skipped) in punching by programming (1) to skip on all cards or (2) to skip selectively by operation of a "skip" key.

SORTER An EAM device which senses punches in tabulating cards and sorts them into pockets according to the position punched in a specific column.

SPLIT (MAILING, SAMPLE) A mailing or sample divided into subgroups for the purpose of testing different questions or procedures.

SPONSOR (OF A SURVEY) The company or department which authorizes and pays for the survey.

SPOT CHECKING Testing the accuracy of an operation, such as coding or punching, by checking samples of the work selected at random.

STABILITY A condition of the sample which is achieved when the increase of sample size does not change the results significantly.

STANDARD DEVIATION A measure of the dispersion of a set of values around an arithmetic mean. In a normal distribution about two-thirds of the individual values fall within one standard deviation above or below the mean, 95 percent within two standard deviations, and 99.7 percent within three standard deviations.

STANDARD INDUSTRIAL CLASSIFICATION See S.I.C. CODE

STATISTICS (1) The science of collecting, analysing, and interpreting numerical data relating to an aggregate of individuals. (2) The data so collected, analyzed, or interpreted.

STORAGE UNIT (COMPUTER) The main internal storage of the computer, or a device (disk, tape, drum) into which information can be entered and from which it can later be retrieved. Synonymous with "memory."

STRATIFIED SAMPLE The result of splitting the universe into smaller populations and then sampling each subpopulation (stratum) separately.

STUB Description (usually on the left) of the horizontal lines of a table.

SUBSAMPLE A sample within a sample. It may be selected by any number of methods, depending on the purpose of subsampling and of the sample design.

SUBSTITUTION The replacement (in a sample) of one or more individuals who could not be reached or induced to answer.

SURVEY Research or examination of a group of individuals, usually by means of a questionnaire.

SURVEY DESIGN The master plan of all phases of a survey, such as sampling, methodology, data-gathering, and data-processing.

SYSTEMATIC SAMPLE A sample selected by some orderly and consistent method, such as taking every nth name on a list.

TAB SHEET A sheet on which hand or machine tabulations are entered.

TABULATE, TAB Counting individual data, such as the answers to questions or questionnaires, and organizing the results in the form of tables.

TABULATOR (1) One who tabulates by hand or machine. (2) An EAM device which reads information from cards and prints out lists, tables, and totals.

TAPE (COMPUTER) A strip of paper or plastic used for the input, storage, or output of data.

TELEPHONE INTERVIEW An interview conducted by telephone (as opposed to a PERSONAL INTERVIEW or MAIL SURVEY).

TEST MAILING See PILOT STUDY.

TEST TABULATION Preliminary hand tabulation of the answers to an open-end question on a sample of the questionnaires, for the purpose of establishing codes.

TOLERANCE A measure of precision of survey estimates that indicates how close they are to the figures which would have been obtained from a complete census.

TRAFFIC STUDY (READER TRAFFIC STUDY) A survey to determine the readership of advertisements and/or editorial matter in a specific issue of a publication.

TRAILER CARDS Auxiliary cards used to augment the capacity of the basic tabulating card in special situations.

TYPE FACE A particular design for the letters of the alphabet used in printing. The type face in which these words are printed is *Electra*.

UNIVERSE See POPULATION.

VALIDATION Checking, by reference to independent sources, that a survey or inquiry is free of bias or distortion.

VAN DYKE A positive print used as a proof before making a plate for offset printing.

VARITYPER (Trademark) A machine similar to a typewriter in which type faces of various styles and sizes can be used.

VERIFICATION (1) Checking with a respondent that he answered a questionnaire and that the answers are correctly recorded. (2) Comparing the answers of survey respondents with those of a sample of nonrespondents. (3) The work performed by the VERIFIER (machine).

VERIFIER A machine by which an operator checks the punches in a tabulating card and which indicates any errors or omissions. It is operated like a keypunch machine.

WAVE   A single mailing, or a group of interviews conducted at about the same time. A survey may consist of several waves.

WEIGHTING   Multiplication of subgroup data by a factor or factors so as to bring their values into proper proportion relative to the population or to other subgroups surveyed.

X COLUMN (PUNCH CARD)   A column automatically punched in the X position to help the keypunch operator make sure that she is on column and has not missed a column or skipped a punch.

XEROX   (Trademark) A copying machine, which uses xerography, a dry, photoelectromagnetic process.

Books on Related Subjects

BROWN, LYNDON O.: *Marketing and Distribution Research*, The Ronald Press Company, New York, 1969.
"Controlling the Computer: Management of EDP Problems," (collection of reprints of articles), American Management Association, New York, 1966–1967.
DEMING, W. EDWARDS: *Some Theory of Sampling*, Dover Publications, Inc., New York, 1966.
DEMING, W. EDWARDS: *Sample Design in Business Research*, John Wiley & Sons, Inc., New York, 1960.
FERBER, ROBERT: *Market Research*, McGraw-Hill Book Company, New York, 1963.
FERBER, ROBERT, D. F. BLANKERTZ, AND S. HOLLANDER, JR.: *Marketing Research*, The Ronald Press Company, New York, 1964.
FERBER, ROBERT (ed.): *Handbook of Marketing Research*. (A comprehensive book on the subject, now in preparation. It will be published by the McGraw-Hill Book Company.)
Glossary of Data Processing and Communication Terms, Honeywell Electronic Data Processing, Wellesley Hills, 1965.
HANSEN, MORRIS H., W. N. HURWITZ, AND W. G. MADOW: *Sample Survey Methods and Theory* (2 vols.), John Wiley & Sons, Inc., New York, 1953.

Kendall, Maurice G., and William R. Buckland: *A Dictionary of Statistical Terms*, Hafner Publishing Company, New York, 1967.
Kish, Leslie: *Survey Sampling*, John Wiley & Sons, Inc., New York, 1965.
Parten, Mildred: *Surveys, Polls and Samples*, Cooper Square Publishers, New York, 1966.
Uhl, Kenneth P., and Bertram Schoner: *Marketing Research Information Systems and Decision Making*, John Wiley & Sons, Inc., 1969.
USA Standard Vocabulary for Information Processing, United States of America Standards Institute, New York, 1966.
Waldo, Willis H.: *Better Report Writing*, Reinhold Publishing Company, New York, 1965.

Index

Index

"About," usefulness of word, 67
Addressing (*see* Envelope, addressing)
Advance notice, 89–93
  printed in a publication, 91, 93
Advantages of mail surveys, 5–10
Advertising effectiveness, measured with "before-and-after" surveys, 220–223, 228
Advertising efficiency, subject of mail research, 17
Advertising penetration, 18, 221, 228, 230
Advertising Research Foundation (ARF), 4, 24, 144, 235, 243, 249
Age groups, 52–53
Agisim, Philip, 100, 146, 150
Air mail, 10, 42, 87, 239
American Association for Public Opinion Research (AAPOR), 254
American Bankers Association (ABA), 122
American Marketing Association (AMA), 24, 141, 150, 151, 213, 243, 249
Analysis:
  outlined in survey design, 23, 25–26, 35
  of survey findings, 199, 216, 223–224

Anonymity of respondent:
  accompanying letter refers to, 102, 105, 112–113, 116–117
  keying prevents promise of, 120, 253
  lack of, when facing personal interviewer, 9
"Anonymous" vs. "confidential," 112–113
  (*See also under* "Confidential")
Answers:
  clear and precise, 66–68
  numerical, 187–189
  single vs. multiple, 182–184, 212
  verbatim tabulation, 182
"Approximately," usefulness of word, 67
Associated Business Publications (ABP), 243, 249
Association of National Advertisers, 249
Audit Bureau of Circulations (ABC), 33
Automated photographic process for transfer of information, 167
Automobile makes:
  Cadillac, 160
  Chevrolet, 54
  Ford, 54, 160, 164
    Mustang, 164

282 Index

Automobile makes (*Cont.*):
  Plymouth, 54
  Rolls-Royce, 59, 115
  Volkswagen, 86, 200
  Volvo, 86
Averages, 201, 209–211, 213
Ayer, N. W., & Son, 3

Bachrack, Stanley D., 150
Base, 184, 198, 200–202, 204, 212–213
"Before-and-after" research, 220–235
Beverage brands:
  Bacardi, 178
  H. & H. Pinch Bottle, 177
Bias:
  causes of: embarrassing the respondent, 63–65
    examples, 65
    fatigue, 63–64
    incentives, improper use of, 94–95, 97–98
    lack of filter question, 63
    language, 241
    question content, 62–66
    question position or order, 65
    questionnaire title, 58–59
    sponsor's name revealed, 61–62, 223, 225
  checked in pilot study, 84, 86
  in coding, 189
  distribution, 5–7
  frame, 30–31
  interviewer, 5, 7–9
  in letter, 102, 115–116
  of the mailing list, 11, 30–31, 251
  nonresponse may introduce, 110, 224, 241
  questionnaire, 37, 61–66, 251
    checked in pilot study, 84, 86
    in corporate-image surveys, 223–224
    in sample, 30–31, 85
  sponsor, 61–62
  subject, 62
  used constructively, 66
Blue Cross Plan, 139
Blue plate signature (*see* Facsimile signature)
Bradt, Kenneth, 128
Breaks (*see* Cross tabulations)
Brennan, Robert D., 100
Bressler, Marvin, 100
Brown, Lyndon O., 4
Brown, Rex V., 36, 149, 151
Budget, inadequate, 11, 13
Bureau of the Budget, 53
Bureau of the Census (*see* U.S. Bureau of the Census)
Bureau of Employment Security, 53
Business and industry as users of mail surveys, 16–19
Business and trade directories, 29

Calculating operations, 160, 198, 208–211
Cannell, Charles F., 21
Card(s):
  master, 199
  verification, 193–194
  (*See also* Mailing cards; Punch cards)
Card cleaning, 160, 194–197, 199
Case history, 12
  requested in questionnaires, 18
Castañeda, Francisco de, 4
Catton, William R., Jr., 150
Census:
  conducted among all members of a population, 27, 30
  cost, 4
  in history, 1
  by mail, 3–4
  Roman, 1
  United States: 1960, 3–4
    1970, 4, 10, 14
    of Business, 15
    of the Population, 15
Census, Bureau of (*see* U.S. Bureau of the Census)
Census figures, United States, 210, 213
Charts, 214, 257–262
Check answers, grouping of, 52–54
Check questions vs. open-end questions, 48–52
Check totals, 201–202
Checking final tabulations, 212–213
Checklist to evaluate mail surveys, 243–249
Church of England, 2
City directories, 28
Class intervals, 200
Classification data, 38, 53, 201
Clausen, John A., 150
Clustering, 6
Code booklet, 184–188, 199
Code sheet, 184
Codes, establishing, 180–184
Codes of ethics, 254
Coding, 160, 171–172, 179–180, 189–191
  by computer, 189
  cost estimate and schedule, 76–83
  and editing instructions, 187–190, 199
Cohen, Louis, 235
Cohen, Reuben, 150
Collator (machine), 198
Columns (*see* Punch cards, columns and positions)
Commerce, Department of (*see* U.S. Department of Commerce)

Index

Common Market, 238
Company recognition study (*see* Surveys, corporate-image)
Completion rate of mail surveys: personal interviews vs. mail questionnaires, 141–142
  (*See also* Response, percentage of)
Computer, 160, 198–199, 201–202
  labeling or addressing, 119, 122–124
  printouts, 198, 202–203, 208
  program, 198–199
  storage units, 198
Concept testing, 16–17
"Confidential," answers to be kept, 112–113, 122–124, 253
  (*See also* "Anonymous" vs. "confidential")
Confidential information required, 11–12
Consistency checks, 160, 194–197, 199
Control, centralized, 6, 10
Control group, 18–19, 222
Coolsen, Frank G., 4
Corporate-image surveys (*see* Surveys, corporate-image)
Cost estimating, 75–80
  checked with pilot study, 84, 87
  forms, 76–81
  in survey design, 23, 26
Cost-saving, resulting in more flexibility, 6, 10
Costs, checking, 80
Counter-sorter, 199
Courtesy, 73, 106
Coutant, Frank B., 213, 218
Cox, William E., Jr., 137
Credit Rating Bureau, 29
Cross tabulations, 160, 201
  as affecting sample size, 35

Dalenius, Tore, 149, 151
Darwin, Charles, 15
Data-gathering procedures, several combined, 20–21, 136, 139–140, 149
Data-processing, 159–218
  electronic (*see* EDP)
Davies, A. H., 254
Decoding, 169, 203–204
Deming, W. Edwards, 8, 14, 36, 150, 202
Demographic data:
  boring to respondent, 57
  on card lists, 28
  sources for breakdowns and classification, 53
Depth interviews used in questionnaire construction, 50
"Dictionary of Occupational Titles," 53
Directories:
  business and trade, 29

Directories (*Cont.*):
  city, 28
  international, 237
  telephone, 11, 28–29, 31, 148
"Directory of Mailing List Houses," 30
Disadvantages of mail surveys (*see* Mail surveys, limitations of)
Distribution:
  bias, 5–7
  frequency, 200
  wider, 5–6
Domesday Book, 1
Donald, Marjorie N., 150
"Don't Know," 69, 189, 197, 201, 210
Dummy tables, 26, 199
Dun & Bradstreet, directories and lists, 29, 237
Dunhill, lists, 29
Duplication of names, 31
du Pont, family, 7

EAM (Electric accounting machines), 198–199, 201
Editing, 160, 176–180
  cost estimate, 76–80
Editor, 178–180
EDP (Electronic data processing), 160, 198–199, 201
Enumerator variance, 8
Envelope:
  addressing, 118–119, 124, 238–239
  opening, 153
  outer (outgoing), 118–119, 122–124
  return (reply), 102, 111, 121–124, 153
    in international surveys, 239–240
  size of, 119
  stamped, 118–119, 121–123
Estimating (*see* Cost estimating)
Ethical standards, 250–254
Evaluation of mail surveys, 243–249
Evans, Franklin B., 14
Examples of possible answers to open-end question on questionnaire:
  biasing, 65
  helpful, 68

Facsimile signature, 116, 123–124
"Family income" responses in mail surveys vs. personal interviews, 8–9
Filter question, 34–35, 184
Findings, proper use of, 253
Follow-up mailings, 129–137, 139–140, 228, 251
  not needed in pilot studies, 87
  sent to every second nonrespondent, 132–133
  (*See also* Waves)

Index

Ford, Neil M., 93
Ford, Robert N., 150
Fowler, Floyd J., 21
Frame, 30–32, 138
  bias, 30–31
Frank, Ronald E., 21
Frankel, Lester R., 100, 150
Franzen, Raymond, 9, 14, 150
Frisbie, Bruce, 191

Gale, Harlow, 3
Galton, Sir Francis, 15
General Electric (GE), 61
Geoffrey, Leon, 202
Gordon, Gerald, 150
Government records as mailing lists, 29
Grouping:
  check answers, 52–54
  numerical answers, 200
  in recaps, 204

Hall, G. S., 15
Hansen, Morris H., 149, 151
Harvard University, 4, 189
Health Information Foundation, 139
Heaton, Eugene H., Jr., 93
Heiskell, Andrew, 26
History:
  of mail surveys, 2–4
  of surveys, 1
Humor, use of, 56
Hurwitz, William R., 149, 151

IBM (International Business Machines Corp.), 168, 202
Illustrations [see Questionnaire(s), illustrations in]
Incentive(s), 94–100, 123–124
  bias, 94–95, 97–98
  checking the effectiveness of, 84–86
  in corporate-image studies, 225, 228
  cost of, 10, 75, 94–95, 99–100
  described in accompanying letter, 102, 115
  in follow-up mailings, 131–132, 134, 257, 259–262
  in international surveys, 240
  money as, 95–100, 121
  promised, 94, 253
  report offered as, 102, 113, 140, 253
  in response-rate statistics, 256–262
  should be small and light, 94, 99
  types of, 95, 240
Income brackets, breaks, 52–53, 210
Income question, 70
Industrial Advertising Research Institute (see Marketing Communications Research Center)

"Industries, Alphabetical Index of Occupations and," 53
International Advertising Association, 24
International mail surveys (see Mail surveys, international)
Interpreter (machine), 197–198
Interviewer(s):
  bias, 5, 7–9
  cannot assure anonymity, 9
  cheating, 7
  cost of, compared with cost of mailmen, 10
  needed, 11–12
  specially trained, 11
  variations attributable to, 8
Interviews (see Depth interviews; Personal interviewing; Telephone interviews)

Jargon, to be avoided, 60–61
Journal (see Periodicals and publications)

Kephart, William M., 100
Keying [see Questionnaire(s), keying]
Keypunch machine, 168
Keypunch operator, 192–193
Keypunching (see Punching)
Kimball, Andrew E., 100, 117, 128
Klein, B., Co., directory of list sources, 30

Labels:
  for mailing-card boxes, 156
  not recommended for mailing questionnaire, 118–119, 122–124
Larson, Richard F., 150
Lazarsfeld, Paul F., 9, 14, 21, 150
Letter(s):
  accompanying, 57, 101–117, 121–124
    avoiding bias, 102, 115–116
    brevity of, 102
    contents of, 102–116
    format of, 116–117
    indicates questionnaire anonymous or confidential, 102, 105, 112–113, 116–117
    personal communication and personalization, 102–106, 116–117, 121–124, 238
    separate from questionnaire, 116–117
    style of, 116
  advance, 84, 86, 91–92
  of certification, 216–217
  follow-up, 131–136
Letter of transmittal [see Letter(s), accompanying]
Levine, Sol, 150
Lockley, Lawrence C., 4

McCandless, Boyd, 150
Machine tabulating, 197–202
McIntyre, O. E., Inc., lists, 29
Madow, W. G., 151
Magazines (*see* Periodicals and publications)
Mail survey(s):
  advantages of, 5–10
  cannot be considered reliable with less than 50% response, 144
  completion rate (*see* Response, percentage of)
  distinctions between mail and other types of surveys, 1, 61
  evaluation of, 243–249
  the first in the New World, 2–3
  history of, 2–4
  hybrid, 20–21
  international, 236–242
  limitations of, 10–14
  time-saving, 6–10
  types of, 15–21
  (*See also* Surveys)
Mailing cards, pulling, 28, 155–157
Mailing list(s), 27–31
  biased (*see* Bias, of the mailing list)
  on cards, 27–28
  of customers and prospects, 29
  duplication of names, 31
  houses, 29
  incomplete, 11, 30
  individual names essential, 30
  international, 237–238
  outdated, 31
  previously used, 31
  problems, 11, 27–31
  testing with pilot study, 84, 86
  unavailability of, precludes mail surveys, 11
Mailing procedures, 118–128
  sequence of operations, 124, 126
Mailings:
  follow-up (*see* Follow-up mailings)
  successive (*see* Waves)
Mark-sense cards, 167
Market Research Society of Great Britain, 254
Marketing Communications Research Center, 24, 243, 249
Massy, William F., 21
Mayer, Charles S., 150, 249
Media surveys, vi, 17
Medians, 210–211, 213
Merk, Gerhard, 21
Method and scope, 215–216
Michigan State University, Bureau of Business and Economic Research, 26
Michigan, University of, 20
Minnesota, University of, 3
Morgan, Arthur J., 21, 249

Morrison, Donald G., 21

*n*th name, every, 32–33
Napoleon, 1
National Association of Home Builders, 98
National Better Business Bureau, 137
National Business Lists, 29
National Committee for an Effective Congress, 140
National Geographic Society, 113
National Opinion Research Center, 189
Neighborhood as a distribution problem, 6–7
Newspapers:
  Christian Science Monitor, 140, 150
  New York Times, 62
  Wall Street Journal, 106
"No Answers," 162, 176, 178–179, 189, 197, 200–201, 210
  counted as "rejects," 184
  distributing, 205
  higher percent in personal interview survey, 8–9
Nonowners, getting replies from, 55–56
Nonrespondents, 13, 138–151
  to mail surveys reached by other data-gathering methods, 20–21, 136, 138–140, 149
  reasons for not replying, 146–147
  reducing number of, 129, 138–142, 149–150
  weighting, 148–149
  what to do about, 147–150
Nonresponse (*see* Nonrespondents)
Nuckols, Robert C., 21
Nuttall, Zelia, 4

Occupation question, 68
"Occupations and Industries, Alphabetical Index of," 53
Open-end questions vs. check questions, 48–52
Organization of American States (OAS), 238
"Other" line, 50, 52, 54, 61

Palmer, O. W., 254
Panels, 19
Participation of reader, 37
Peabody Museum of American Archaeology and Ethnology, 4
Percentaging, 160, 201, 208–209, 213
Periodicals and publications:
  American Sociological Review, 14, 21, 150
  Atlantic, 19
  Banking, 128
  Barron's, 91

286 Index

Periodicals and publications (*Cont.*):
  Business Week, 251
  Christian Science Monitor, 140, 150
  Foreign Affairs, 62
  Fortune, 114, 143
  Harper's, 19, 143
  Journal of Advertising Research, 93, 100, 117, 137, 150–151, 235
  Journal of the American Statistical Association, 150, 202
  Journal of Applied Psychology, 150
  Journal of Marketing, 4, 100, 117, 128, 150, 218
  Journal of Marketing Research, 21, 36, 93, 100, 137, 243, 249
  Journal of Psychology, 14, 150
  Journal of the Royal Statistical Society, 2, 4, 21
  Life, 61
  Look, 61
  Marketing/Communications, 100
  Media/scope, 21, 243, 249
  National Geographic, 148, 150, 236, 240, 242
  New York Times, 62
  New Yorker, 148
  Newsletter of the World Association for Public Opinion Research, 242
  Newsweek, 251
  Oil and Gas Journal, 29
  Printers' Ink, 100, 128, 137
  Public Opinion Quarterly, 14, 21, 93, 100, 128, 150, 191
  Reader's Digest, 61
  Time, 14, 251
  Time International, 225, 240
  Wall Street Journal, 106
Personal interviewing:
  clustered, 6
  completion rate, 141–142
  of individuals hard to reach, 7
  interviewer bias, 5, 7–9
  of nonrespondents to mailings (*see* Nonrespondents, to mail surveys reached by other data-gathering methods)
Personal involvement of respondent, 60, 105–106, 130
Personalizing [*see* Letter(s), accompanying, personal communication and personalization]
Philip II, 2
Pilot study (pilot mailing), 55, 84–88
  cost and time, 87–88
Politz, Alfred, 66, 150
Politz, Alfred, Research, Inc., 141
Politz-Simmons method, 149
Polk, R. L., & Co., directories, 28
Polls, newspaper straw, 3

Ponton, W.S., lists, 29
Poor's Directory, 29, 228, 237
Population (*see* Universe)
Postage:
  cost of, 10, 42, 75–76, 239
  international, 236, 239–240
  use of stamps instead of metered mail, 118–119
Postcard:
  advance, 89–90
  advance and reminder, checking effectiveness of, 84–86
  mailed along with the questionnaire, 120–121
  reminder, 130–132
Pratt, Robert W., Jr., 150
Precoding, 71–72, 171–172
Premiums [*see* Incentive(s)]
Presentation of findings [*see* Report(s), presentation]
Printing:
  letter, 116
  questionnaire [*see* Questionnaire(s), printing]
Probability sample (*see* Sample, probability)
Product testing, 17, 20
Projection, 160, 211, 213
Publications (*see* Periodicals and publications)
Pulling mailing cards (*see* Mailing cards, pulling)
Punch cards, 167–175, 192–202
  cleaning, 194–197
  columns and positions, 168–171
    number needed for numerical answers, 187
  correcting errors, 196–197
  interpreted, 168
  skip field, 193
  trailers, 170–171
  verification, 193–194
  [*see also* Card(s)]
Punching, 160, 167–175, 192–198
  alphabetic, numeric, symbols, 168
  errors, 193–194
  margin of error, 72
  single vs. multiple, 169–170, 192

Questionnaire(s):
  appearance of, easy to answer, 37, 39, 48, 123–124
  bias, 37, 61–66, 84–86, 223–225, 251
  blanks, 153–155
  cannot be structured, 11–12
  checklists (*see* Questions, check)
  color of, 40, 122–123
  comments, how to ask for, 73

Questionnaire(s) (*Cont.*):
  completeness and relevance of, 37–39
  construction of, 37–74
    corporate-image surveys, 221, 223–224
    with data-processing in mind, 38, 71–72
    different in mail surveys, 42
  controls, built-in, 72–73
  courtesy, 73
  described in accompanying letter as short and easy to answer, 102, 111
  difficult, 11–12
  distributed by hand, 20
  folding of, 42, 119, 121
  format of, 39
  illustrations in, 40–41
  inserted or printed in publications, 20
  instructions, notes and explanations, 63, 65, 68, 70–71
  interesting, 57–61
  keying, 28, 119–120, 123–128, 131
  language (wording) used, 60–61
  layout of, 45–49, 71–72, 123, 171–175
  length of, 12, 39, 122–124, 139–140, 256–257
  master, 172–175, 187, 192, 195–196, 199
  number to be mailed, 33–35
    in pilot study, 85
  pages: number of, 39, 122–124, 256–257
    size of, affecting response rate, 256–257
  paper, 40, 42, 122–123, 239
  pretesting, 74
  printed on same page as letter, 116–117
  printing, 42–44, 124–125
  sectionalizing, 48, 69–70
  sequence of subjects, 38, 69–70
  serializing, 191
  structuring, 11, 72, 223
  title, 58–59
  translating, 241
  typesetting, 42
Questions:
  bias of content and position, 62–66
  check, 38, 45, 162
    answers to be punched without coding, 172
    vs. open-end, 48, 50–53
  checked in pilot study, 84, 86–87
  confidential, 55
  difficult, 54
  eliciting precise and unambiguous answers, 66–68, 123
  filter, 34–35, 184
  frivolous or trivial, to be avoided, 56
  income, 70

Questions (*Cont.*):
  in international surveys, 241–242
  introductory, 58–60
  numbering, 48
  numerical, 52–53, 164
  occupation, 68
  open-end, 45, 48–52, 162, 180–181, 187
    in international surveys, 242
  order of (*see* sequence *below*)
  phrasing, 38
  ranking, 68–69, 224
  rating, 68–69, 228–229
  readership, 70, 227
  rotated, 63–64
  sequence, 38, 65, 69–70
  skipping, 55–56
  strain on memory, 54
  wrong, 54

Random numbers, table of, for sample selection, 32
Random sample (*see* Sample, random)
Ranking, 68–69, 224
Rating, 68–69, 228–229
Readership question, 70, 227
Readership traffic study, 18
Recapping (recaps), 160, 166, 199–208
  test tabs, 184
Recognition studies, 219–235
Refusals, 11, 153–155
Rejects, in machine tabulation, 184
Reliability:
  ascertainable, 31
  degree of, 22, 24–25
  impaired by budget limitations, 13
Reminder postcard, 130–132
Replies:
  percentage of (*see* Response, percentage of)
  thoughtful, 6, 9–10
  truthful, 6, 8
Report(s):
  contents of, 215–216
  format of, 216–218
  offered as incentive, 102, 113
  outlined in survey design, 23, 25–26
  presentation of, 213–218
Representativeness, 139, 142–146
Reproducer (machine), 198
Reproducing data from the mailing card, 28
Research findings, investigating published material, 22, 24
Research objectives, 22–25, 221–223
Research organizations, 25
Respondent, not the addressee, 11, 13

Response:
　percentage of: analyzed by first vs. second wave and incentives used, 257–262
　　analyzed by size and number of pages, 256–257
　　consideration in sample design, 34
　　in corporate image surveys, 224–228
　　how to achieve high, 122–124, 139–142, 149–150
　　increased by advance notice, 89–91
　　increased with incentives, 94–100
　　in international surveys, 240
　　low, occasional usefulness of, 145
　　minimum standard, 144–145
　　progress made, 3–4
　　tables and charts reflecting experience, 255–262
　　tested with pilot study, 84, 86, 88
　　representative, 142–145
　　speed of, 10, 131, 262–263
Response rate (*see* Response, percentage of)
Returns:
　checking in, 152–158
　percentage, rate of (*see* Response, percentage of)
Richmond, Samuel, 150
Robinson, R. A., 95, 100, 128, 137, 146, 150
Rotation, 63–64

Sample:
　bias, 30–31, 85
　checking against known distribution, 33
　definition of, 23, 25
　probability, 11, 31, 33
　random, 32–36, 85, 138, 142, 180–181, 224
　　in pilot study, 85, 88
　size, 33–35
　　as affected by cross tabulation, 35
　　no magic in large numbers, 33
　stratified, 34
Sampling, 31–36, 238
　design, 31–32
　error, 33, 35–36
　systematic, 32–33
　　avoiding obvious starting point and interval, 32
Scaling system, 70
　corporate-image surveys, 223–224, 228, 232–234
Scheduling, 81–83
Scoble, Harry M., 150
Scott, Christopher, 21
Semon, Thomas T., 150
Sharp, Harry, 21
Sheldon, department store lists, 29

Simmons, Willard R., 150
Simmons, W. R., & Associates, Inc., 141, 150
Simon, Raymond, 117
Skip field in a punch card, 193
Sorting questionnaires, 160–161
Special delivery, 134–136
Speed of response, 10, 262–263
Sponsor:
　bias, 61–62
　ethical considerations, 250–252
Stability, 35, 181, 224
　distinguished from representativeness, 143
Stafford, James E., 93
Stamps (postage) used, 118–119, 121–124, 239–240
Standard Industrial Classification (SIC), 28, 53, 155
Statistical Abstract, 53
Statisticians needed, 32–33
Stock, J. Stevens, 150
Stratified sample, 34
Subgroups, 34, 198
Subsample, 34, 146, 201
Subscribers to publications, used as mailing lists, 29, 237
Suchman, Edward A., 150
Sudman, Seymour, 191
Supervision of editing, coding, tabulating, 165
Survey Research Center of the University of Michigan, 20
Surveys:
　on advertising, 17–18
　"before-and-after", 220–235
　for business and industry, 16–19
　competitive, 61–62
　consumer, 16–17
　corporate-image, 219–235
　　case histories, 225–235
　of dealers, 91–92
　design, 22–26
　industrial, 16
　low response, occasional usefulness of, 145
　method decided on, 23, 25
　multiple, 18–19
　objectives (*see* Research objectives)
　readership, 17–18
　timing, 23, 26, 75–83, 222–223
　tracking, 223
　(*See also* Mail surveys)
Systematic sampling, 32–33

Tables:
　column headings, stubs, line headings, 201, 204, 212
　layout, 201–202

Index

Tabulating, 159–208
  brands, 164
  consideration in constructing the questionnaire, 38, 71–72
  hand, 157, 159–166
  machine, 159–160, 197–202
  reason questions, 164–165
  specifications, 199–202
Tabulations:
  bases (*see* Base)
  marginal, 199–200
  outlined in survey design, 23, 25–26
  test, 157, 180–185, 187
  (*See also* Cross tabulations)
Techniques needed to achieve research objectives, 23, 25
Telephone directories, 11, 28–29, 31, 148
Telephone interviews:
  compared with mail survey, 9–10
  individuals hard to reach, 7
  of nonrespondents to mailings, 20, 136, 139–140
Telephone introduction of mail questionnaire, 91
Tepping, Benjamin J., 202
Test mailing (*see* Pilot study)
Testing several variables, 85
Thomas' Register, 29, 237
Time available, insufficient, 11, 13
Time as a cost factor, 80–81
Timing:
  in corporate-image surveys, 222–223
  in cost estimating and scheduling, 75–83
  in survey design, 23, 26
Title and position, 68, 204
Totals, 200, 204, 213
Trailer cards, 170–171
Translating for international surveys, 241
Typesetting questionnaires, 42

Undeliverables, 152–153, 155
Underrepresentation of poor or rich families, 6–7

United Nations, 213, 237–238, 240
U.S. Bureau of the Census, 4, 14–15, 40, 53, 167
  evaluation of mail technique, 4, 8, 10
  study of card punching errors, 193–194
U.S. Bureau of Internal Revenue, 115
U.S. Department of Commerce, 4, 14–15, 29, 53, 238
U.S. Department of Labor, 53
U.S. government, largest user of mail surveys, 15
Universe:
  in corporate-image surveys, 221–222
  defined in survey design, 22–24
  represented by respondents, 142
  sampled without clustering, 6
Usefulness of information checked with pilot study, 84, 87

Van Doren, Lawrence N., 128
Variables tested in pilot study, 85
Verification of punched cards, 193–194
Verifier (machine), 193

Waisanen, F. B., 93
Watson, John J., 100, 117, 137
Waves:
  second, 130–134
    patterns of response rates, 257–262
  third, 134–136
  fourth and successive, 136–137
  trend established from, 130, 148–149
Weighting, 34, 211
Weighting the nonresponse, 148–149
Western Union Company, The, 30
Westinghouse, 61
Word association, 224, 234
World Association for Public Opinion Research, 242, 254
Wotruba, Thomas R., 100

X column, 172, 193